Other, non-Ripper, writing by the author:

"There is almost a sensuousness of impulse and verbal attack in Stephen Senise's use of language and a richness of imagery and sincerity of presentation that is truly convincing."

PETER SKRZYNECKI (OAM)

FALSE FLAG

JACK THE RIPPER

STEPHEN SENISE

Acorn Independent Press
London

Dedicated to the descendants of Shem and to Lucia Lorenza.

سلام שלום

Salam Shalom

Remembering

Martha Tabram (1849-1888)
Mary Ann Nichols (1845-1888)
Annie Chapman (1841-1888)
Elizabeth Stride (1843-1888)
Catherine Eddowes (1842-1888)
Mary Kelly (c.1863-1888)
Alice McKenzie (c.1849-1889)

Rest In Peace

In honour of the pioneers,
Bob Hinton, Stephen Wright (†2000), Garry Wroe and Chris Miles.

And when Eurybiades lifted up his staff as though to strike him, Themistocles said: "Smite me if you will, but listen."

The Life of Themistocles, Plutarch

CONTENTS

False flag:

A ruse. Designed to deceive in such a way as to make certain activities appear as though they are being carried out by other entities, groups, or nations.

A *false flag* operation is one conducted by one party and made to appear as though it were the actions of another.

Collated from multiple sources

Jewbaiter, Jew-baiter:

Someone who hates and would persecute Jews.
Synonyms: anti-Semite.

Webster's Dictionary

More than just an anti-semite, an anti-semite that constantly takes his views into the public.

Urban Dictionary

Judenhetze:

Systematic persecution of the Jews, Jew-baiting, from Juden-, combining form of *Jude* Jew + *Hetze* pursuit, persecution, incitement to hatred, malicious propaganda.

Oxford Dictionaries

ACKNOWLEDGEMENTS

Thanks are made mindful of the time, effort and advice of all those who have so kindly been able to assist; and to the staff of the State Library of New South Wales (including the Mitchell Library), State Records New South Wales, Richmond-Tweed Regional Library, National Library Of Scotland (Maps), British Library (Collections & Services), Salvation Army Heritage Centre (William Booth College, London). Also, to *Ripperologist: The Journal of Jack The Ripper, East End & Victorian Studies*, for helping publish some of my preliminary and ongoing research.

In appreciation.

Illustrations, maps and sources

Images from various editions of the *Illustrated Police News* reproduced with the assistance and permission of the British Library Board. Images from *Punch* and *Famous Crimes* reproduced with the permission of the British Library Board. Images from the Bathurst gaol record, reproduced with permission of State Records New South Wales. The image of the Victoria Home For Working Men is reproduced with the assistance and permission of the Peter Higginbotham-Mary Evans Picture Library. The image of the entrance to Darlinghurst gaol (1887) is reproduced with the permission of the Mitchell Library (State Library of New South Wales). The image of the RMS Ormuz (*Illustrated London News*, 14 May 1887) is from the author's collection. The illustration of the discovery of Elizabeth Stride's body, is from the from the *Pictorial News* edition of 6 October, 1888; that of the corner of Duke Street and Church Passage is from the *Building News* of 21 August, 1908. The historical image of the Great Synagogue is sourced courtesy of the *Casebook: Jack The Ripper* photo archive (Ryder, Stephen P. [Ed.]); and permission has been sought, for the image featuring the building which housed the old Princess Alice pub. The photograph of the author standing outside of the former Darlinghurst gaol was taken by Lucia Lorenza (December 2017). The photograph of Christ Church school, was scouted by Lucia Lorenza and taken by the author (November 2016).

Maps reproduced with the assistance and permission of the National Library of Scotland: George Washington Bacon map of London (1886), and Ordnance Survey map of London (revised 1894). Reynolds map of London (1882) is in the public domain.

Whilst every effort has been made to appropriately credit and reference the images, maps and sources that help form part of this study, the author apologises for any oversight which he would be happy to correct in future editions.

AUTHOR'S NOTES

They were killed during 1888's 'Autumn of Terror'. Residents of London's East End, Mary Ann 'Polly' Nichols, Annie Chapman, Elizabeth Stride, Catherine Eddowes and Mary Kelly. Among students of Jack The Ripper's crimes, they are the generally accepted, or canonical, victims. That assessment might be traced back to a now famous 1894 report by Sir Melville Macnaghten of the Metropolitan Police Criminal Investigation Department and eventually Assistant Commissioner. In it, he opined that "the Whitechapel murderer had 5 victims – & 5 victims only".

In doing so, he echoed police surgeon Dr Thomas Bond who had been brought in to provide a medical overview of the case at the height of the Ripper scare in late October 1888. In his judgment, the five had all died at Jack The Ripper's hand. Dr Bond's opinion would later come to include another victim, Alice McKenzie, who was struck down during the following year.

A spate of murderous assaults on women in London's East End from 1888 to 1891 comprised a police file covering the Whitechapel series. It was made up of the canonical five plus another six non-canonical victims. Opinion as to the status of these six has always been, and continues to be, in a state of flux. The most prominent among them is Martha Tabram. Alice McKenzie is the other non-canonical victim most often considered when contemplating possible other attacks perpetrated by this infamous serial killer.

A result of this overlap is that the terms 'Whitechapel murderer' and 'Jack The Ripper' became metonyms, somewhat interchangeable, once the latter's name entered the story in October 1888. For simplicity's sake, and because it is the name by which he came to be most recognised, 'Jack The Ripper' has been adopted earlier than the chronology strictly dictates in the pages that follow.

Anti-Semitic language contained in era-specific media reports and literature:

These give an idea of the pervasiveness of anti-Jewish prejudice in parts of continental Europe, and within some segments of British society, in the late-19th century and first half of the 20th. The Judeophobia outlined in this study forms part of the architecture of the Ripper tale and deals with an ugly and unsavoury, broader historical reality: what in 1898 Emile Zola famously denounced as "the scourge of our time" and nothing short of an "obsession". For readers with a greater interest in this aspect of the story, endnotes provide references to many texts offering opportunities for further reading.

Toponymy:

In an effort to maintain a consistent and easily recognisable spelling for Austro-Hungarian towns referenced in Victorian era media reports, the standard form used during that period has been adopted in this work. These usually mirrored official German language place names.

Unfortunately, apart from larger towns and cities, eg. Vienna and Cracow (today's Krakow, Poland), these tended to vary considerably from report to report. Different spellings have been reproduced as-is when part of a contemporary article, but standardised within the body of the work for the sake of clarity.

Autopsy references:

Descriptions of the injuries and mutilations suffered by the victims have been dealt with in no greater detail than deemed relevant to the narrative. For more detailed accounts, interested readers are directed to post-mortem reports freely available online.

INTRODUCTION

> "But I don't want to see the police," I protested. "What I wish to do, is to go down into the East End and see things for myself. I wish to know how those people are living there, and why they are living there, and what they are living for. In short, I am going to live there myself."
>
> Jack London, *The People Of The Abyss* (1903)

The year 1888 was to become synonymous with Jack The Ripper. His brief time in the spotlight would cast attention, not only on his crimes, but the stage on which he came to prominence: London's East End. Protagonist and backdrop thus became an infamous combination: murder and mayhem.

Gaslight falling on swirling fog. Cherubic Cockney street urchins. Hansom cabs and ladies of the night. An almost kitsch diorama that has curtailed and contained our understanding, not only of the scene of Jack The Ripper's crimes, but also the crimes themselves.

In reality, the air in that part of London would have been laden with the smell of sourdough and bagels, Warsaw sausage, gefilte fish and smoked beef[1]. If you listened carefully above the din, you might have understood that the voices were not always those of the capital's native poor. In many neighbourhoods around Whitechapel, they were more likely speaking Yiddish and their owners wearing a black hat, sporting long hair and a beard[2]. "A fragment of Poland torn off from Central Europe and dropped haphazard into the heart of Britain," as one journalist from the *Jewish Chronicle* would describe London's "ghetto" at the turn of the century, with its "ringleted Pole" and "beshawled women... its hunger, its humour... (and) the grand passion of the chosen people"[3].

The following is not just your usual detective story, for all that it contains a front-line suspect and important new information from government archives, only now come to light. The infamous murders that took place in Whitechapel toward the end of the 19th century have for too long been wrapped within the tight constraints of a whodunit; hamstrung like one of the mad doctors or other cackling suspects of popular legend confined belatedly to the Victorian insane asylum in the dead of night.

It is accepted today that police detectives chasing the serial murderer of 1888 could well have used a modern profiler-psychologist to aid them in their work. There has been no shortage of modern case studies looking at the evidence to try and piece together a better such understanding. On the one hand immensely worthwhile, cracking the case has proven stubbornly elusive. It is the contention flowing from research presented here, that a greater degree of sociological detective work has also been needed in order to flush out what happened during the course of the world's most notorious murder spree, and why events transpired as they did. Particularly undervalued has been the demographic shift then under way in the ethnic make up of the East End's population and the social reverberations set in motion.

These broke upon an environment where, less than a generation earlier, Great Britain's Jews had gained full legal emancipation after an incremental process going back decades[4]. The national debate that accompanied it had provided an opportunity for benighted, racially motivated charges to be aired against the Jewish community, alleged foreignness and moral failings among the more prominent[5]. But such arguments would pale in comparison to what was to come, when pogroms in Russia from 1881 set off a migratory wave crashing on British shores that had very practical effects, particularly on the streets and neighbourhoods of London's eastern slums.

Which is why Jack The Ripper is part of a bigger story. It is told here with a view to help unfurl a real world explanation of the bloody events commencing in 1888 and the aim of laying to rest the ghosts of a hitherto partly imagined, certainly out of focus, landscape. Gaining a deeper understanding of the case now depends on breaking the rustic-quaint thrall of Victorian East London, as popularly understood, and for the study of this notorious episode to rise above the inkblot test it has from time to time been prone to resemble. Until then, we remain strangers in a foreign land.

In the pages that follow, there has been a focus on contemporary sources, in particular, the many newspapers that were flourishing during a nascent epoch of more popular style journalism. The thesis proposed here, for the first time in the 130 year case history, is that in consuming their contents, the modern era's first and most notorious serial killer became a veritable media monster.

Pack away the Cluedo set. What follows is a look through a window of forgotten history. Prepare for the unimaginable: someone uniquely sinister staring back.

Monday, 12 November 1888. Capital to an empire.

The Thames flowed impassive while the day and the autumn ebbed. This year, the chill seemed to express the spreading fear which had taken hold of one part of town, over in Whitechapel, in the impoverished east. There, depravity had taken on unique, physical form, and preyed.

The inquest into the murder of another victim had just wound up, and what the newspapers had been reporting for days, was official: the mutilation visited on this latest, poor woman had been horrific. Savage.

It was then, that a casual labourer wandered into the thin, triple story, red brick and stone building on the corner of a bustling East End thoroughfare. It was home to the Commercial Street police station. The man had a contribution he wanted to make to the investigation.

Inspector Abberline was soon summoned. The information at hand was dynamite.

CHAPTER 1

OF JEWISH APPEARANCE

Let us turn aside, into the Whitechapel Ghetto, where they most do congregate.

Simon Gilbert (born Simon Gelberg in 1869, London)
journalist & editor, *Jewish Chronicle*

In 1887, the great metropolis of London had been the setting of Queen Victoria's golden jubilee procession, celebrating the monarch's 50 years on the throne. "No one ever, I believe, has met with such an ovation as was given to me... The cheering was quite deafening and every face seemed to be filled with real joy. I was much moved and gratified," wrote the Empress in her diary.

For the purpose of the royal script, it was just as well the official procession had stuck to a six-mile route around the streets of the city and affluent West End. In Whitechapel, that slum abutting the eastern edge of the city, north of the docks, there was little to get excited about. Unemployment had been critically high for years, at times reaching up to 70% within some mainstay industries. Living conditions were among the most squalid in the empire and life expectancy, low. Referring to a previous Victorian generation, an oft-quoted statistic from neighbouring Bethnal Green placed the average age of death among the labouring class at 16[6].

From 1873 to the mid-1890s, Great Britain's economy had been mired in the original Great Depression, the 'Long Depression'. In the midst of it, during November 1887 in Trafalgar Square, about two and half thousand police and troops clashed with tens of thousands of marchers who wanted an end to unemployment and a change of government policy in Ireland. This violent, political flare-up would become known as 'Bloody Sunday', with the East End having made its fair contribution by providing both eager protesters and organisational impetus. Much of the fuel, had come courtesy of an inexhaustible supply of hardship and want in the lives of the long-suffering people residing in this most neglected part of the capital.

Conducting an enquiry into living conditions in London's eastern environs, philanthropist Charles Booth had been horrified by the deprivation he had found. It saw him embark on his great sociological study and mapping of London's poverty, published in 1889 as *Life & Labour of the People*.

Another contemporary social reformer was William Booth, founder of the Salvation Army. Decades earlier, he had begun his life's mission of bringing hope and Christian succour to the poor of East London. By the late 1880s, he lamented the work still to be done:

> The foul and fetid breath of our slums is almost as poisonous as that of the African swamp... a population sodden with drink, steeped in vice, eaten up by every social and physical malady, these are the denizens of Darkest England amidst whom my life has been spent[7].

The use of exotic imagery was not simply literary flourish on the part of Booth. An intimate of East London's problems, he was tapping into the notion of this periphery as an outpost of empire "in some distant territory"[8], a quasi-foreign *terra incognita*[9].

The East End in those years was where misery, already well established, had made the company of tens of thousands of eastern and central European Ashkenazi Jews fleeing poverty, persecution and worse. Mainly, but not exclusively, they came from Russian Poland following a new Czar's return to an openly anti-Semitic political program starting in 1881. Jews from Germany and Austria-Hungary joined the migration, many of whom were also ethnic Poles fleeing Bismarck's edict expelling them from Prussia in 1886.

A special report in the *Lancet* in 1884 harked back to the very commencement of this modern day exodus, which set off an overcrowding problem that would effect Whitechapel for decades to come as more and more refugees made their way to safety:

> … night after night, wagon loads of poor Jews were brought up from the docks, where they had just arrived still panic-stricken from Russia. Starving and penniless, glad to have escaped with their lives, they thronged the poor dwellings of Fashion-street and neighbourhood[10].

Arrived on British shores, the newcomers found a long established Jewish community which considered itself English and very much at home. The differences between the two sets of co-religionists were quickly evident, the same *Lancet* report referring to the newcomers as "thoroughly foreign... eastern" Jews, "Poles in their instincts, customs and predilections".

By 1888 Nathan Adler, Chief Rabbi of the British empire, had warned continental co-religionists eyeing London as a haven that things were dire. "There are many who believe that all the cobblestones of London are precious stones, and that it is the place of gold. Woe and alas it is not so."[11]

A few years earlier the Board of Guardians for the Relief of the Jewish Poor had put out their own advisory: "We beseech every right-thinking person among our brethren in Germany, Russia and Austria to place a barrier to the flow of foreigners"[12].

Such pleas did little to stem the tide of Jewish refugees arriving in London. At this time, the East End's population stood at about 420,000[13], or nearly 500,000 if a bigger net is thrown around the surrounding areas. Of those, 33,000[14][15]might loosely have been referred to as practising Jews. A significantly higher figure was referenced by Charles Booth for the years 1886-87, which included non-practising Jews, but he seems to have left out those residing in nearby Stepney and Poplar: "I get about 45,000 ...concentrated in great numbers particularly in Whitechapel"[16]. Even that may have been a conservative estimate.

Other figures, of anywhere between 60,000 and 106,000, were also current with a degree of reliable corroboration at around 60,000 to 61,0000 covering the period 1888 to no later than 1893[17]. Beatrice Webb, who had helped her cousin Charles Booth with his research into East End poverty, described these statistics in particular as "the most authoritative figures" in an essay, 'The Jews Of East London'[18].

"Two things alone defy the immortal gods – figures and the past," the British Prime Minister, Sir Robert Peel had said half a century earlier. Doubly warned by his maxim, it might be taken as a mild advisory while sifting through the old data, trying to arrive at definitive numbers[19]. What can be said with certainty is that in many neighbourhoods abutting the city, around Spitalfields, Jews constituted a majority. In Whitechapel as a whole, Booth's numbers boasted 28,790 in a population of 73,518[20], though these statistics were as much as two years out of date by mid-1888, and Jewish refugees were arriving in the East End at a rate of as many as 10,000 per year, according to some testimony[21].

Consistent with that, an agent of the Charity Organisation Society (Whitechapel Committee) reported his opinion that the native British element in the district of Whitechapel constituted as little as half the population: "Some of the streets that were occupied by British workpeople have been entirely cleared, and are now occupied by Jews"[22]. By the end of the century, anywhere up to 100,000, possibly more, had made their home in and around Whitechapel[23]. Many others would find temporary residence there on the way to other parts of the United Kingdom or before continuing their journey to other parts of the empire or the United States. "Strangers in a strange land... worse off than they were before," some would even return home[24].

The new arrivals were entering what must have at times appeared like a dog-eat-dog environment, just as they thought they had come upon their deliverance. Beatrice Webb wept for the new arrivals as she saw them disembark:

> For a few moments it is a scene of indescribable confusion. Cries and counter-cries; the hoarse laughter of the dock loungers at the strange garb and broken accent of the poverty-stricken foreigners; the rough swearing of the boatmen at passengers unable to pay the fee for landing. In another ten minutes eighty of the hundred newcomers are dispersed in the back slums of Whitechapel; in another few days the majority of these, robbed of the little they possess, are turned out of the free lodgings destitute and friendless.[25]

Indeed, the first few steps on arrival at the London docks could prove particularly hazardous. Swindlers of all kinds, including those who spoke in the refugees' own tongue, were ready to pounce on the ship-weary newcomers or "greeners"; overcharging them to carry luggage, taking them to overpriced and dishonest lodging houses, selling them worthless travel tickets, and tricking unescorted girls into prostitution. In 1885, Constance Rothschild Battersea founded the Jewish Association for the Protection of Girls and Women as a response.

Another charitable institution, the Poor Jews Temporary Shelter was opened in 1886 at number 84 Leman Street*. There, a migrant could stay up to 14 days and receive two meals a day, although no money was doled out. Those who could afford it were expected to pay. The shelter's sponsors, indeed the Anglo-Jewish community more broadly, were mindful of not inadvertently encouraging the sea of humanity arriving at the docks lest it be misconstrued that philanthropy equated a "provision being made for the large influx of foreign Jews to the East End"[26]. It was a defensive but very real political consideration. One social historian born of Jewish immigrant parents, would describe the period and its socio-political pressures in a study a century later, noting:

---

* Division H headquarters for the Metropolitan Police, which would play an important part in the Ripper investigation, was at number 76.

1888 was the year that the 'problem' of foreign immigration finally broke surface, and the old scapegoat, the Jew, was available in all his vulnerability.[27]

Many British-born East Enders, and others besides, viewed the refugees as competitors for already limited resources and blamed them for transforming the character of the neighbourhoods in which they settled. The flip side was that the new arrivals found much that was familiar in their new surroundings, including Jewish schools, cemeteries, places of worship, Russian vapour baths, kosher butchers, bakeries, restaurants, political clubs, coffee houses and institutions, both charitable and social. In the British-born Samuel Montagu, Whitechapel even boasted a member of parliament of the Jewish faith from 1885 to 1900.

Yiddish was the informal lingua franca among most of the Jewish residents and there were theatres, newspapers, publishers and booksellers catering to the flourishing use of the Judeo-German tongue in East London – often described as a dialect of German. The following contemporary report is typical:

> On the walls and other available spaces, one sees advertisements in Yiddish, and enterprising tradesmen go in for Yiddish handbills. There are Yiddish clubs and gambling-halls, and little Jewish lodging-houses without end.[28]

Visitors to the East End often cited language as one of the first indications that they "must be in some far-off country whose people and language" seemed very different. A good example is the response of "Mrs Brewer" in a piece entitled 'The Jewish Colony In London' in an 1892 edition of *Sunday Magazine*:

> The names over the shops were foreign, the wares were advertised in an unknown tongue, of which I did not even know the letters, the people in the streets were not of our type, and when I addressed them in English the majority of them shook their heads. This being so I tried German,

which succeeded up to a certain point; but to have reached their hearts and brains I must have had a knowledge of Yiddish...[29]

In particular, the language was the mainstay of the many Jewish political radicals agitating in East London[30]. Near the corner of Greenfield Street and Commercial Road, the *Evening Standard* described one of their typical meeting places:

> Bills in each of the windows, in Hebrew characters, inform the Yiddish public and passer-by that 'here can be had coffee', also what they spell *tie,* tea, and *aller ort von refreshments* which every one will easily construe to mean all kinds of refreshments. This is a coffee-house much patronised by the great bulk of the poorer East End Anarchists and Socialists who live in the district.[31]

Practically around the corner was one of the main Yiddish language newspapers, the socialist *Arbeter Fraint* at 40 Berner Street, situated behind the International Working Men's Educational Club, which had taken control of the paper in 1886. One of Jack The Ripper's canonical victims, Elizabeth Stride, would be found murdered in its courtyard at the height of the murder spree.

The *Arbeter Fraint* had begun operations in Fort Street in 1885, not far from another of the early radical Yiddish language newspapers, the *Polishe Yidl*, originally published from offices in 137 Commercial Street, starting in 1884.

A few minutes walk from Fort Street, in Bell Lane, there was the Free Jewish School. By the end of the 19th century it would become one of the biggest elementary schools in the world. Between 1880 and 1900, it is estimated that one third of all London's Jewish children would pass through its doors, helping to absorb and Anglicise thousands of the refugees into British society. It was a task both strands of the education system, Jewish and gentile, took very seriously. The great paradox was that at least in the early phases of learning, this process had to be conducted in Yiddish. There can be no better example than the case of one of the local English board schools, Christ Church School in Brick Lane, whose student population was about 95% Jewish by the late-1880s. The teachers had to learn Yiddish to be able to communicate with their pupils as a first step in the children's Anglicisation[32].

In less than a generation, the Head of H (Whitechapel) Division, Superintendent William Mulvaney, would press for a cadre of Yiddish speaking policemen[33]: "it would be very desirable to have members of the Service who could speak this language"[34]. The Home Office quickly agreed with a modest such scheme, and training of some members of the Metropolitan Police "to qualify themselves for the effective discharge of their duties among the alien population" had begun by 1903[35]. By that late stage, realities on the ground had long meant that many a police constable had picked up some degree of fluency in the tongue. The *Daily Mail* referred to them as "burly bi-linguists" in an article entitled "Yiddish-Speaking Policemen":

> The need to understand Yiddish... is felt by most of the East End police... "Most of us," said a sergeant yesterday "understand a lot of their 'lingo'"... One such constable was found in the Commercial road... "Macht fiss," said the young constable, occasionally varying this, when the crowd got out of hand, with "Gay aweck". To an English crowd he would have said, "Pass along, please," and "Nah, then, git out of it".[36]

By 1888, entire neighbourhoods had taken on a distinctive character replete with the exotic aromas of what must have seemed to the locals, a bewildering culinary tradition. In 1888, a parliamentary select committee would hear evidence of some streets in Whitechapel where most shops and stalls were in the hands of foreigners, primarily "Russian and Polish Jews"[37][38]. Several blocks, around Wentworth and Commercial streets, reflected this shifting demographic reality more than most. By the time of George Arkell's 1899 map of *Jewish East London*, the area would be at the epicentre of Jewish settlement to the tune of 95-100% of the inhabitants. It was a neighbourhood that would play a central geographic role in the Ripper saga.

Henry Dejonge, a long time Jewish resident of the East End who made his living as an interpreter and doing minor legal work, told the committee that Wentworth Street, in particular, had seen some drastic changes to its make-up over the past eight years and was much "altered":

Committee:	What do you mean by altered?
Dejonge:	It has become foreign
Committee:	They were English?
Dejonge:	Yes
Committee:	And it has changed?
Dejonge:	Yes
Committee:	What has become of the English?
Dejonge:	They have been driven to Mile End and other places
Committee:	And their place has been taken by what?
Dejonge:	Russian and Polish Jews

His testimony was corroborated by another witness who appeared before the select committee, police Superintendent Thomas Arnold, Head of H (Whitechapel) Division who in various ways explained the departure "of our own population from the localities which are now inhabited by the foreigners"[39].

The witnesses seem to have been describing an early example of that demographic effect which in the next century might have been labelled 'white-flight', where inner-city areas become home to a new underclass, with the former residents moving to outer ring suburbs. In 1895, the newly arrived future editor of the *Arbeter Fraint* newspaper, Rudolph Rocker was aware that, "the influx of Jewish immigrants from Russia and Poland had gradually displaced the old inhabitants, and this unsavoury part of London had become the home of the Jewish working class"[40]. A few years earlier, in 1892,

Dr Robert Billing, Bishop Suffragan for East London and Rector of Spitalfields, noted that: "I know that during the last four years whole streets have become entirely occupied by Jews, foreign Jews, where there was not a Jew before"[41]. It was a reality that in coming years would make its mark in popular fiction, in novels such as Walter Wood's *The Enemy In Our Midst* (1906). In this work, the protagonist, native born casual labourer John Steel is advised early on by a policeman to:

> Clear out of this district. It isn't fit for a Christian Englishman to live in, an' your about the only one of 'em left. I can't give it a name but it ought to be called either Young Germany or the New Jerusalem.

Indeed, the term 'East End' of London had come to express more than just local geography, it had come to include the ethnic dimension, and Whitechapel, "London beyond Aldgate", was described akin "to a foreign town"[42]. In years to come, the travel writer Henry Vollam Morton would express the effect in similar vein during a brief visit to these neighbourhoods[43], at the end of which he commented, "I caught a penny omnibus back to England"*. Such poetic license, however, was prone to give way to hyperbole or worse. Taking issue with the influx of Jewish immigrants, a letter appearing in the *Times* in July 1887 inveighed against "pauper foreigners" who were accused of, "...successfully colonising Great Britain under the nose of Her Majesty's Government"[44].

At times, this urban topography told a story of two communities facing off rather than integrating:

> The assertion of Jewish territoriality was contested street by street by an indigenous population that was alarmed by the

---

* For a more contemporaneous report, in similar vein, see *The Alien Invasion*, by William Henry Wilkins (Methuen & Co, 1892), Chapter 2, 'The Increase And Extent': "In Whitechapel... It is easy to imagine oneself to be in a foreign city... That particular quarter of London is like being in the Ghetto of a continental city".

inflationary influx on rented accommodation... The trend, though, was towards complete segregation at the residential scale; streets tended to become all Jewish or remain all English[45].

Charles Booth described the effect in the years leading up to the Ripper story:

... each small street or group of houses tend to become entirely Jewish. They congregate together; whole blocks of buildings and whole streets are recognised as theirs.[4647]

The British-born population were not just curious observers to the transformation that was occurring at street level. Disruptions to the housing market brought on by rapid immigration caused more than dismay or despair, and spilled over into unrest. In some streets, the prevailing mood was that of a *"Judenhetze"* – ominously to actively anti-Jewish[48]. Some modern students of the period contend that much of the resulting street violence directed against the Jewish community was borne primarily of this clash for territory[49].

The Reverend H. A. Mason, Vicar of All Saints, Stepney, testified to the influx of Jewish newcomers and the "ill-feeling" that existed between them and the native-born population they were seen as supplanting[50]. Booth went further in describing such tensions, and as he put it, the "absorption of (the) district by Jews"[51]:

English remain in streets & courts which are wholly English... there is a mixture of English & Jews in some streets but friction & quarrels the inevitable result. The repulsion felt of one for the other is mutual.

As the displacement of the indigenous underclass transformed the area, tensions became palpable:

The Jews' alien status and the higher rents which accompanied them incited severe hostility when they settled in a new street as the Jewish quarter gradually spread out. Sensing that they would soon be submerged, some of the English and Irish inhabitants moved out at once. Others remained behind to give vent to cold or hot hostility, whether by calculated snubbing or, at times, by stones thrown and windows broken.[52]

Impugning the newcomers played its part in churning this social clash: it was said that they dragged down wages, could live on less and in poorer accommodation with less space, which pushed up rents and generally lowered living conditions and increased overcrowding. Such sentiments and the economic grievances on which they rested could be crudely whipped-up and were heard at anti-Jewish rallies, which were common from the mid 1880s[53] and echoed all too frequently in the press[54]. Social historian William Fishman, an *enfant du quartier,* referred to it as, "rhetoric derived from the lowest common denominator – the irrational hatred festering in the mind of the slum dweller... (and) by 1888 prejudice had broken surface"[55].

It had been building for years. In 1886 a letter writer to the *Pall Mall Gazette* had already described the new arrivals as a "pest and a menace to the native born East-Ender" and responsible for the area's "distress"[56]. In Spitalfields, in particular, and Whitechapel more broadly, Englishmen were depicted as being in a perilous situation as they competed for accommodation and more besides with the "scrapings of Russia and Poland"[57]. Writing as John Law, novelist Margaret Harkness captured the feeling of the moment in her 1888 novel *Out Of Work*:

> Why should they come here I'd like to know? London ain't what it used to be; it's just like a foreign city. The food ain't English; the talk ain't English. Why should all them foreigners come here to take our food out of our mouths, and live on victuals we wouldn't give to pigs?

Starting with the 1888 Trades Union Congress, organised labour called for strict legislation against the immigrants who they blamed for stealing their members' jobs. In the logic of these attitudes, the employment of an immigrant was equal to, "a betrayal of the English working man"[58]. It was not unknown for the language of class concern to become merged with anti-Semitic references, implicit and overt. In 1891, the pages of the *Labour Leader* inveighed against England's most famous family of Jewish bankers by using easily recognisable such commentary, alluding to classic parasitic, blood imagery on par with the worst examples emanating from the continent:

> The Rothschild leeches have for years hung on with distended suckers to the body politic of Europe. This family of infamous usurers... This blood-sucking crew has been the cause of untold mischief and misery in Europe during the present century, and has piled up its prodigious wealth chiefly through fomenting wars... Wherever there is trouble... and men's minds are distraught with fear of change and calamity, you may be sure that a hook-nosed Rothschild is at his games...[59]

Not all such commentary was wrapped in the vitriol of prejudice. Locally, Bishop Billing, who had worked among the poor for 20 years as Rector of Spitalfields, appeared to repeat genuine economic concerns when he wrote of the newcomers and the brewing social situation:

> It is contended that they injuriously compete with our own people... because of the glut they cause in the labour market, and because of their readiness to accept wages and to be content with conditions of living which are unacceptable, and something more than merely unacceptable, to the Englishman.[60]

Even the *Jewish Chronicle* aired opinions that were sympathetic to the native working class, mindful, like Bishop Billing, of underlying economic conditions:

Although a Jew, I am also an Englishman, and as such cannot fail to sympathise with the many hardships of our much tried English working classes; and can therefore, fully understand their just feeling of anger at seeing the work that should be theirs given to foreigners, thereby keeping them half starved.[61]

Fundamentally, the notion of Jews as an imposition on the East End community was widely held. Much of the friction could be traced to a very specific industrial reality: the 'sweating system', which was based on a wide network of sweatshops which exploited cheap, usually Jewish, labour for long hours in often unsanitary and unsafe environments. The following report in the socialist newspaper, the *Commonweal* in April 1888, was based on the official testimony of a tradesman* knowledgeable of the system's workings, and sheds light on the conditions endured by many of those caught in its grips:

...the sweating rooms were almost invariably very dirty and overcrowded, both as regarded sleeping rooms and often as regarded workrooms. He had found beds in underground cellars, and many times persons slept in the workrooms and took in lodgers. The place was generally unhealthy, and the atmosphere very detrimental, especially to child life. In one room there were six persons at work, and the cooking and working were going on in the same place. Cleanliness was never thought of at all. He had known eighteen persons living in one room about 9 ft. by 15 ft. The sweating was generally in Spitalfields, Whitechapel, and Commercial Road.

In turn, the already precarious conditions of British labour were considered at risk. An editorial in the *East London Advertiser* from 3 March 1888 summed up the pervading, if simplistic, sentiment:

The swarms of foreign Jews who have invaded the East London labour market, are chiefly responsible for the

---

* Mr William Hoffman; before the House of Lords select committee on the Sweating System, 17 and 20 April, 1888.

sweating system and the grave evils which are flowing from it – the brunt of the hardship... (falling) with tenfold severity upon the English man and woman.

In this climate, Jewish immigrants were often viewed as making their way at the expense of any hope of the native working class improving their lot, as well as taking away from them the small inducements that made life's struggle bearable. The immigrants would never be popular in Britain, opined one journalist, Samuel Jeyes, "since they succeed, if not in taking the bread out of English mouths, at least in reducing the margin of wages which might be spent on beer and gin and they are naturally... detested."[62]

By November 1887, cabinet minister Charles Ritchie, representing the electorate of St George's-In-The-East, had warned the Prime Minister, Lord Salisbury, that the immigration issue needed to be faced without delay[63]. As pressure mounted, the would-be politician and vehement campaigner against Jewish immigration, Arnold White, led a delegation to the Home Secretary in December. A self-styled authority on the East End, he had that year published his great polemic about East London's woes, *Problems Of A Great City*. A parallel work of his, *The Modern Jew* (1899), might best be described as a racist diatribe. In it, he suggested it was "high time for other nations to smite the Chosen People hip and thigh and to join Holy Russia in her artless effort to revenge the tragedy of Calvary".

It would be within the context of such a political lead-up that by early 1888 two parliamentary committees of enquiry were quickly dispatched to investigate what amounted to the 'foreign Jewish question': a House of Commons Select Committee on Emigration & Immigration (Foreigners), and a House of Lords Select Committee on the Sweating System. The latter was charged with looking into "the East-end of London" specifically, as part of its terms of reference. A close ally of White's, the Earl of Dunraven, would fill the role of chairman for the Lords' committee. White would appear as a witness before both the select committees. The crux of his evidence might succinctly be summed up in his own words from his attendance on 8 May:

The poor Russian Jew laughs at what he hears of English poverty and scanty fare. He has a false notion that the English artisan is generally overfed, and easily discontented, and that the Jew can live easily where an Englishman would starve.

The *Pall Mall Gazette* of 9 May 1888 was enthusiastic in support of his efforts: "Mr White's evidence will confirm all that we have urged as to the wisdom of not allowing this country to become the rubbish-bin of European labourers". Or as John Colomb, Conservative Member for the East London constituency of Bow & Bromley had put it a few months earlier, "I object to England with its overcrowded population, being made a human ashpit for the refuse population of the world"[64].

The editor of the *Pall Mall Gazette*, William Stead, a pioneer of the tabloid style, had also tried to pre-empt the two committees. Writing on 7 May 1888, and using language thematically not unlike White's, he was adamant:

It is by no means improbable that a crusade against the foreign paupers in our midst will rapidly come within the range of practical politics. The invasion of England is unquestionably a matter of grave alarm. It has gone on until the enemy is already in possession of the capital... We shall be surprised if the combined result of the Sweating and Immigration Committee is not to place some check upon the invasion of England.

Often overlooked is the extent to which these two high profile parliamentary select committees had a geographic focus on Whitechapel. Besides the Lords committee's terms of reference singling out the East End, the local member of parliament Samuel Montagu was on the House of Commons' select committee on immigration; and on the 3rd of July 1888 the Lords requested that he be granted special and ongoing leave to attend their own meetings, which was granted.

The conclusions of the first committee reports, both delivered at the end of July, vindicated the Jewish population in a way. Acknowledging the complexity of the issue, they did not recommend checks on immigration straight away as many had hoped, but proposed instead to continue to meet and gather information, effectively postponing an outcome and keeping the issue alive[65]. In that sense, they offered little by way of curbing sentiments on the streets of the East End. These would remain decidedly hostile, as the Jewish community was only too aware.

A testament to that were the comments of one irate workman, interviewed by the *British Weekly* at the same time the select committees had started deliberating. The government didn't care, the worker thundered:

> If we broke the heads of fifty Jews down here in Whitechapel something would be done to prevent this immigration.[66]

Unrealised expectations that the select committees would recommend firm curbs on immigration gave renewed fuel to flickering anti-immigrant fires that were prone to spark into life in the East End in those years[67]. Two such organised examples had been the founding by Arnold White and the Earl of Dunraven of both the Society for the Suppression of the Immigration of Destitute Aliens and an Association for Preventing the Immigration of Destitute Aliens, in 1886 and 1891 respectively.

While the latter had as its secretary, William Henry Wilkins, whose idea it was that the association should serve to protect British labour "from the hordes of destitute Jews", the former society could boast, at least nominally, not only cross-party, but even cross-confessional support[6869].

While it may have been politic for such social issues to be handled with the occasional veneer of philanthropic impartiality, under the surface as well as out on the street, the racial question was bubbling away, stoked by those willing to garner political capital. The practice was not the exclusive purview of rabble-rousers, would-be nationalists or hack journalists. Things could and did spill over into mainstream politics. Samuel Montagu MP, a practising Orthodox Jew, was on the receiving end of his fair share[70][71]. Though English born, when he entered politics elements of the press took to referring to him as "the Hebrew candidate", with attacks featuring clearly anti-Semitic references[72]. When one of Montagu's opponents missed out on being elected in 1886, he blamed "the ignorance and partisanship of Jewish electors"[73]. Rumour mongering was a less overt method employed against him. On one occasion in 1892, he was forced to take to the press to confront a whisper campaign that claimed he was planning to build a block of flats to be tenanted exclusively by Jews. It was one of many attempts to defame him during his 14 years representing Whitechapel in parliament[74].

The 'Irish Question' is one example of a national debate becoming contaminated by East End demographic tensions as it played out locally. When Montagu, a Liberal, spoke sympathetically in favour of Home Rule to local party delegates at the Jewish Working Men's Club in Alie Street on 6 June, 1888 he reminded them of their own national history of oppression. His party-political opponents quickly accused him of stirring up prejudice among his co-religionists "against their Anglo-Saxon brethren"[75].

To local Conservatives opposed to greater autonomy for Ireland, the issue was worth more than just hurling barbs of reverse-racism at Montagu, and seems to have been employed in a cynical exercise to try and garner local Jewish support to advantage. On 6 July, at a gathering of local Primrose League Conservatives in Goulston Street, media reports were cited from a Trades Council conference in Cork earlier in the year that had unanimously demanded the town's Jews be banished. The delegates across the Irish Sea had referred to Jews as "vampires" and "crucifying gypsies" to be exterminated[76]. With a notable Irish population resident in the East End, not to mention broader political implications, the warning to local Jews was clear: "they should not soil their hands by any such alliance"[77]. Tongue-in-cheek commentary a few months earlier in the *St James's*

Gazette had said much the same thing (see appendix i), and in its coverage of the Primrose League meeting, the *East London Advertiser* leant its support to the political tactic adopted by the local Tories. It also repeated details of the inflammatory Irish reports[78], though it is unlikely that Jewish members who attended the meeting needed to be manipulated to feel any more uneasy at the rising tide of anti-Semitism.

It is worth noting that in a few short months, Goulston Street would be the location where Jack The Ripper would leave an infamous piece of graffito directed against the Jews. English press coverage of the Cork Trades Council episode and Primrose League meeting in July are also telling because they provide a glimpse of common racial narratives swirling around at that moment.

It starts to become clear why, as early as October 1884, the *Polishe Yidle* had warned of the potential for a "bloody and terrible affair" of Russian-like proportions in Brick Lane off Commercial Street*. The same editorial described the attitudes of the native born population towards their Jewish neighbours:

> … do the English like the Jews? The answer is No! Go any Sabbath afternoon to Whitechapel and stand for a few moments in a doorway near where some of the English workers lounge with their pipes in their mouths, and you will hear, every time a Jew passes by, the loving call 'Bloody Jew!'... Look in the eyes of the passing Englishmen and can't you discern the look – which is already half indicative of a pogrom?[79]

In 1887, the Yiddish language *Die Tsukunft* carried reports of "ordinary people" tormenting the newcomers that eventually escalated into "a great fight between Jews and locals" on successive Saturdays, first in Brick Lane and then Church Lane[80]. A decade

---

*Many present-day references for this citation incorrectly point to another East End Yiddish language newspaper as the source, *Die Tsukunft*, and a date of 1879. But *Die Tsukunft* did not get under way until November 1884, having taken over from the *Polishe Yidl*. The editorial above is from one of the very last editions of the *Polishe Yidl*, that of 3 October 1884.

and a half later, little seems to have changed according to testimony heard at the Royal Commission on Alien Immigration: "Frequently late of a Saturday night you see some of the 'boys', as they call them, pummelling into the aliens"[81].

The picture was consistent with evidence provided to the ongoing Commons select committee on immigration in 1889 by Superintendent Arnold, who testified that the "lower order... British roughs" were known to assault passing Jews[82]. A more economically determinant analysis proposed that much of the, "... mindless Jew-bashing, reported by police and others, is better understood as an expression of defensive territorialism that came most readily to the poor and politically marginalised classes"[83]. Someone who might have been sympathetic to such a take, but was caught in the thick of it, was the anarchist Sam Dreen. He would one day write for the Yiddish language *Arbeter Fraint* and recalled arriving at the docks as an adolescent from Russia in 1899. It was a familiar tale: "We walked through a rough area, where the inhabitants hated immigrants and threw stones at us all the way to Leman Street"[84].

His editor, the Yiddish-speaking gentile Rudolph Rocker had arrived in East London on new year's day 1895 and soon began frequenting political meetings at a pub located on the same street where Jack The Ripper's canonical second victim, Annie Chapman, was found murdered. Despite the numerical superiority Jews enjoyed in Hanbury Street, attitudes towards them remained decidedly hostile[85]. Writing over half a century after events, Rocker could still describe the atmosphere of those days, as when evoking the following scene:

> At the Whitechapel end of Hanbury Street was the public house, the Sugar Loaf, where the Jewish comrades held their weekly meetings in a back room. There was no separate entrance, so we had to go through the pub, which was not pleasant, because there were always several drunks there, men and women, who used foul language and became abusive when they saw a foreigner.[86]

All out physical attacks on the newcomers, "Jew-baiting and Jew beatings", were not uncommon[8788]. On the eve of Jack The Ripper's 'Autumn of Terror', the *East London Observer* reported an incident involving Leah Ginski of 11 Boyd Street. The young woman had been sitting outside her front door when approached and called a "Jew bastard!" before being physically attacked and sustaining injuries[89]. The assault took place a stone's thrown from the International Working Men's Educational Club in Berner Street where another of Jack The Ripper's canonical victims would be found murdered in a few months.

In April 1888, a group of Torie toughs disrupted a socialist gathering in Bethnal Green, shouting insults at those they described as "dirty foreigners". When one of the speakers tried to engage a bully in the discussion, he was struck with a blow to the jaw and the assailant's exclamation of "I'm an Englishman, I am!"[90].

These sentiments and their antecedents would coalesce in more formal fashion in May 1901 with the establishment of the British Brothers League. Launched in the East End[91] with the aim of "restricting immigration of destitute foreigners"[92], within months the league would boast a membership of 6,000 mainly factory workers and the unemployed. Their rallies were well attended and regularly featured high profile speakers like William Evans-Gordon, the MP for the East End electorate of Stepney, and one of the league's main organisers.

Though there was a reluctance by some of the league's leadership to embrace an overtly anti-Semitic position, there is little question that stopping the immigration of foreign Jews was the point of the campaign and racism was rife within its ranks[93]. The league's founding president, William Stanley Shaw, once lamented a future London becoming "a Jewish city on the Thames"[94], while the *East London Observer* went so far as to distance itself from the movement, citing concerns about anti-Semitism[95]. When anti-Jewish riots broke out in Ireland in the early months of 1904, the league passed a resolution in support of the virulent anti-Semite, Father John Creagh, whose sermons had sparked the 'Limerick pogrom'. The British Brothers League thanked the firebrand preacher:

…for the noble work he had undertaken to prevent a class of undesirable aliens who have received the hospitality of the Irish race from demoralising the nation and bringing misery into the homes of our Irish Brothers and Sisters through their inborn instinct of greed, usury and arrogance.[96]

In subsequent years there would be notable anti-Jewish disturbances in south Wales (1911) and Leeds (1917)[97]. On 23 September 1917, street fighting broke out in the East End, in Bethnal Green, between nativist elements and Jews, resulting in "an excitable crowd" of some 5,000 people cornering the Jewish inhabitants of Blythe and Teesdale streets who were forced to seek refuge indoors. Stones were thrown and windows broken before police managed to restore order. An arrest was subsequently made when someone tried to lead his companions onto further action: "There's another gang of f-----g Jews," he shouted before being arrested[98][99].

Less than a generation on, the East End would be regarded a stronghold of the British Union of Fascists and would host its leader, Oswald Mosley, at public speaking events[100]. Such colloquiums could trace their genesis to anti-Jewish rallies prevalent during the mid-1880s[101]. The social historian William Fishman, born in London in 1921 and having lived through the period *in situ*, was in no doubt when describing this link between what he called, the "legacy of racism" and its bearing on "local support for Mosleyite Fascism in the 1930s"[102].

Of an earlier generation to Fishman, author Arthur Goldberg had similarly joined the dots. Born and raised in the East End, he left home for South Africa in 1876 and returned in old age. Writing his autobiography in 1936, at the height of local strutting by English Blackshirts, he recalled his childhood:

Oh! there was Jew-baiting in the East End then, as now, but in those days it was not considered of sufficient news value to be mentioned in the papers. There was no sort of ceremonial made of it, with banners and crudely worded pamphlets and young men dressing themselves up in quasi-military uniforms. They just did it single-handed, if they felt like it... Christian versus Jew.[103]

This was the sentiment and landscape of the East End street in the decades to 1900 and beyond. So much so, that in 1886 the *Pall Mall Gazette* had polemicised about a "Judenhetz(e) brewing in East London"[104], and in 1887, of a coming "anti-Jewish riot in the East End"[105]. In the same year, the *Times* reproduced a letter of Arnold White's warning of "the chapel bell... set a-ringing by a few Jews being done to death in Whitechapel"[106].

Courtesy of Jack The Ripper, such dire prognostications were about to move inexorably closer.

End of Chapter 1 notes:
East End population statistics and demography

Booth's population figures and number of Jewish residents 1886-87, based on Registration Districts & School Board divisions		
	population	Jewish residents
Whitechapel	73,518	28,790
Bethnal Green (included as part of Hackney)	127,641 (not included in Tower Hamlets total)	2,580 - 5,000 (Booth's estimates cited at different times)
St. George's-in-the-East	47,578*	5,880
Stepney	62,063	not specified
Mile End Old Town	110,321	7,750
Poplar	166,393	not specified
Tower Hamlets total population	459,873	-
East End Jewish population[§]	-	45,000 - 47,420

* more accurate figure as published in *Life & Labour of the People* Vol II

Author's comment (i): I have attempted to arrive at an estimate of the East End population to allow a better geographical reflection of setting, rather than just relying on the figure for Tower Hamlets cited in *Life & Labour of the People*. As Booth himself alluded to, the idea of an East End should allow for some degree of statistical input from Bethnal Green (which the raw Tower Hamlet figures do not reflect). Accordingly, I have shifted the geographic focus slightly to

---

[§] While Booth's figures make for an authoritative, baseline estimate, they were quickly rendered out of date by the fast pace of demographic change taking place in the East End by 1888. Further, many of the newer arrivals would not have been reflected in the official figures, given the disorganised, furtive nature of their arrival and domicile in England.

the north at the expense of the easternmost, outlying district, Poplar. This exercise seems not entirely dissimilar to Booth's, when he tried to work out the Jewish population's presence in the "East End": he included Bethnal Green but appears to have left out not only Poplar, but Stepney as well. The effect has been to create a slightly greater centre of gravity around Whitechapel. My estimate for the total East End population is 421,121, including Whitechapel, Saint George's-in-the-East, Mile End Old Town, Stepney and Bethnal Green; or 498,625, if including Poplar.

Author's comment (ii): For a broader discussion on why the School Board numbers had proved invaluable to both Booth and Arkell as a good means of extracting reliable statistical data, see *The Jew In London: A Study Of Racial Character And Present-Day Conditions*, C. Russell & H.S. Lewis (1901) pp. intro – xxix, xxxiv-xxxvi.

Snapshot: Christ Church school, Brick Lane, as it still stands today. By 1888 the teachers had to learn Yiddish to communicate with their students.

CHAPTER 2

JUDENHETZE

> If you would understand the immortal agony of Jewry, go into the East-End colony.
>
> Simon Gilbert

It was 3.40am on Friday, 31 August 1888. The faintest glow from a none too nearby street lamp helped illuminate the gloom. Barely sufficient, it managed to reveal the outlines of a woman lying next to the gutter in front of a gateway. The first passers-by to come upon her, considered whether she may have been a drunk passed out by the side of the road.

The scene was notable, not simply as a cruel metaphor for a moment in time and place, but because the woman had in fact been murdered. Jack The Ripper's first canonical victim lay on the slender pavement of this narrow, cobbled street called Buck's Row, a hundred yards parallel and back from a major thoroughfare, Whitechapel Road.

Police would later identify her as Mary Ann "Polly" Nichols, a 42 year-old alcoholic who helped earn her living on the streets. An autopsy would reveal she had sustained two savage cuts to the throat, the second down to the vertebrae. Significant mutilations to her abdomen and comparatively lesser ones to the sexual organs were noted. Beat police and nearby watchmen had heard nothing, nor local residents.

Barely a week later and still reeling from Nichols' slaying, an indignant East End would wake to news of another outrage on Saturday, 8 September. The mutilated body of canonical second victim, Annie Chapman, had been found shortly after 6.00am in the back yard of a house at 29 Hanbury Street.

There was much that united the two women in life as in death. Chapman, like Nichols, belonged to a class for whom survival was a daily challenge. She too was a drinker who resorted to prostitution to get by and was in her forties[107]. The most conspicuous similarity was the manner in which they had met their violent deaths. Chapman's throat had sustained a double slashing of such severity that the police's H Division surgeon Dr George Bagster Phillips opined "an attempt had been made to separate the bones of the neck"[108]. Indeed, the head had been nearly severed from the body. She had been disembowelled, the sexual organs attacked, and the pelvic organs, including the womb, had been taken.

Witness evidence would prove somewhat less than tangible. On the one hand, Chief Inspector Donald Swanson in charge of the overall investigation noted that, "inquiries did not supply the police with the slightest clue to the murderer"[109]. Whereas, Coroner Wynne Baxter believed that local resident, Elizabeth Long, had made an important sighting of Chapman with a "foreigner", whose face she admittedly did not see, about half an hour before the body was found. Testimony by Albert Cadosh, resident at number 27 next door, and John Richardson, a tradesman whose mother lived in the building itself, provided some degree of circumstantial support for Mrs Long. The medical evidence, however, backed by the police[110] suggested that Chapman had already been dead an hour or more, "hence the evidence of Mrs Long which appeared to be so important to the Coroner, must be looked upon with some amount of doubt, which is to be regretted," reads an official Home Office document prepared by Swanson[111].

If officialdom was somewhat out of sync in its own impressions of the most recent murder, things were exponentially worse on the streets of Whitechapel. There, fact and rumour – as would become only too apparent – made little pretence of existing in hermetically distinct isolation, and it was not unknown for the media to add to the confusion. To be fair, newspapers often reported gossip for what it was, like when the *Star* produced the following report on the day that Chapman's body was found.

> ...all sorts of rumours were flying about. The woman living next door declared that this morning there was written on the door of No. 29, "This is the fourth, I will murder sixteen more and then give myself up." There was no basis for this story, however, there being no chalk mark on the door except "29."[112]

The example is a good one. Other newspapers had picked up on variations of the same story and printed it as fact. In reality, the press could be just as prone to feed the scuttlebutt as feed off it, even if it was only to tear down a straw man, or raise one in its place. For instance, in laying to rest the supposed importance of an innocuous leather apron found near the scene of Chapman's murder (or possibly, a piece of it[113]), the *Pall Mall Gazette* fuelled already existing embers of speculation about a ghoulish "Hebrew" menace stalking the neighbourhood:

> One report has it that the leather apron found near the place where the body lay, belonged to a man whose name is unknown, but who is nicknamed "Leather Apron".[114]

The rumour mill had been alert to 'Leather Apron' within days of the murder of Polly Nichols, as his media 'debut' at about that time attests[115]. This is from the *Pall Mall Gazette* edition of September 8, the day Chapman was killed:

> He is five feet four or five inches in height, and wears a dark close-fitting cap. He is thickset, and has an unusually thick neck. His hair is black, and closely clipped, his age being about thirty-eight or forty. He has a small black moustache. The distinguishing feature of costume is a leather apron, which he always wears, and from which he gets his nickname. His expression is sinister, and seems to be full of terror for the women who describe it. His eyes are small

and glittering. His lips are usually parted in a grin which is not only not reassuring, but excessively repellent. He is a slipper-maker by trade, but does not work. His business is blackmailing women late at night. A number of men in Whitechapel follow this interesting profession. He has never cut anybody, so far as is known, but always carries a leather knife, presumably as sharp as leather knives are wont to be. This knife a number of the women have seen. His name nobody knows, but all are united in the belief that he is a Jew or of Jewish parentage, his face being of a marked Hebrew type. But the most singular characteristic of the man is the universal statement that in moving about he never makes any noise. What he wears on his feet the women do not know, but they agree that he moves noiselessly. His uncanny peculiarity to them is that they never see him or know of his presence until he is close by them… "Leather Apron" never by any chance attacks a man.

Was the street talk surrounding this sinister character, and its reporting, an indication of what was in the offing? As news spread of Chapman's murder, simmering social tensions on the street quickly came to the fore. Cries of "down with the Jews" were soon heard, giving way to signs of something worse, akin the warnings issued by the *Polishe Yidl* in 1884 and the *Pall Mall Gazette* in 1886. The *East London Observer* reported[116]:

A Riot against the Jews

On Saturday in several quarters of East London the crowds who had assembled in the streets began to assume a very threatening attitude towards the Hebrew population of the district. It was repeatedly asserted that no Englishman could have perpetrated such a horrible crime as that of Hanbury-street, and that it must have been done by a Jew - and forthwith the crowds proceeded to threaten and abuse such of the unfortunate Hebrews as they found in the streets.

Covering the same disturbance, the front page of *Lloyd's Weekly* gave a more in-depth perspective:

As the day advanced and the Jewish East-End crowds congregated around the scene of the murder, and its neighbourhood became more leavened with English working men, the excitement grew; and, unfortunately, owing to the rumours about the individual "Leather Apron," took a rather nasty turn. Bodies of young roughs raised cries against the Jews, and many of the disreputable and jabbering women sided with them. This state of things caused several stand-up fights, thus putting a further and serious strain on the police, many of whom began to express their fears of rioting.

Describing the scene in the district last night, a correspondent says: - The excitement in Hanbury-street and the surrounding neighbourhood still continues, and extra police have been employed to keep a course for the traffic of the evening, but in this they are very much hampered by noisy crowds of men and boys crying "Down with the Jews." Sometimes there is a show of resistance, but the strong force of police on the spot are equal to the occasion, and promptly separate assailants. Just as our correspondent was writing a gang of young vagabonds marched down Hanbury-street shouting "Down with the Jews!" "It was a Jew who did it!" "No Englishman did it!". After these the police were prompt, and whenever there was a stand they quickly, and without ceremony, dispersed them. There have been many fights, but the police are equal to it, as men are held in reserve under cover, and when there is a row they rush out and soon establish order. As the night advances the disorderly mobs who openly express antipathy to the Jews increase, and a request has been forwarded to headquarters for extra men.[117]

A man named John Pizer, a second-generation Polish Jew, was eventually found hiding with family in Mulberry Street and arrested on suspicion of being the dreaded 'Leather Apron'. When he appeared at the inquest into Chapman's murder he rationalised his decision to lay low. He'd had no choice, he told coroner Baxter: "I should have been torn to pieces". By this time, and without fear of contradiction he could also boast, "I have been released, and am not now in custody – I wish to vindicate my character to the whole world". With which Baxter could but agree: "I have called you partly in your own interest in order to give you opportunity of doing so"[118]. Pizer's alibi to police had proven unassailable, which did not mean he could do without their protection to get home from the inquest and past the waiting mob outside[119].

There were other things that no amount of police protection could defend from, like a barb spoken by a magistrate in an unrelated case the day after Pizer's release: "The Pole has no business in this country. He is taking the bread out of the mouths of Englishmen"[120]. Which was a slightly more emphatic flight of fancy from the bench than coroner Baxter's, who in summing up, expressed the opinion that Chapman's murderer may have exhibited "Judas-like approaches".

As if things weren't bad enough in these fever-pitched days, an ominous report appeared in the *Star* dealing with the old fable of 'Jewish ritual murder', a catch-all anti-Semitic slander that referred to the supposed ritual slaughter of Christians by Jews. Child martyrs, like William of Norwich and Little Saint Hugh of Lincoln, were two local examples of the blood libel historically levelled at Jews in England, continental Europe and beyond. Chaucer's *Canterbury Tales* loosely captured one such episode of medieval propaganda in 'The Prioress's Tale', which directly referenced the latter case, possibly inspired by the former[121]. "'My throte is kut unto my nekke boon', Seyde this child". This racist conspiracy theory was still receiving qualified support as late as 1853, when one newly published work explained that the young St William had fallen during, "a time when the Jews were powerful in our land… a martyr to their hatred of the Christians"[122].

That the blood libel had survived into modern times among segments of the English population is confirmed by reports from Bradford in

January and February 1889, involving the case of murder victim John Gill:

> Among the more ignorant inhabitants of the district where the victim lived there is a belief that the crime is the work of the Jews, this being due to a partial survival of the old and gross superstition which credits the Jews with the sacrifice of Christian children at Christmas time.[123]

Interestingly, first reports immediately made a parallel to the East End murders, though they were unrelated:

> The epidemic of murder and mutilation which has spread consternation in the East-end of London has at length broken out in the provinces, and although the crime discovered on the morning of the 29th ult. at Bradford has, from the methods of the assassin and the sex of the victim, apparently no direct connection with the Whitechapel outrages, there can be little doubt that the mind of the culprit has been strongly influenced by recent occurrences in the metropolis.[124]

Brought to bear in the context of rising social tensions, it is not difficult to see how a killer's rampage could have acted as a lightning rod and brought new life to an old lie. Though it is hard to pinpoint exactly when during Whitechapel's 'Autumn of Terror' the accusation had re-surfaced, it is likely to have emerged from lingering folk memory[125], possibly reinvigorated by recently arrived gentile migrants hailing from the continent. But whatever role may have been played by an infusion from beyond the British Isles, there is evidence it had proven a resilient local echo, even putting aside the synchronous Bradford case.

The influential Orientalist, Sir Richard Burton, had been ready to publish a work as early as 1887, if not many years earlier, containing a section titled 'Human Sacrifice Amongst The Sephardim Or Eastern Jews'. Through a combination of circumstance and wise counsel it did not go to print in his lifetime, not until 1898. Thanks to behind the scenes negotiations and legal manoeuvrings, in part involving the Board Of Deputies For British Jews, much of the more offensive material was omitted when it was eventually published in an altered and abridged form as *The Jew, The Gypsie and El Islam.* This did not stop revived attempts to publish the work in its totality, on and off, for more than a decade. The episode serves as an indication that the issue was controversial, but equally, a current one[126].

By 1900, a group of conscientious English Catholics had become so concerned that they wrote to Pope Leo XIII requesting a public repudiation of the blood libel. The eminent petitioners were led by Herbert Vaughan, Cardinal-Archbishop of Westminster, and included Lord Russell of Killowen, Lord Chief Justice of England and previously Attorney General (1886 and 1892-94). Their enlightened appeal fell on deaf ears. Worse, the Holy See tore down their hopes with a cutting concluding advisory that "ritual murder is a historical certainty"[127][128][129].

In the lead-up to the 'Limerick pogrom' of 1904, Father Creagh could make use of the ritual murder accusation to reach out to his congregants as he railed against the Jews in one of his sermons:

> Nowadays they dare not kidnap and slay Christian children, but they will not hesitate to expose them to a longer and even more cruel martyrdom… to fasten themselves like leeches and to draw our blood when they have been forced away from other countries.[130]

Some academics researching the period in British history, including Sara Libby Robinson, have noted the tendency for anti-immigrant rhetoric to stray into terrain replete with classic anti-Semitic motifs. At their core, these contained expressions of blood imagery: of Jews being portrayed as blood-suckers, parasites and vampires. Indeed, readers would have found it impossible to read this far without having picked up on the theme. In her research, Robinson honed in on one aspect: "the fundamental connection between Jews and vampires is blood, specifically blood libels"[131].

For the local Jewish community, fear of the libel unleashed in the present anti-immigration and increasingly anti-Semitic environment had been lurking in the shadows since the beginning of the 1880s. While there had been earlier cases, at least three famous international episodes had featured in the British press during this period, beginning in 1881 with the Fornaraki Affair (Alexandria, Egypt / Corfu, Greece); though it was the Tisza-Eszlar (Hungary, Austria-Hungary) and Ritter cases (Galicia, Polish Austria-Hungary) which would reverberate loudest and longest. No doubt, media coverage which was want to repeat references to accused "Jewish butchers"[132] and other blood imagery, unintentionally played its part in reanimating the folk fable as court proceedings dragged on for years through legal twists and turns. There is no question that, to varying degrees, the details of these cases were aired well and truly.

Where British editorialising touched on the reports they usually gave little to no credence to the substantive charge, and short thrift was the response sometimes provided by the foreign correspondents themselves. On occasion, however, and to the great chagrin of London's Jewish community and many right-minded people besides, they could be less than clear-cut in refuting the libel[133]. One such example comes courtesy of the *Globe*'s coverage of the Fornaraki case, on 18 April 1881:

> …if it be true that *vox populi vox Dei*, then one should surely pause before exonerating the Jews of Alexandria of every suspicion of guilt.

On this occasion, to make matters worse, the *Globe*'s Cairo correspondent raised another episode in the sad catalogue of ritual killing accusations[134]: that levelled against the Jews of Damascus in 1840 for the alleged murder of the 62-two-year old Sardinian, Father Thomas. Though the men accused were all proven to be innocent, it was nevertheless an infamous case that had taken decades to die down in press coverage across Europe and the popular mindset[135].

Another example of a less than wholehearted rejection of the blood libel was found in the *Spectator*'s coverage in 1883 of the Tisza-Eszlar case. The 14-year-old female victim had allegedly had her throat cut by Jews inspired by religious ritual for the purpose of collecting her blood:

> The ancient and extraordinary charge against the Jews of sacrificing human beings in their Passover rites has been revived in Hungary. A girl named Esther Solymosi was recently murdered, or supposed to be murdered, at Tisza Esslar, and certain Jews were accused of cutting her throat in the synagogue... The charge looks prima facie ridiculous, and derives its whole importance from its recurrence from time to time in widely separated countries and in nearly every century. We have read much apologetic Jewish literature but have never seen a reasonable explanation either of the charge, or of what is much more wonderful, the persistent popular belief in it. If that has any foundation, which is most improbable, there must exist embedded in Judaism a cabalistic sect which has preserved through ages some dark tradition of the efficacy in extreme cases of human sacrifice.[136]

The last sentence in the report had an almost word for word resonance with the notably qualified dismissal of the libel, as famously uttered by Czar Nicholas I. In 1835, he had said that, "among the Jews there probably exist fanatics or sectarians who consider Christian blood necessary for their rites"[137].

Another piece of coverage from 1883 pertaining to the Tisza-Eszlar case, entitled "The Trial Of Hungarian Jews" appeared in the *Times*. It reported dispassionately on the prosecution's case which, "undertook to prove, from the Talmud, that ritual murder was held lawful among the Jews"[138], but in the process, the libel got a very distinguished airing as it had in its pages previously[139] and would in future. Foreign-based correspondents reporting on these cases often fell into the trap of simply relaying the latest developments uncritically, inadvertently giving equal weight to both sides of the argument. Even putting aside the absurdity represented by the blood libel, the prosecution cases were prone to basic inaccuracy and contradiction, but were able to provide a degree of sensationalism that sober refutation by the defence could not always do. Ultimately, correspondents were limited to reporting these cases as they played themselves out, without necessarily weighing up the validity of legal argument or providing moral commentary. Occasionally, readers were left in no doubt about the mendacious flight of fancy entailed by the charges, sometimes not. Then there were those times when they seemed to give a degree of legitimacy to the ritual murder accusation, as happened at the height of the 'Autumn of Terror', creating great controversy in the process, as will be discussed in chapter 4.

These reports from the early to mid 1880s sparked organised and immediate responses from London's Jewish leaders in concert with the local Jewish press. One unintended consequence was the resulting public to and fro, which managed to further air the issue; and in the case of the *Spectator,* dig its heels in while maintaining it did not believe in the veracity of the blood libel.

The following excerpt is from a piece that defended its earlier reporting of the Hungarian trial and was written in response to criticisms from the Jewish community. The more it tried to make its argument, the less it seemed to succeed:

THE MURDER AT TISZA ESSLAR

Jewish contemporaries are quite annoyed because we recently suggested, a propos of the trial at Tisza Esslar, that if evidence were ever produced in favour of the absurd libel on them that Christian victims were slaughtered at the Passover, it might only indicate that some Cabalistic sect with a traditional faith in human sacrifice was embedded among their people. We intended to suggest a defence unassailable by evidence as to special cases, but they accuse us of "philosophic dislike" to Jews, and readiness to receive accusations against them. They are entirely mistaken. We have no more dislike for Jews than for Arabs or Parsees, or any other Oriental people – dis-liking only the Jewish desire to remain separate, yet cease to be thought so – and have immense respect for the intellect, the fortitude, and the philanthropy of the higher men of the race... Here is a quiet community, dwelling for years, it may be centuries, among the Hungarians – who, again, are accustomed to see among them a medley of races – and yet exciting such hatred, that the moment a Christian girl disappears they are suspected of murdering her, and entire classes help to eke out the "blood accusation"... There must be fear, dread, of the Jews in Tisza Esslar, or hatred could hardly rise so nearly to insanity, and we should like to know what the root of that fear is. The Jewish Chronicle will not tell us, we dare say, but perhaps other witnesses, who know Hungary well, will. Is there not in Hungary, Roumania, and South Russia, mixed up with the dislike for Jews as separatists, and the envy of them as accumulators, a distinct belief that they among mankind are specially sorcerers, and can inflict disease by wishing it? Such a belief prevails among many Mussulman peoples, and it may well have wandered North and West, kept up by the Jewish traditional knowledge of medicine, their legendary lore, and their strong temptation when powerless – under wrong to invoke the Powers above to avenge them. Such a belief would account for much, if not all, of the popular credulity, among peoples who in their habits of mind still retain the deep impress of the East.[140]

The polemics and controversy surrounding the case certainly ensured it made its mark in the British media. In fact, over the course of the 1880s Tisza-Eszlar was the cause célèbre that via one reference or another, just would not die. Elements of it reappeared in the press up to and including the height of Jack The Ripper's murder spree, long after those accused had been acquitted. When in late March 1888, flooding in the wine growing town of Tokaj, Hungary, hit the newspapers, its own renown was trumped by its geographic proximity to the, "...village of *Tiszaeszlar*, chiefly known from the trial of the Jews accused of murdering a Christian girl"[141]. And on 22 September, just weeks after the East End's anti-Jewish riot, newspapers carried reports of the suicide of Hungarian police officer Andreas Recsky, "implicated in the Tisza-Eszlar trials, when a number of poor Jews were accused of having butchered" Esther Solymosi[142].

The other widely reported case from Austria-Hungary was that of an accused Polish Jew named Moses Ritter, which hit the press in 1882, though it originally dated to 1881. Media coverage such as the following was carried widely and did not cease, even after Ritter was finally acquitted in 1886 after having been condemned to death on three separate occasions.

SENSATIONAL CRIMINAL TRIAL

VIENNA, Oct. 10. (1884) - A protracted and sensational criminal trial, almost rivalling the celebrated Tisza Eslar case in the public interest which it has excited, was concluded at Cracow to-day. The accused, a Jew, named Ritter, and his wife, and one Strachlinski, a Polish Christian, were charged with the murder of a Christian girl whom Ritter had seduced. It was alleged that Ritter, finding the girl was *enciente**, determined in accordance with a Jewish superstition, which regards illicit union of a Hebrew and a Christian and the issue thereof as unholy, to destroy both her and her unborn child. Accordingly he enticed the girl into a cellar, and, with the assistance of his wife and Strachlinski, murdered her in the most brutal manner with an axe. The prisoners then dissected the body and distributed the remains in various hiding places... Portions of the body were discovered in a brook. Inquiries were instituted, resulting in the arrest of Ritter and his confederates. Strachlinski made a full confession, but afterwards withdrew it, alleging it had been extracted by torture. The prisoners were tried and convicted

---

* pregnant.

at the assizes at Rzeszou, Ritter being sentenced to death, and the other prisoners to penal servitude. Against this sentence they appealed on technical grounds, and a new trial was ordered which commenced at Cracow at the beginning of last week. It is alleged that the funds for the defence have been provided for by some rich Jews in this city. Seventy-two witnesses were examined, and the trial finished today. The three prisoners were convicted, and sentenced to death, amidst a scene of the greatest excitement.[143]

Such dangerous contextual parameters having been established in lead-up years, it is understandable that within days of Chapman's murder Jewish voices should want to nip in the bud whispers of "blood guiltiness", as did the *Star*'s "Jewish Correspondent" in the edition of 11 September 1888 and the *Jewish Chronicle* a few days afterwards. It also confirms that rumours relating to the ritual murder charge were current[144], keeping in mind the time lag that was involved before registering in the press. From the *Star:*

THE JEWS AND THE MURDERS.

What a Jewish Correspondent says of Their Horror of Blood.

If the panic-stricken people who cry "Down with the Jews" because they imagine that a Jew has committed the horrible and revolting crimes which have made Whitechapel a place to be dreaded know anything at all of the Jewish horror of blood itself, they would pause before they invoked destruction on the head of a peaceful and law-abiding people. Of course, there is little danger of our having in civilised London a recurrence of scenes enacted in the East - in Greece, in Turkey, and in Asia Minor! It is only in recent years that the scandalous superstition known as the "blood accusation" has been exploded by the light of inquiry. Some years ago, in the countries mentioned, many a Jewish Community was plundered, outraged, and massacred to satisfy a bloodthirsty mob eager for revenge, because a Christian had been discovered dead in a field or on the banks of a river. It was thought by the rude population that the Jewish festival of Passover necessitated A HUMAN SACRIFICE, and that in order to propitiate their God the Jews seized a Christian and put him to death... That the beast who has made East London a terror is not a Jew I feel assured. There is something too horrible, too unnatural, too un-Jewish I would say, in the terrible series of murders for an Israelite to be the monster. There never was a Jew yet who could have steeped himself in such loathsome horrors as those to which publicity has been given in *The Star*. His nature revolts at blood-guiltiness, and the whole theory and practical working of the Whitechapel butchery are opposed to Jewish character.

The *Jewish Chronicle*:

NOTES OF THE WEEK.

Without doubt the foreign Jews in the East End of London have been in some peril - though happily averted - during the past week owing to the sensationalism of which the district has been the centre. There has been forcibly brought home to us *the genesis of the anti-Jewish outbreaks which still occasionally occur abroad, and which were not unknown in England in ancient times*. It is so easy to inflame the popular mind when it is startled by hideous crime, that sensation-mongers incur a fearful responsibility when they add to the excitement by giving currency to every idle rumour.[145] (author's italics)

Not only Jewish voices were speaking up, aware that murmurs of blood libel were currency during these heady days. Another chastising report, from the *Daily News,* seemed to be saying as much. Concerned for the safety of the Jewish community, it is only hinted at, not daring to mention its name. It was published on the same day as the *Star*'s report on 11 September:

There is good reason why... the public acceptance of the maniacal theory should be endorsed and encouraged. There is positive danger in the growth of any other opinion at present in Whitechapel. As we have said, the mutilation of bodies... is foreign to the English style in crime. There is a disposition at once, therefore, to set down such atrocities to the credit of some ill bred and ill nourished foreigner from the lowest dens of vice in Europe. So, in Whitechapel, there was arising a murmur of ugly foreboding for some of the foreign element there. Sheer rumour of the silliest kind was beginning to take an odious precision, and there was arising in the East End a Judenhetze more abhorrent than that which abroad is due to religious fanaticism.[146]

On the streets of Whitechapel, such rumour would have easily merged and become subsumed within the urban myth of 'Leather Apron' and a more general, panicked anti-Semitism of which John Pizer's woes were symptom, as indeed the following report demonstrates. Any suspicion that the above cited articles were trying to pre-emptively forestall the charge of Jewish ritual murder, rather than responding to rumours already current, is laid bare in the following early report from the *Pall Mall Gazette*. It was printed on 8 September, the same day Chapman was murdered, and pre-dates other reports, Jewish or gentile by several days:

The excitement in the vicinity is intense, and *unfounded rumours are flying about*. One report has it that the leather apron found near the place where the body lay, belonged to a man whose name is unknown, but who is nicknamed "Leather Apron," and evidently known in the district... Looking at the corpse no one could think otherwise than that the murder had been committed by a maniac or wretch of the lowest type of humanity. Indeed, we should have to go to *the wilds of Hungary or search the records of French lower peasant life before a more sickening and revolting tragedy* could be told.[147] (author's italics)

If it was less than clear that this sober piece was alluding to whispers of blood libel by its oblique reference to "unfounded rumours are flying about" intertwined with Jewish bogeyman "Leather Apron", then the guarded reference to Tisza-Eszlar* and feudal times puts it beyond doubt. In fact, the two news items, that of the *Daily News* and the *Pall Mall Gazette,* are close enough reflections of one another to corroborate the story they were trying ever so cautiously to report: that a very specific, racist type of rumour was abroad in Whitechapel.

If the media had been contained in their understandable desire to tiptoe around accusatory talk of blood libel on the streets of London to that point then all bets would soon be off. Both the Ritter and Tisza-Eszlar cases were about to reverberate loudly, as Jack The Ripper made a pronouncement he wanted everyone to hear clearly: he was a Jew. Supposedly. Thus would speak a serial killer, to all apparent intent confirming one body of strongly-held popular opinion that, "no Englishman did it"[148].

---

* a village at the foot of the rugged Carpathian mountains in eastern Hungary, *ie* the very "wilds of Hungary".

End of Chapter 2 notes:

Der Proceß

In 1948, the events surrounding the Tisza-Eszlar trial would feature in a German language film brought to the screen by director Georg Wilhelm Pabst, a Bohemian native born in 1885 and one of the early masters of German cinema. Described as "a strong indictment of anti-Semitism", the film *Der Proceß* (The Trial) won best director and best actor awards at the 9th Venice Film Festival[149].

In taking the prize, Pabst beat some notable entries, namely Roberto Rossellini's *L'Amore* and Laurence Olivier's *Hamlet*.

CHAPTER 3

BLAMED FOR NOTHING

Where there is a breaking away from the rigid doctrines of political economy as taught by capitalist mouthpieces, it is largely due to the influence and to the new light of Socialism shed around his English shopmates by the refugee workmen. Are we then to allow the issues at stake in the (class) struggle between the robbers and the robbed to be obscured by an anti-foreigner agitation?

Conspicuous in urging restrictions on foreign labourers, stands Mr. Arnold White, who thinks a Jew-hunt possible in the East End, and is fearful lest, as he told a Government official lately, the patience of certain Irish cockneys should be exhausted and they take the matter into their own hands.

'The Blarsted Furriners'*
Commonweal, 28 April 1888

John Pizer must have still been looking over his shoulder when in the early morning hours of the last Saturday of September 1888, the twin murders of Elizabeth Stride and Catherine Eddowes set London reeling. If the racial genie was not already out of the bottle, then Jack The Ripper had just tried to put the question beyond doubt. In the time it would take him to kill these latest victims and escape, he would boldly announce an anti-Semitic narrative as a means of incriminating the easiest of scapegoats. The locations of these two murders would offer a parallel subtext.

---

* Over two editions, 28 April & 5 May – the editorial (by Frank Kitz) offered a general criticism of Arnold White's anti-Semitic and anti-socialist views, before zeroing-in on a more detailed critique of his testimony before the parliamentary select committees.

The attack on Elizabeth Stride occurred inside the entrance of a yard, from which premises the Yiddish language radical newspaper *Arbeter Fraint* was printed and published. Immediately adjacent, and sharing the yard at 40 Berner Street was the International Working Men's Educational Club, which owned the newspaper. It was a focal point for local Jewish radicals. Approaching 1am, 20 to 30 people were still in the building fraternising and singing after the conclusion of the evening's lecture, "Why Jews Should Be Socialists".

Only fifteen minutes earlier, by his own estimate, Israel Schwartz a Hungarian immigrant, had turned off Commercial Road making his way south on his way home. The scene that greeted him as he walked down Berner Street would see him become one of the case's most important witnesses as he came upon the scene of a stocky man assaulting a woman in the gateway of Dutfield's Yard. Dreading involvement, possibly not grasping that the woman was engaged in the opening throes of a life battle, "Schwartz... became alarmed and ran away"[150]. He crossed to the other side of the street where he noticed a man lighting a pipe, and kept going. As he extracted himself from the situation, the woman's assailant shouted out "Lipski", a local anti-Semitic epithet, while the man with the pipe ran in Schwartz's same direction for some distance. Metropolitan Police Inspector Fredrick Abberline, in charge of detectives on the ground in Whitechapel, explained Schwartz's account after questioning him closely, with a friend of the Hungarian's acting as interpreter[151]:

...since a jew named Lipski was hanged for the murder of a jewess in 1887 the name has very frequently been used by persons as mere ejaculation by way of endeavouring to insult the jew to whom it has been addressed, and as Schwartz has a strong jewish appearance I am of the opinion it was addressed to him as he stopped to look at the man he saw ill-using the deceased woman.[152]

That Abberline's underlying assumption was correct is verified in a report of the previous year by the Yiddish language *Die Tsukunft*:

When an ordinary person kills a person everything is quiet. It will not occur to anyone to call another person by the name of a murderer. But when Lipski is sentenced to death, the ordinary people taunted other Jews 'Lipski'![153]

Police suspected the man with the pipe to be a bystander or passer by[154], not dissimilar to Schwartz in that regard. To cover all bases, including the possibility that he may have been an accomplice of the assailant, a search of the neighbourhood was undertaken to enquire after any residents by the name of Lipski, without result.

Schwartz and the man with the pipe having left the scene, Louis Diemschutz the club's steward, made his way toward Dutfield's Yard, having turned into Berner Street from Commercial Road at 1am with his cart and pony. Arrived at destination, he tried to manoeuvre through the gates but his pony shied. When he descended and lit a match, the darkness revealed a woman's body inside the gateway. He dashed into the club to raise the alarm and to confirm that his wife was safe. Running back out with a comrade, Isaac Kozebrodsky, he ran into the street in search of help.

By 1.16am, a doctor was on the scene in the person of Dr Blackwell, who had consulting rooms at 100 Commercial Road. Stride had suffered a double knife wound to the throat, one of which had been sufficiently severe to cause death. According to one witness who had arrived on the scene before the doctor, her throat had been "fearfully cut" with a "great gash in it over two inches wide"[155]. Dr Blackwell would opine that Stride "could not have been dead more than twenty minutes"[156], consistent with a timeline based on Schwartz's and Diemschutz's witness statements.

These in turn dovetailed with other testimony. Morris Eagle (or Siegal) who had delivered the evening's lecture had passed through the yard's gates at about 12.40am, after returning from escorting a friend home. He had noticed nothing untoward. The entrance area was so tight that he most likely would have, darkness notwithstanding, if only by stumbling over the body had it been there. Joseph Lave, a temporary lodger at the club, had much the same to say:

I came out first at half-past twelve to get a breath of fresh air. I passed out into the street, but did not see anything unusual. The district appeared to me to be quiet. I remained out until twenty minutes to one, and during that time no one came into the yard. I should have seen anybody moving about there.[157]

One long-held view and the most reasonable is that Diemschutz interrupted the murderer before he could do much more than kill Stride, which explains the absence of mutilation. In a review of the medical evidence, Dr Thomas Bond advised police that "the discovery appears to have been made immediately after the deed"[158]. Indeed, early witness observations, including Mrs Diemschutz's, that blood from the victim was still flowing, suggest Stride was not long dead in those first minutes after the alarm went out. It implies that the steward's arrival on the scene may not only have given the killer pause, but possibly corralled him in Dutfield's Yard, there being no other way out but through the narrow gate or via the high risk, roundabout route of the club building.

There is every chance that while Diemschutz raced inside to alert his comrades, Jack The Ripper was hiding in the gloom waiting for the right moment to slink away*. Diemschutz had not noticed anybody departing the scene as he had approached his destination from the vantage of his cart. Neither had Leon Goldstein moments earlier who had taken the same route on foot, glancing up at the club as he passed by. A neighbour, Fanny Mortimer who resided at 36 Berner Street, had stood at her door "nearly the whole time between half past twelve and one o'clock... and did not notice anything unusual"[159] consistent with witnesses from the club. It is conceivable then, that Jack The Ripper may still have been lurking in the darkness when Mrs Diemschutz's screams brought club patrons spilling into the yard, possibly taking the opportunity to vanish into the crowd and away.

---

* A possibility raised by Diemschutz himself at the inquest, in an extended response to a question by Inspector Reid.

Mortimer, Diemschutz and Goldstein's testimony, taken together, add weight to the assumption that Jack The Ripper was still at work when the club steward pulled up in his cart and pony. It suggests a very real possibility that the murderer was not just distracted by one Jewish man in Israel Schwartz before he killed Elizabeth Stride, and interrupted by another in Louis Diemschutz before he had a chance to mutilate her, but that he may well have been lucky not to fall prisoner to a milling crowd of Jewish socialists.

Given the stealth and apparent control exhibited in the cases of Nichols and Chapman, Stride's was a less than perfect, almost botched attempt, which nearly seems to have cost the murderer dearly. In part, it may have contributed to what unfolded next: an enraged response against those he held responsible for losing his grip on the situation.

It was, however, a calculated anger in at least one respect. Demonstrating a local's savvy, he must have been aware of that invisible blue line dividing the territories of the Metropolitan from the City Of London police forces, and which ran down Middlesex Street. Of Jack The Ripper's crimes, all but one would be committed within the jurisdiction of the Metropolitan Police. The murder he was about to launch into would be the only one committed just within city bounds, born of that exigency of throwing possible police pursuers off his trail. Having poisoned the well, the hop across the border to the relative safety and calm afforded west of Middlesex Street made sense, and the murder sites were close enough one to the other: a 12-minute walk or so.

Mindful of the morning's first murder literally at the door of a Jewish radical club, unfolding events on that fateful early morning, provide an insight into the killer's thinking. Within the hour of his deadly assault of Stride, he would strike in Mitre Square situated practically behind London's Great Synagogue. No surprise then, that as per events at the International Working Men's Educational Club, the witnesses were Jewish.

Joseph Lawende, Joseph Hyam Levy and Harry Harris were leaving the Imperial Club in Duke Street, directly opposite the synagogue, a minute or so before 1.35am. Across the road, on the corner of Church Passage, which ran along the synagogue's southern side leading to Mitre Square, they saw a man and a woman talking quietly and paid them scant attention but for Levy's quip to Harris, "Look there, I don't like going home by myself when I see these sort of characters about".[160]

At 1.44am, City police constable Edward Watkins, patrolling his beat, entered Mitre Square. It would be in its gloomiest, southern-most corner where a macabre scene awaited him.

>...I turned sharp round to the right, and flashing my light, I saw the body in front of me. The clothes were pushed right up to the breast, and the stomach was laid bare, with a dreadful gash from the pit of the stomach to the breast. On examining the body I found the entrails cut out and laid round the throat, which had an awful gash in it, extending from ear to ear. In fact, the head was nearly severed from the body. Blood was everywhere to be seen. It was difficult to discern the (extensive) injuries to the face for the quantity of blood which covered it...[161] (author's parentheses)

The first medico on the scene was Dr George Sequeira, from a renowned family of physicians of Sephardic origin and who resided nearby at 34 Jewry Street. He had arrived at 1.55am and estimated "life had been extinct... very few minutes – probably not more than a quarter of an hour".[162]

A later autopsy would reveal that Eddowes had died from the effects of her throat having been cut. Extensive mutilations had been performed after death, consistent with PC Watkins' layman's observations described above. Her womb and a kidney had been taken. The areas around the groin and rectum had suffered stabs and cuts.

Mitre Square's list of potential witnesses included a couple of watchmen, one a former policeman, plus a resident serving police officer, but nobody had heard or seen a thing. Included to the list must be patrolling police officer PC James Harvey, who arrived but did not enter Mitre Square via Church Passage and Duke Street at 1.41am or soon thereafter. PC Watkins' beat had previously brought him into Mitre Square at 1.30am, from the opposite direction to Harvey's, from Mitre Street, less than a quarter of an hour before making his grim discovery. And yet he had observed nothing untoward. As per elements of his previous murders, Jack The Ripper seems to have come and gone with a considerable degree of stealth.

It is worth considering whether he might have gauged this element of his success in Mitre Square against the frustration of events in Berner Street. Was it, in part, the tension of this paradox that helped launch the extraordinary act of bravura and spite which the evening was about to reveal?

At 2.55am, one street east, back across that political blue line marking a return to Metropolitan Police territory, PC Alfred Long's beat brought him past the entrance of the stairwell of the Wentworth Model Dwellings in Goulston Street. There he discovered the bloody and dirty portion of a woman's apron. It would later be confirmed that the item had been cut from what Eddowes had been wearing. A few feet above PC Long's discovery, on the jamb of the archway was chalked a message in small, barely inch-high letters[*]:

The Juwes are the men that Will not be Blamed for nothing

The murderer had used the material to wipe his hands or knife and discarded it while appearing to follow a trajectory which had brought him back into the East End, and presumably closer to safety.

Subsequent enquiries would clear those living in the tenements leading from the stairwell, numbers 108-119 Goulston Street, "occupied almost exclusively by Jews"[163]. For this last reason, the potential clue threw up a dilemma for the police, as explained by superintendent Thomas Arnold, Head of H (Whitechapel) Division:

---

* About 2.0 cm or 0.8 of an inch.

...in consequence of suspicion having fallen upon a Jew named 'John Pizer' alias 'Leather Apron' having (allegedly) committed a murder in Hanbury Street a short time previously, a strong feeling existed against the Jews generally, and as the Building upon which the writing was found was situated in the midst of a locality inhabited principally by that Sect, I was apprehensive that if the writing were left it would be the means of causing a riot and therefore considered it desirable that it should be removed...[164] (author's parentheses)

Despite some to-and-fro, the Metropolitan police came to the conclusion that the message was too incendiary to be left until sufficient light permitted it to be photographed. Nothing less than rubbing out the offensive graffito was called for. It was so important a decision that while Metropolitan Police Commissioner Sir Charles Warren raced to the scene to make a determination first-hand, a detective had already been sent ahead by Arnold armed with a wet sponge, posted and at the ready.

It would be a decision oft criticised at the time, especially by the press, and to the present day. But mindful of the tinderbox racial tensions in Whitechapel, it was one that Warren approached with a justifiable degree of circumspection:

> ...after taking into consideration the excited state of the population of London generally at the time, the strong feeling which had been excited against the Jews, and the fact that in a short time there would be a large concourse of the people in the streets and having before me the Report that if it was left there the house would likely to be wrecked (in which from my own observation I entirely concurred) I considered it desirable to obliterate the writing at once, having taken a copy... I do not hesitate myself to say that if the writing had been left, there would have been an onslaught upon the Jews, property would have been wrecked, and lives would probably have been lost, and I was much gratified with the promptitude with which Superintendent Arnold was prepared to act in the

matter… It may be realised therefore if the safety of the Jews in Whitechapel could be jeopardised… by the question of the spelling of the word Jews, what might have happened to the Jews in that quarter had the writing been left intact.[165]

Much speculation has surrounded the chalked message over the years, including one mainstay interpretation that it was a plain case of the writing being left by a bitter and defiant Jewish Ripper complete with a peculiar (mis)spelling of the word Jews – a semantic issue which was about to take on a life of its own, as alluded to above by Warren. Parallel to this line of argument has been criticism of the police for precipitously wiping away a vital clue, which in turn has provided fuel to conspiracy theories of varied stripe.

Another view is that Jack The Ripper discarded the bloodied half-apron on his way past and by chance it happened to land near an already present, unrelated, anti-Semitic graffito – but were that the case, why the small letters? What also belies such a simple interpretation is that on PC Long's previous pass by the Wentworth Model Building at 2.20am, he testified that the apron piece "was not there"[166] nor had he noticed any graffiti, as he would tell the inquest into Eddowes' murder.

His testimony has corroboration by a second officer, provided by City Police Detective Constable Daniel Halse:

At twenty minutes past two o'clock I passed over the spot where the piece of apron was found, but did not notice anything then.[167]

DC Halse's inquest evidence is important too for his observation that the graffito looked "recently written":

It looked fresh, and if it had been done long before it would have been rubbed out by the people passing.[168]

The detective constable makes a practical point but he may also have been alluding to the fact that in a neighbourhood and building

79

inhabited principally by Jews, a piece of anti-Semitic writing would not have lasted long – the less trafficked, early morning hours may well have been the only fortuitous moment to get away with delivering such an offensively themed scrawl.

Also in favour of its authenticity, is the quasi-cryptic content of the message itself with its accusatory theme. Subtextually, complementary messages come through as well. They speak of the murderer's ire as a result of the botched attempt in Berner Street and those he blamed: Diemschutz and the Jewish comrades from the socialist club. It would also seem to give fuel to an illusionary fire: the blood libel charge, as indeed the events of the double-event more broadly do. Fundamentally though, it is difficult for this author to extract the graffito from its contextual surroundings, specifically, to the anti-Jewish riots which had followed Chapman's murder three weeks earlier. In other words, Jack The Ripper wanted to convey the impression that the rioters had been correct in blaming the murders on the Jews; and that a defiant, now crowing, Jewish culprit was at work: "The Juwes are the men that Will not be Blamed for nothing".

Consistent with what he was trying to achieve, the half apron was left underneath the graffito as the murderer's way of authenticating the message. No need for bogus letters* in red ink to newspaper editors signed Jack The Ripper, or other such "practical jokes" as Inspector Henry Moore dismissively referred to the full gamut of so-called 'Ripper correspondence'§ [169]. Chilling and effective, when he had something to say, the killer had his own way of presenting his credentials like none other: near the crime, at the time. Why else,

---

* On 1 October, the name 'Jack The Ripper' would hit the press and give the 'Whitechapel fiend' a new moniker, forever more etched into history. Police released correspondence purportedly by the killer, but later understood to be the work of an enterprising journalist - likely, Thomas J. Bulling of the Central News Agency.

§ An FBI report prepared in the centenary year of the murders by renowned profiler John Douglas warned that letters allegedly received by authorities purporting to have come from the Jack The Ripper needed to be seen in the broader context of their rarity within the annals of serial murder: "in summary I would not put emphasis on the communiqués".

take the high risk of carrying a damning piece of evidence on his person all the way to Goulston Street?

The police seemed in little doubt: from Moore, who thought the message was "undoubtedly by the murderer"[170], to Assistant Commissioner of the Metropolitan Police Sir Robert Anderson who thought it "the only tangible piece of evidence ever obtained"[171]. Major Henry Smith, the Acting Commissioner of the City force, believed it was "probably" genuine and left as a ruse "to throw the police off the scent, to divert suspicion from the Gentiles and throw it upon the Jews"[172].

In a confidential report to the Home Office dated 6 November 1888, Sir Charles Warren mirrored what was, or would become, the general consensus of his colleagues regarding the authenticity of the graffito and Smith's interpretation of the killer's intent, when he wrote:

> … writing on the wall in Goulston Street evidently written with the intention of inflaming the public mind against the Jews[173].

An insightful accompanying report by Chief Inspector Swanson goes into greater detail and underscores the point:

> Upon the discovery of the blurred chalk writing on the wall, written, – although mis-spelled in the second word, – in an ordinary hand in the midst of a locality principally inhabited by Jews of all nationalities as well as English, and upon the wall of a common stairs leading to a number of tenements occupied almost exclusively by Jews, and the purport of the writing as shown at page 3 was to throw blame upon the Jews, the Commr. deemed it adviseable to have them rubbed out. Apart from this there was the fact that during police enquiries into the Bucks Row and Hanbury Street murders a certain section of the Press cast a great amount of suspicion upon a jew named John Piser,

alias, "Leather Apron", as having been the murderer whose movements at the dates and hours of those murders had been satisfactorily enquired into by Met. Police, clearing him of any connection, there was also the fact that on the same morning another murder had been committed in the immediate vicinity of a Socialist Club in Berner Street, frequented by Jews, – considerations, which, weighed in the balance with the evidence of chalk writing on the wall to bring home guilt to any person were deemed the weightier of the two.[174]

Though this part of Swanson's report provides justification for the expunging of the graffito, there are also outlines of a racial narrative coming into focus, hinting at the killer's broader strategy. It may be wishful thinking to imagine that the report's author was overly mindful of it at the time of writing, but to the Jewish community the racial overtones were clear. For everything else that may have been theorised about Jack The Ripper's purported correspondence over the years, the only two near-indisputable pieces of communication to have come from him focused exclusively on a racial narrative. The first sprung from his own lips when he used the local anti-Semitic slur ("Lipski") heard by Israel Schwartz near the entrance of premises operated by a well-known Jewish club and newspaper. The second, in the form of the anti-Semitic graffito, scrawled subsequent to fleeing the scene of his second murder of the morning behind the Great Synagogue. Unsurprisingly, an editorial in the *Jewish Chronicle* at the time of the Eddowes inquest came to the conclusion that: "There are not wanting signs of a deliberate attempt to connect the Jews with the Whitechapel murders."[175]

Indeed, that somebody was trying to frame the Jews while fanning community tensions elicited a concerted response by some of the Jewish community's most prominent, and eventually came to include Sir Charles Warren, a gentile. What had sparked the stream of high profile intercessions had been an incorrect report on 12 October in the *Pall Mall Gazette,* and echoed by many of its competitors:

The language of the Jews in the East End is a hybrid dialect, known as Yiddish, and their mode of spelling the word Jews would be "Juwes". This the police consider a strong indication that the crime was committed by one of the numerous foreigners by whom the East End is infested.

That the press were on the wrong track can be seen by Warren's extraordinary act of publicly wading into the debate and contradicting such assertions via a press release in subsequent days. His actions are also indicative of how aware police were were of the social temperature in the street and their ongoing concern that fresh anti-Jewish rioting might break out:

> With reference to a statement in various journals that the word "Jews" is spelt "Juwes" in the Yiddish jargon, the Commissioner of Police has ascertained that this is incorrect. It is not known that there is any dialect or language in which the word "Jews" is spelt "Juwes."[176]

Warren had been spurred to action after seeking advice from Acting Chief Rabbi Hermann Adler, who on 13 October wrote to him concerned that "… in the present state of excitement it is dangerous to the safety of the poor Jews in the East to allow such an assertion to remain uncontradicted"[177]. Adler refuted the claims categorically:

> I was deeply pained by the statements that appeared in several papers today, the 'Standard', 'Daily News', etc., that in the Yiddish dialect the word Jews is spelled 'Juewes'. This is not a fact. The equivalent in the Judao-German (Yiddish) jargon is 'Yidden'… I am convinced that the writing emanated from some illiterate Englishman who did not know to spell the word correctly…[178]

Adler was preaching to the converted with Warren, as his subsequent media statement would make clear, and who on the same day had himself written a minute for the Home Office stating the police's belief that:

...the last murders were obviously done by some one desiring to bring discredit on the Jews and Socialists or Jewish Socialists.[179]

A few days later, Whitechapel MP Samuel Montagu was putting a near identical argument to the *Pall Mall Gazette* and its readership:

...if the 'handwriting on the wall' was done by the monster himself, can there be any doubt of his intention to throw the pursuers on a wrong track while showing hostility to the Jews in the vicinity.[180]

As if foreseeing the limitations of such svelte logic, the police authorities had quickly determined that they would take no chances: not only had the murderer's message been expunged, in short order they reinforced the main East End police stations with the presence of an extra 50 constables at each. Acknowledging the very real possibility of fresh anti-Jewish rioting breaking out, the press could but agree with such foresight – for all their other criticisms of the police[181].

In such and various ways, Jack The Ripper's grand plan was determining both the official response and the subsequent conversation. The piper, calling the tune, and a killer's strategy, on perfect display.

End of Chapter 3 notes:

A further note on the geography of the 'double-event'

There would be a meaningful geographic echo six months after 'the double-event' underscoring the link between the two murder sites and, in turn, to Jewish life in East London. Like the administrative line that divided the territory of the Metropolitan from City police forces, London's Jewish community had its own, less formalised, internal territorial divisions.

The International Working Men's Educational Club and the Great Synagogue represented different poles of philosophical standpoint; two world views in less than harmonious rapport. The Berner Street club with its own Yiddish language newspaper produced on-site, was a significant base of operations for East End Jewish activists of the left.

The Great Synagogue, like the *Jewish Chronicle*, formed part of a more mainstream, established Anglo-Jewry. The temple's location in Duke Street reflected the urban topography of another epoch in the history of London's Jews and a broader patchwork cut from both Sephardic and Ashkenazic cloth, "Portuguese" and "German"[182]. Anchored slightly closer into the city than the most recent migration, this was the traditional heartland of the Anglo-Jewish community dating back centuries. In Israel Zangwill's 1892 novel *Children Of The Ghetto: A Study Of A Peculiar People,* he calls its pious leadership "these aristocrats of the Ghetto… within a stone's throw of the 'Duke's Place' edifice"[183]. Conscious of ongoing political campaigning by their class antagonists on the Jewish left, they saw their own good standing in English society potentially jeopardised by the efforts of what they were prone to dismiss as rabble-rousers.

In between these two political markers, lay the fluid mass of recently arrived migrants, in large part observant, among them the outright Orthodox in the practice of their faith, but by no means a monolithic bloc. It was over these newly arrived Jews, the victims of the sweating system and unemployment, that the disparate approaches would clash on Saturday, 16 March 1889, in what the *Jewish Chronicle* would record as an event, "quite unparalleled in the history of the Jews in London"[184].

At 12.30pm on that Sabbath, anywhere up to 3000 protesters began to head off from their marshalling point outside the International Working Men's Educational Club as part of a "synagogue parade". The organisers and participants were seeking to protest against the inequities of capitalism and Rabbi Hermann Adler's refusal of their earlier request to preach a sermon sympathetic to the unemployed and those trapped in the grip of the sweating system.

When the procession arrived at the Great Synagogue replete with banners in Yiddish and English and a German marching band, a force of as many as 60 City police were waiting and barred their entrance. A leadership delegation from among them then sought to meet with Rabbi Adler, but weary of political entrapment he had wisely handed over the reins to a colleague and was not in attendance. With their hand stayed, the leaders of the march sought permission to hold an open air meeting in Mitre Square, adjacent. Police turned down the request with advice that such an assembly would not be permitted, nor would it "in any part of the City"[185]. Doubly thwarted they had to be content with an alternative venue back in the East End. The demonstrators moved off, and as they commenced making their way to the Mile-End 'Waste' the band struck up La Marseillaise:

Tod jader Tyrannei!
Die Arbeit werder frei!
Marsch, marsch
Marsch, marsch!
Und wärs zum Tod!
Denn unserer Fahn' ist roth![186]

Having arrived at destination, speeches were delivered and a resolution endorsed and circulated in Hebrew* and English:

---

* More likely, in Yiddish, using Hebrew script.

That this meeting of unemployed and sweated London Jewish workers of both sexes, strongly condemns the Delegate Chief Rabbi, Dr. Hermann Adler, for refusing to comply with the courteous request of the Committee of the Jewish unemployed to preach a sermon at the Great Synagogue, having special reference to our position and prospects; further, we render our protest against the practice of labour sweating indulged in by certain members of the Jewish community. In consequence of the indifference of the rich Jews in not telling us, through the Chief Rabbi, how to improve our miserable condition, we clearly see that they are unwilling to assist us in ameliorating our position; we, therefore, call upon our fellow workmen not to depend upon the rich classes, but to organise in a strong body to strike for the abolition of the capitalistic ruling.[187]

By some accounts, the successful motion seems to have been received with less than rapturous support. The tepid response may have been a portent of what was to come. By the time the meeting concluded, some of the many observers and mockers the march had picked up along the way, to and from the city, seem to have become a problem:

…the leaders returned to their club in Berner-street, where they were followed by an immense concourse of people, some hissing and hooting them.[188]

Arriving back at the International Working Men's Educational Club, they found that the police were already in attendance with a strong force and either expecting trouble or, according to a report in an anarchist journal[189], ready to mete it out. Up to 300 people were eventually congregated outside, and tensions become strained. Though details are hazy, police got what they were expecting when fighting broke out and spilled inside the club, with several club members arrested including Louis Diemschutz and Isaac Kozebrodsky, who it will be recalled, had both become involved in events on the night of Elizabeth Stride's murder.

The synagogue parade episode is a telling one. It reinforces the proposition that Jack The Ripper knew his neighbourhood and what made it tick, its sinews and exposed nerves. It adds another level of understanding to his decision to cross police jurisdictions in the course of the double-event. Undoubtedly, he was intent on avoiding the Metropolitan Police by heading to Mitre Square, but in so doing he also found a second location where he could incriminate the Jews by topographical association after botching the first attempt in the courtyard of the International Working Men's Educational Club. The full gamut of Jewish expression, radical and righteous, was thus caught in his inculpatory net: the most recent migration and its forerunners, held equally to account, and a written message in Goulston Street to match the verbal one ("Lipski") delivered in Berner Street.

Author's comment: At one point in the Berner Street melee Mrs Diemschutz tried to rescue her husband from the clutches of the police, armed with a broom. The couple must have been very committed to one another. Recalling the night of Liz Stride's murder, the first thing that Louis Diemschutz did on discovering the prostate woman's body was to hurry inside to assure himself that his wife was safe. On this occasion it seems Mrs Diemschutz showed an equal amount of concern for her husband.

CHAPTER 4

RITUAL MURDER REDUX

This London Ghetto of ours is a region where, amid uncleanness and squalor, the rose of romance blows yet a little longer in the raw air of English reality; a world which hides beneath its stony and unlovely surface an inner world of dreams, fantastic and poetic as the mirage of the Orient where they were woven, of superstitions grotesque as the cathedral gargoyles of the Dark Ages in which they had birth.

Israel Zangwill, born London 1864
Children Of The Ghetto: A Study of A Peculiar People (1892)

Dangerous currents as these were for the Jewish community and its leadership, they were part of a bigger tide that had surged forth in the first days after the double-event. On 2 October, the blood libel burst its banks, this time without the constraints and feints which typified previous media references.

Two days after the double murder of Stride and Eddowes, the *Times* published an inflammatory piece by its Vienna correspondent referencing the famous Ritter trial. It would be the first of three related pieces by the *Times* in the space of what would drag out to roughly three weeks. The article itself became a hot news item, with the essential points of the story repeated in coverage which spanned newspapers the length and breadth of Britain, popping up for several weeks afterwards:

THE WHITECHAPEL MURDERS VIENNA, OCT. 1.

With reference to the recent atrocious murders in London, attention may be called to a crime of an exactly similar kind which preoccupied the public in this country for nearly three years. A Galician Jew named Ritter was accused in 1884 of having murdered and mutilated a Christian woman in a village near Cracow. The mutilation was like that perpetrated on the body of the woman Chapman, and at the trial numbers of witnesses deposed that among certain fanatical Jews there existed a superstition to the effect that if a Jew became intimate with a Christian woman he would atone for his offence by slaying and mutilating the object of his passion. Sundry passages of the Talmud were quoted which, according to the witnesses, expressly sanctioned this form of atonement. The trial caused an immense sensation, and Ritter, being found guilty, was sentenced to death. The Judges of the Court of Appeal, however, feeling that the man was the victim of popular error and anti-Semitic prejudice, ordered a new trial upon some technicality. Again a jury pronounced against Ritter, and once more the Court of Appeal found a flaw in the proceedings. A third trial took place, and for the third time Ritter was condemned to be hanged, but upon this the Court of Appeal quashed the sentence altogether, and Ritter was released, after having been in prison 37 months. There is no doubt that the man was innocent, but the evidence touching the superstitions prevailing among some of the ignorant and degraded of his co-religionists remains on record and was never wholly disproved.[190]

Because the story had appeared in the pages of British journalism's most prestigious flagship, while at the same time becoming newsworthy itself, it had created parallel tracks of legitimacy down which the ritual murder story was propelled. The upshot was that the blood libel was repeated again and again, in newspapers London and nationwide.

The *Pall Mall Gazette*, an evening newspaper, jumped into action on the same day. Its response is a good example as it spanned the full gamut of the media's reaction by taking opposing positions and on at least one occasion, in the same edition. On page four, under "Occasional Notes":

We hope that Dr Hermann Adler will lose no time in publishing a conclusive refutation of the absurd story telegraphed to the *Times* from Vienna as to the sanction alleged to be given by the Talmud to the crimes of the Whitechapel murderer. We utterly refuse to believe for a single moment that the Talmud in any of its isolated texts contains any words which by any possibility could be construed as amounting to a promise to a Jew who has broken the seventh commandment of absolution if he also breaks the sixth. The feeling against the Jews is quite strong enough in the East-end already without adding to it this groundless calumny.[191]

Then on page seven, it canvassed various theories including the following, whose wording was nearly identical to the *Times* article which had apparently caused such editorial affront as recently as three pages previously:

OBEDIENCE TO THE TALMUD - Among certain fanatical Jews there exists a superstition to the effect that if a Jew became intimate with a Christian woman he would atone for his offence by slaying and mutilating the object of his passion. Sundry passages of the Talmud are said to sanction this form of atonement.[192]

Not needing prompting from the *Pall Mall Gazette*, Rabbi Adler was already on the case, and together with Dr Moses Gaster, the Sephardic Chief Rabbi from nearby Bevis Marks synagogue, they were preparing individual but equally irate letters to the *Times* to refute the ritual murder charge. Both were duly published the next day. The arguments contained in the two letters are summarised by the following press report that made use of Gaster's arguments while quoting Adler:

The Whitechapel murders are so unparalleled in their horror that the wildest theories are afloat as to their perpetrator. The fact that there is a considerable Jewish population in the district has led to the revival of some of the anti-Semitic slanders that have so strange a vitality. The Vienna correspondent of the Times has made himself responsible for the repetition of certain charges made during the notorious Cracow murder trial. "There is no doubt," he says, "that the man was innocent; but the evidence touching the superstitions prevailing among some of the ignorant and degraded of his co-religionists remains on record, and was never wholly disproved." The particular superstition here referred to is an atrocious form of the "blood accusation." We have on several occasions shown the baselessness of this medieval fable... exposed the charge of human sacrifice which credulity, at once ignorant and cruel, has brought against the Jews. It has been a favourite weapon in the hands of the persecutor... These falsehoods formed the chief pretext for the long, bitter, and deadly persecutions of the Jews by which medieval Christendom were disgraced. They have reappeared in recent years in such cases as the Tisza Esslar trial. If the anti-Semites were not for the most part ignorant fanatics, they might be reminded that they are merely reviving... cruel falsehoods... Dr. HERMANN ADLER, and Dr. M. GASTER have each written to the Times protesting against this revival of the blood accusation. There is, of course, no justification in the "Talmud" for the charge. "I can assert without hesitation," says Dr. ADLER, "that in no Jewish book is such a barbarity even hinted at. Nor is there any record in the criminal annals of any country of a Jew having been convicted of such a terrible atrocity."... It is the duty of all who have the opportunity to protest against the false scholarship and false witness upon which the Judenhatze has to rely.[193]

The *Jewish Chronicle* waded in too, with editorials holding the *Times* to task for lending its "respectable... columns to such suggestions which are the work of ignorance if not of malice"[194]. Nor could it help but note the broader and obvious implications:

This telegram (from the *Times*' Vienna correspondent) appears to us as dangerous a piece of composition as could be imagined. Of course it is not correct... The impropriety and injustice of the libel is only equalled by the danger involved in telegraphing it... no one knows what an excited mob is capable of believing against any class which differs from the mob-majority by well-marked peculiarities. Many English and Irish workpeople at the East End are inflamed against the immigrant Jews by the competition for work and for houses, by the stories of the sweaters and the sweated. If these illogical and ignorant minds should come to believe in the report heedlessly spread by a writer who is obviously not quite just, nor well-informed himself, the result might be terrible.[195] (author's parentheses)

For all the attempts over the course of a fortnight by the *Jewish Chronicle* and others to set the record straight, the *Times* returned to the story on 16 October with updates from both sides of the argument, effectively throwing the blood libel a lifeline. The opening third of this latest article provided a quick re-cap of the Ritter affair, repeating the ritual slaying charges expounded in the original piece. The next part consisted of a rebuttal of those points based on a letter recently received from Dr Josef Samuel Bloch, a Talmudic specialist and Jewish member of the Austrian parliament. Bloch had risen to fame during that other cause célèbre, the Tisza-Eszlar case, by taking to task the arguments presented at trial by the Catholic 'academic', August Rohling, previously considered an authority on 'Jewish ritual slayings' but whose career did not survive Bloch's assault on his anti-Semitic fantasies.

Where the second *Times* article got itself into more trouble was in the concluding paragraph, effectively giving the last word on the matter to the case for the affirmative and validating the claims made in its original article:

Another correspondent, however, who also writes from Vienna, affirms, as a lawyer of more than 20 years' standing, that our Vienna correspondent was virtually correct in his statement of the case. He declares that, whatever may be the reading of the Talmud, the superstition in question was clearly proved at the trial as existing among the low-class Jews of Galicia. The Ritters, he says, were acquitted because the only witness against them died in prison, and the rest of the evidence was meagre and incomplete.[196]

What needs to be kept in mind is that this latest instalment from Vienna was playing out in a news environment in which the contents of the Goulston Street graffito had become public knowledge several days previously. It becomes ever clearer why Police Commissioner Warren had taken the extraordinary step of wading into the media sphere by refuting the alleged Yiddish spelling of the word "Juwes".

Showing little of Warren's sensitivity or good judgement, the second *Times* article had the effect of beginning another round of media references to the Ritter and Tisza-Eszlar cases and the blood libel, beginning with the *Evening News* which reproduced the latest *Times* article in full on the same day.

But such reporting had never really ceased, reverberating for weeks after the Vienna correspondent's original piece and becoming subsumed with a report from the *London Standard*'s Vienna correspondent on 9 October. In the latter, it was Bloch who made reference to a superstition which also came up at the Ritter trial supposedly current among German thieves who believed in the special powers of stupefying candles made from the internal organs of mutilated women. A red herring, it had the effect of acting as yet another catalyst for references to the case and its central premise, the blood libel.

Finally cognisant, on 25 October, the *Times* decided to try and bring discussion on the subject to a close with a concluding refrain that, "We cannot allow this subject to be discussed any further in our columns". Summarising the contents of its two previous articles, it placed the blood libel on record yet again, for what would be the last time as far as the pages of its newspaper were concerned:

Dr. Bloch denied, and our other correspondent affirmed the existence among the low-class Jews of Galicia of a superstition such as would account for the mutilation of the body of the woman for whose murder the Ritters were tried, and, it has been suggested, for the mutilations in the case of the Whitechapel murders.

While sticking to its guns, it did make an important admission towards the end. It conceded that "the Ritters were finally acquitted by the Supreme Tribunal on the merits of the case, and not because the only witness against them had died in prison", contrary to what had been attested in its article of 16 October and implied in the one of 2 October.

If the staff at the *Times* had hoped their editorial edict would help quell discussion, it would take only one day to disabuse them of their optimism. The hydra they had helped create would not be so easily tamed. The next day, 26 October, there were new reports[197] from Vienna, thereafter carried widely in the London and British press, about a case from Leskau in Moravia, Austria-Hungary. Repeated under variations of the same screaming headline, "REVOLTING MURDERS IN MORAVIA", they describe the case of two sisters, great beauties by all accounts, aged 17 and 19, found by a peasant in the forest. They had been killed and "frightfully mutilated".

The particulars of those mutilations contain a detail overlooked in the 130 years since Jack The Ripper stalked the streets of Whitechapel, and whose importance will become apparent in the following chapter:

> The elder sister was shot through the temple and her two breasts were cut off. The younger sister was shot in the breast and neck, while a wooden stave pierced the lower part of the body, running into the ground.

Exotic eastern European setting notwithstanding, Jews were rightly spared any mention. Though "plebeian" was one adjective used, the suspects were described in non-ethnic, non-religious terms. A saving grace. Which does not mean an English readership exposed to repeated media references about lower-class Jews supposedly being in the thick of murders involving the mutilation of Christian women would have been able to make such a fine distinction by that late stage. In that sense, the Leskau news items were not stand-alone articles. An established context had been provided in preceding days, weeks and months by a series of reports as telegraphed by the Vienna correspondents, then repackaged, followed-up and polemicised. The textual parameters and touchstones in the reports that covered the Ritter, Tisza-Eszlar and Leskau affairs, were effectively the same. The *Daily Telegraph* made one obvious link, referring to the latest atrocity as "a horrible double murder, recalling in some of its revolting details the Whitechapel mysteries"[198].

English language newspapers overseas[199] were still reprinting that phrase and recycling the Leskau articles for time afterwards, following new impetus provided by events soon to play out in the East End. They wouldn't be the only ones to find inspiration from the Moravian reports. Someone sinister was also reading the 'papers. In matter of fact, he was taking notes for future reference. Jack The Ripper had already demonstrated he knew how to work a narrative, and he was not letting go.

End of Chapter 4 notes:

London Magnet, **25 June 1883**

SENSATIONAL TRIAL IN HUNGARY

The trial of the Jews accused of having murdered Esther Solymosi, on the eve of the Jewish Passover last year, began on Tuesday before the Court of Justice of the Szaholcz County. Nyiregihaza, the chief town of the county, situated near the Tokay vineyards, has a population of 25,000, mostly Magyars, and in itself presents nothing worthy of note, has played no part in the history of Hungary, and does not possess a single stately edifice. Its streets are, like those of most small towns in Hungary, straight, broad, unpaved, and bordered principally by low thatched houses. With the exception of the numerous officials, the greater part of the population are farmers, some of them, however, being employed in winter as artisans, selling their wares to the neighbouring peasants. The Jewish inhabitants are either shopkeepers, peddlers, or usurers. They all belong to the orthodox party, and remain in the darkest superstition. Most of them wear "kaftans" reaching down to the ankles, and have an insuperable aversion to cleanliness. Trial by jury exists, in Hungary only for Press offences, and so the case is heard before an assembly of Judges and as the accused have the right of appealing first to the Royal Table (Court of Second Instance), and then to the Royal Curia, it may drag on for years. Herr Szeiffert, who has charge of the case, is the third Public Prosecutor mixed up in it. The-first shot himself, the anti-Semitic party asserting that he had been bribed by the Jews; and the second was recalled owing to the violent attacks made upon him in a Buda-Pesth journal. The President of the Court is Herr Kornis.

Soloman Schwarz, 37, butcher – the office of Jewish butcher is a religious one, and often held together with that of priest and teacher; Abraham Buxbaum, 20, schoolmaster; Leopold Braun, 27, butcher; Herman Volner, 36, "workman without domicile," as he describes himself *i.e.,* beggar; Joseph Scharf, 41, Synagogue beadle; Adolphus Junger, 58, Jew, landowner in Eszlar; Abraham Braun or Brenner, 37, workman; Salomon Lustig, shopkeeper; Lazar Weiszstein, 56, farmer; and Emanuel Taub, 28, Synagogue servant. The four first named are accused of having murdered Esther Solymosi, and the six following of being accomplices. Besides these, there are five others accused of having dressed the body of a grown up girl in Esther Solymosi's clothes, in order to deceive the friends of the missing girl. In opening the proceedings, the President stated that what the Court had to decide was whether a crime had been committed; and, if so, whether the accused were the guilty parties.

This case, it may be remembered, arose from the disappearance of a young peasant girl of Christian faith, called Esther Solymosi, three days before the Jewish Passover of 1882. Up to this day the case has remained a complete mystery, and the allegation that she has been murdered by Jews rests upon the evidence of two boys, one five and the other 14 years old, sons of Joseph Scharf, the Synagogue beadle of Tisza-Eszlar. In order to explain the strong feeling that exists on the subject, it may be well to mention that just one year before – namely, at the time of the Jewish Passover in 1881– a serious anti-Jewish riot took place at Kieff in Russia, and this was followed by severe persecution at Balta, and other places in the south of Russia. The agitation was spread all over Hungary by agents of the Berlin Juden-hetze, who worked on the superstition of the Hungarian peasantry, by reminding them of the old charge against the Jews, that they must have the blood of Christian, and, if possible, of a Christian girl, to celebrate the Passover. This superstition, which is to be traced to the times of early Christianity in Rome, where it was used against the Christians by the Romans, has in fact never died out in Hungary, and whenever a Christian servant girl, wilfully or otherwise, disappeared from the house of her Jewish employers during the time of the Passover, it was always believed by the peasantry that the girl had been murdered for religious purposes, and many cruel persecutions resulted, although not one authentic case of such murder has ever been proved. So much being premised, it is easy to understand what followed after the disappearance of Esther Solymosi. Several weeks after the full description of her person and clothing had appeared in every newspaper, the body of a girl was fished out of the River

Theiss, near Tisza-Eszlar, in clothes exactly answering to those of the missing girl. It was asserted at the time that the post-mortem examination proved to a certainty that the body could not be that of Esther Solymosi; and the circumstance that it was dressed in Esther's clothes, or in clothes strongly resembling them, only added to the already existing mystery, and naturally suggested that the murderers wanted to pass off a dead body, taken, perhaps, from a hospital, as that of the girl.

The latest addition to the very voluminous evidence, however, throws doubt on this view, for Professor Hofmann, of Vienna University, who has thoroughly investigated the affair, testifies that, judging from age, height, and special marks, the body may have been that of the missing girl. The importance of this is obvious, for, if the story of the two boys is true, Esther Solymosi's throat was cut in the Synagogue, and it is admitted that in the case of the body found in the river, death had been produced by suffocation. The Act of Accusation sets forth the following narrative of alleged facts. On April 1st, 1882, three days before the Jewish Passover, Esther was ordered by her mistress to go to a neighbouring village to buy some painter's colours. She started on her journey at half-past eleven in the morning, and on her way she met her sister Sophie, and spoke to her. She duly arrived at the small general shop, where she bought some red and blue colour and lamp-black. On her way home she again met her sister Sophie, but did not stop, saying she must hurry home, as the colours – which she showed her sister – were wanted at once. At two o'clock on that evening Esther had not reached home, and, accordingly, her mistress went to look for her, first at her mother's house, and then at her aunt's, but could find no trace of her.

The case, was, of course, much talked about, and eventually, owing to rumours of what had been said by the two sons of Josef Scharf, the district magistrate opened an investigation, but this only took place in the beginning of May, nearly a month after the girl had so mysteriously disappeared. The boy Samuel Scharf, five years old, simply stated that his father and several other Jews, including a butcher, had murdered her at a morning rehearsal of the hymns and prayers which were to be used during the Passover. His elder brother, Moritz Scharf, however, gave the following details: – On the day in question, at 11 a.m., he went to close the doors of the Synagogue, but four men whom he names, sent him away, saying that they had not yet finished their prayers. As Moritz went back to the beadle's house he saw Esther Solymosi passing up the village street, and his father ordered him to call her in to arrange the candlesticks on the wardrobe, it being Saturday, on which day religious Jews do no kind of work.

The girl entered the room and placed the candlesticks as desired. At this moment the beggar Volner came in and asked her to come into the Synagogue and do some service there, probably of the same kind. Esther went, and when she had gone about a quarter of an hour the boy, who had gone out again into the courtyard, heard terrible cries coming from the building. He hastened to the Synagogue, but finding the door locked from inside, he looked through the keyhole, and states that he saw Esther Solymosi on the floor, partly undressed, two of the men holding her down, while the third cut her throat right through with a knife such as is used by the Jewish butchers. Two earthenware vessels were, he adds, held under her throat to catch the blood, which was then poured into a larger vessel. This done, the girl was dressed again, and placed in the Synagogue vestibule, where he observed four other Jews, who surrounded the body that nothing more could be seen. The boy goes on to say that he hurried to the room of his parents and related what he had seen, but was silenced by his mother, who peremptorily bade him hold his tongue. An hour later the beggar Volner came into the room and told the boy to shut up the Synagogue. This he did, seeing nothing of the body nor any blood-spots. This story differs from that related by the younger boy in some important points, the latter having accused his own father of participation in the murder. A woman living in the neighbourhood of the Synagogue declares that at the time in question she heard three or four appalling screams for help coming from the Synagogue, and several others testify to the same effect. On the other hand, the time mentioned by the boy Moritz does not coincide with the evidence of the girl's mistress and of the shopkeeper, or of her sister.

On June 18, the body already spoken of was found in the river. On this point also there is some strange evidence. Some raftsmen have confessed that on June 7, when they were passing the village of Kerecseny, they were spoken to by an old acquaintance, a Jewish raftsman called Smilovics, who asked them whether, for good pay, they would carry a body which would be handed to them on a certain day at a certain place. The bargain was concluded, and on June 11 they actually received a body from Smilovics, and, at the same time, a dark woman, of between 30 and 35, handed to them a bundle of clothes, and ordered them to dress the body in them. Smilovics helped with the dressing, and especially dictated how the clothes must be put on. A handkerchief, containing red and blue colour, was placed in the left hand of the corpse, and then the body, with the clothes and the colour, was again put in the water, where it remained several days attached to the raft, after which time the men produced it, saying they had just found it in the river. This is all that is known or alleged regarding the most mysterious affair.

On Tuesday, the Public Prosecutor in opening the case vehemently attacked the Judges who presided at the preliminary investigation, accusing them of having delayed the trial and disturbed the peace of the dead, thus causing public commotion and riots. The President repelled these attacks, saying that the Judges had only done their duty. The prosecutor announced that he intended to call 138 witnesses. The first to give evidence was the mother of Esther Solymosi, who simply repeated the story of the disappearance of the girl, and stated that until the boy Samuel Scharf made his revelation she had supposed that her daughter had fallen into the Theiss. Moritz Scharf, the eldest boy and the principal witness for the prosecution, then entered the witness-box. He is a fine lad of about 14. Like most Jewish lads, however, his exact age cannot be ascertained, as the Rabbis often omit to register the birth of male children, so that they may avoid military service. He related with great self-possession and without the least hesitation the story of how his father enticed Esther Solymosi into the Synagogue, where he saw her being murdered and the blood collected into an earthen vessel. All the accused were here brought into the hall, and, amid a scene of the highest excitement, the boy identified Salomon Schwarz, Leopold Braun, Abraham Buxbaum, and his father Joseph Scharf, as the actual murderers.

Scharf hereupon declared that he could no longer bear to hear his son make such statements, and demanded that the boy, who he says, had evidently learnt his story by heart, should repeat it in German, as he would not dare to lie in his mother tongue. In whatever district they are the mother tongue of these Eastern Jews is a sort of German *patois*. The other defendants joined in this demand, but the boy refused to speak in German. After the Public Prosecutor had cross-examined him without shaking his evidence the defendants requested that the boy should be confronted with his mother but at this point the President adjourned the trial. The accused were led back to prison amid dense crowds of spectators, who, like the newspapers of the district are intensely anti-Semitic. The Burgomaster has issued a proclamation exhorting the inhabitants to maintain order.

CHAPTER 5

NO ENGLISHMAN

> This is the real enemy, the invader from the East, the Druze, the ruffian, the oriental parasite; in a word: the Jew.
>
> George Bernard Shaw, 1856-1950
> *London Morning Post*, 3 December 1925

What unfolded next was an episode as macabre as it was just about unimaginable. If English sensibilities had been offended previously by the nature of the murders occurring in Whitechapel, then a ghastly discovery on the morning of Friday, 9 November 1888 would provide an extra dimension of shock and outrage.

Not even the passing of half a century could blunt its impact on Walter Dew, a 25-year-old Detective Constable with the Whitechapel Division in 1888. Recounting the relevant anecdote in his memoirs, *I Caught Crippen*, Dew describes it as, "the most gruesome memory of the whole of my police career":

> If I remember rightly it was between ten and eleven o'clock in the morning that I looked in at Commercial Street police station to get into touch with my superiors. I was chatting with Inspector Beck, who was in charge of the station, when a young fellow, his eyes bulging out of his head, came panting into the police station. The poor fellow was so frightened that for a time he was unable to utter a single intelligible word.
>
> At last he managed to stammer out something about "Another one. Jack the Ripper. Awful. Jack McCarthy sent me."

Mr. McCarthy was well-known to us as a common lodging-house proprietor.

"Come along, Dew," said Inspector Beck, and gathering from the terrorized messenger that Dorset Street was the scene of whatever had happened, we made him our pilot, as we rushed in that direction, collecting as many constables as we could on the way.

The youth led us a few yards down Dorset Street from Commercial Street, until we came to a court approached by an arched passage, three feet wide and unlighted, in which there were two entrances to houses which fronted on Dorset Street. The place was known as Miller's Court.

Leaving the constables to block Dorset Street and to prevent anyone from leaving the court itself, Inspector Beck and I proceeded through the narrow archway into what might be described as a small square. It was a cul-de-sac, flanked on all four sides by a few mean houses.

The house on the left of the passage was kept by McCarthy as a chandler's shop, while one room of the houses on the right was rented by a girl named Marie Kelly.

McCarthy's messenger was by this time able to tell a more or less coherent story. He told us that some of the neighbours had become alarmed at the non-appearance that morning of Kelly. They had spoken about it to McCarthy, and he had sent the youth to find her.

The door of her room was locked, but the lad looked through a broken pane of glass in the only window in the room which faced the wider part of the court, and had seen something which froze the blood in his veins and sent him helter-skelter to the police station.

The room was pointed out to me. I tried the door. It would not yield. So I moved to the window, over which, on the inside, an old coat was hanging to act as a curtain and to block the draught from the hole in the glass.

Inspector Beck pushed the coat to one side and peered through the aperture. A moment later he staggered back with his face as white as a sheet.

"For God's sake, Dew," he cried. "Don't look."

I ignored the order, and took my place at the window.

When my eyes had become accustomed to the dim light I saw a sight which I shall never forget to my dying day.[200]

"The poor fellow," who burst into the police station overwhelmed and speechless was Thomas Bowyer. At 10.45am, he had been sent by his boss, John McCarthy, to collect the rent from a tenant in arrears. She was the "Marie Kelly" of Dew's memoirs, a French affectation she adopted for her real name, Mary Jane Kelly, and she was Jack The Ripper's canonical fifth victim.

Bowyer would tell the inquest into her murder of knocking at her door again and again without reply. He next put his, "hand through the broken pane and lifted the curtain… (and) saw two pieces of flesh lying on the table"[201]. Concerned possibly that his eyes betrayed him, he looked a second time and "saw a body lying on the bed and blood on the floor"[202]. In reality, the body itself might have better been described as the scattered remains. In the language of the Vienna correspondents, Kelly had been "butchered", "frightfully mutilated". The landlord, McCarthy, picks up the story. It makes for difficult reading:

> When I looked through the window the sight I saw was more ghastly even than I had prepared myself for. On the bed lay the body, while the table was covered with lumps of flesh. Soon Superintendent Arnold arrived, and instructions to

burst the door open were given. I at once forced it with a pickaxe and we entered. The sight looked like the work of a devil. The poor woman had been completely disembowelled. Her entrails were cut out and placed on a table. It was these that I had taken to be lumps of flesh. The woman's nose had been cut off, and her face was gashed and mutilated so that she was quite beyond recognition... Her liver and other organs were on the table. I had heard a great deal about the Whitechapel murders, but I had never expected to see such a sight. The body was covered with blood and so was the bed. The whole scene is more than I can describe. I hope I may never see such a sight again.[203]

At the autopsy, police surgeon Dr Thomas Bond determined that the mutilations were far more extensive than anything outlined by layman observations such as McCarthy's. So much so, that officially determining she actually was Mary Kelly rested foremost on a rather precarious identification provided by her one-time partner Joseph Barnett. He recognised her, courtesy of her eyes and hair alone[204]. Her heart was unaccounted for, and according to some suggestions, the killer had "carried it away"* [205]. And in a crucial point of convergence with the Leskau reports of the previous fortnight, the autopsy confirmed a gory detail. It was one a sensational press was unlikely to pass up, just as the killer had hoped: "the breasts had been cleanly cut off"[206]. In fact, he had placed them carefully where police and medical examiners could not fail to notice: one next to Kelly's right foot and the other under her head. She was the first and only victim to be so mutilated.

Owing to various reasons, among them, the extensive nature of the mutilations and the passage of time before medical opinion was brought to bear, "...it is difficult to say with any degree of certainty the exact time that had elapsed since death" warned Dr Bond in a

---

* "... it is still confidently asserted that some portions of the body of the deceased woman are missing", *Times*, 13 November 1888; see also Dr Bond's post-mortem report, "Heart absent", MEPO 3/3153, ff. 10-18.

report of the post-mortem examination[207]. It would prove an overture to a debate that continues to this day. But after his introductory caveat, Bond opined that: "1 or 2 o'clock of the morning would be the probable time of the murder" and he was "pretty certain" in his reasoning. Broadly consistent with that estimate, some witness evidence deemed important by the police threw open a window stretching to a few hours later. At least one of Bond's colleagues present at the autopsy, Dr George Bagster Phillips, was quoted in the *Times* adding a few hours again to the later time frame suggested by witnesses[208]. At the inquest, on Monday 12 November, Dr Phillips attributed the cause of death to the severing of the right carotid artery. Kelly's throat had been cut, but Phillips did not elaborate much further before proceedings began winding down.

Earlier, testimony was heard from the murdered woman's fellow Miller's Court resident Mary Ann Cox, which indicated that Kelly was in her room, alive and well as late as 1am, or not too long thereafter, having heard her singing 'Only A Violet I Plucked From My Mother's Grave When A Boy'[209]. Another resident, Catherine Picket, who did not appear at the inquest, corroborated Cox, as did the landlord McCarthy. The *Illustrated Police News* reported that "the last thing he had heard of her was at one o'clock Friday morning, when she was singing in her room, and appeared to be very happy"[210].

But maybe this wasn't the last word on the subject, or from Kelly. At the inquest, evidence was heard from another Miller's Court resident, Elizabeth Prater, who was awoken by her kitten Diddles, some time between 3.30am and 4am. It was her belief that she had heard the cry of "murder" at about that time or possibly a bit later. Sarah Lewis who was staying with friends at number 2 Miller's Court also thought she heard a cry, shortly before 4am which seemed to be "coming from the direction of the deceased's room"[211]. As it was a common enough thing to hear about the neighbourhood, both women ignored it.

As for suspects, during her evening's comings and goings Cox had seen Kelly at between a quarter to midnight and midnight in the company of a short, stout man, 5ft 5in tall, wearing a billycock hat. He had a fresh complexion, clean shaven chin, sandy coloured whiskers and carrotty moustache. He carried a can or pot of beer and Kelly was "very much intoxicated"[212], consistent with those who claimed to have seen her at various pubs earlier in the evening.

For a while, her description of the man would be treated as a piece of "principal evidence"[213]. Indeed, the *Daily Telegraph*'s 13 November edition covering the previous day's inquest thought it could observe the outlines of two emerging threads by way of suspect identification in the wider case, and referenced a grab-bag of purported, garbled and legitimate sightings. The first: broadly consistent with Cox's identification. The other: variously described as a "dark foreign-looking man". Historian and student of the murders Philip Sugden put it best in reference to this latter possibility: "No; for credible evidence that the Ripper may have been a Jew the police had to wait for George Hutchinson"[214]. Cox's evidence was about to be trumped.

It was 6pm on Monday, 12 November. The inquest had concluded earlier in the day with a verdict of wilful murder against some person or persons unknown. It was only then that into Commercial Street police station wandered, "a young man named George Hutchinson, who declared that he had seen Kelly at 2a.m... in the company of a man... the exact opposite in appearance of the man seen by Mrs Cox"[215]. He may well have waited three full days and the business end of a fourth, but he had quite a story to tell. It is preserved in full in the official record[216]:

> About 2 am 9th I was coming by Thrawl Street, Commercial Street, and saw just before I got to Flower and Dean Street I saw the murdered woman Kelly. And she said to me Hutchinson will you lend me sixpence. I said I cant I have spent all my money going down to Romford. She said Good morning I must go and find some money. She went away toward Thrawl Street. A man coming in the opposite direction to Kelly tapped her on the shoulder and said something to her. They both burst out laughing. I heard her say alright to

him. And the man said you will be alright for what I have told you. He then placed his right hand around her shoulders. He also had a kind of a small parcel in his left hand with a kind of strap round it. I stood against the lamp of the Queen's Head Public House and watched him. They both then came past me and the man hid down his head with his hat over his eyes. I stooped down and looked him in the face. He looked at me stern. They both went into Dorset Street I followed them. They both stood at the corner of the Court for about 3 minutes. He said something to her. She said alright my dear come along you will be comfortable. He then placed his arm on her shoulder and gave her a kiss. She said she had lost her handkerchief he then pulled his handkerchief a red one out and gave it to her. They both then went up the court together. I then went to the Court to see if I could see them, but could not. I stood there for about three quarters of an hour to see if they came out they did not so I went away.

Description age about 34 or 35, height 5ft 6 complexion pale, dark eyes and eye lashes slight moustache, curled up each end, and hair dark, very surly looking dress long dark coat, collar and cuffs trimmed astracan. And a dark jacket under. Light waistcoat dark trousers dark felt hat turned down in the middle. Button boots and gaiters with white buttons. Wore a very thick gold chain white linen collar. Black tie with horse shoe pin. Respectable appearance walked very sharp. Jewish appearance. Can be identified.

The surviving, official case notes show Inspector Abberline believed in the truth and importance of Hutchinson's statement after having interrogated him personally. On the same evening that the witness had come forward, Abberline wrote the following report:

He informed me that he had occasionally given the deceased a few shillings, and that he had known her about 3 years. Also that he was surprised to see a man so well dressed in her company which caused him to watch them. He can identify the man and arrangement was at once made for two officers to accompany him round the district for a few hours tonight with a view of finding the man if possible.

Hutchinson is at present in no regular employment, and he has promised to go with an officer tomorrow morning at 11.30 a.m. to the Shoreditch mortuary to identify the deceased. Several arrests have been made on suspicion of being connected with the recent murders, but the various persons detained have been able to satisfactorily account for their movements and were released.[217]

On the next day, the 13th, the media were already publishing elements of Hutchinson's story. By the 14th, it was reported that the Central News Agency had interviewed him and his name was linked publicly for the first time directly to the account. Immediately, and to and varying degrees thereafter, his statement was viewed juxtaposed, almost in opposition, to the suspect described by Cox. The *Echo* lays out the situation in its edition of the 13th: "The police are *embarrassed* with two definite descriptions of the man suspected of the murder" (author's italics).

The same edition also latched onto early doubts about the degree of value with which the new evidence provided by Hutchinson was being treated by the police: "The importance which they then attached to it has since suffered diminution."

It might have been understandable. Hutchinson's soon to be published media version (see appendix ii) elaborated further on the police statement to the point of stretching his words to nearly twice the length and, in some quarters, credulity along with it. While every other plausible sighting ranged between fleeting and to the point, his read like a screenplay, prompting one modern sceptic to describe Hutchinson's suspect as, "the perfect villain... totally theatrical"[218].

It wouldn't take the arrival of the present era for doubters to start picking his story apart. Almost immediately legitimate questions started being aired in the press, beginning with the same *Echo* edition of the 13th, before his name was even in the public domain:

From latest inquiries it appears that a very reduced importance seems to be now - in the light of later investigation - attached to a statement made by a person last night that he saw a man with the deceased on the night of the murder. Of course, such a statement should have been made at the inquest, where the evidence, taken on oath, could have been compared with the supposed description of the murderer given by the witnesses. Why, ask the authorities, did not the informant come forward before? As many as fifty-three persons have, in all, made statements as to "suspicious men," each of whom was thought to be Mary Janet Kelly's assassin. The most remarkable thing in regard to the latest statement is, that no one else can be found to say that a man of that description given was seen with the deceased, while, of course, there is the direct testimony of the witnesses at the inquest, that the person seen with the deceased at midnight was of quite a different appearance.

On the 15th, it was the *Star* that reported along similar lines. It seems almost to be repeating Hutchinson's suspect identification, tongue-in-cheek:

Another story now discredited is that of the man Hutchinson, who said that on Friday morning last he saw Kelly with a dark-complexioned, middle-aged, foreign-looking, bushy-eyebrowed gentleman, with the dark moustache turned up at the ends, who wore the soft felt hat, the long dark coat, trimmed with astrachan, the black necktie, with horseshoe pin, and the button boots, and displayed a massive gold watch-chain, with large seal and a red stone attached.

As we have already said, the only piece of information of any value which has yet transpired is the description given by the widow Cox of a man - short, stout, with a blotchy face and a carroty moustache - who at midnight on Thursday went with the murdered woman into her room.

Then on the 16th, the *Morning Post* too asked whether it was wise to put too much store in Hutchinson at the expense of Cox's identification:

Many persons competent to form a reliable opinion upon the matter still believe that Cox accurately described a man who was in the company of the woman Kelly, and therefore they question the wisdom of the police in relying exclusively upon Hutchinson's information.

On the 17th, it was the turn of the *London Graphic* to make some salient points about Hutchinson's suspect:

It is true that on this last occasion a man has given a very precise description of the supposed murderer. The very exactitude of his description, however, engenders a feeling of scepticism. The witness in question admits that at the time he saw him he did not suspect the person he watched of being the Whitechapel assassin; yet, at two o'clock in the morning, in badly-lighted thoroughfares, he observed more than most of us would observe in broad daylight, with ample time at our disposal. A man who in such a hasty survey notes such points as "a pair of dark 'spats,' with light buttons, over button boots," and "a red stone hanging from his watch-chain," must possess the eyes of a born detective.

As late as a week after Hutchinson came forward, the debate between which candidate should be given pre-eminence, Cox's or Hutchinson's, remained inconclusive as far as the *Echo* was concerned. It did not speak well for Hutchinson that his fuller account, supposedly closer to the time of the murder, was at best seen on equal terms with Cox's:

The police have not relaxed their endeavours to hunt down the murderer in the slightest degree; but so far they remain without any direct clue. Some of the authorities are inclined to place most reliance upon the statement made by Hutchinson as to his having seen the latest victim with a gentlemanly man of dark complexion, with a dark moustache. Others are disposed to think that the shabby man with a blotchy face and a carrotty moustache described by the witness Mary Ann Cox, is more likely to be the murderer.[219]

The inferred unease that underpinned some of these reports was almost immediately echoed all the way across the Atlantic by Washington's *Evening Star*. In its edition of 14 November, it welcomed Hutchinson's involvement, but with a pinch of salt and a cutting advisory: "it would be just as well to keep a sharp eye upon Hutchinson himself"[220].

What these reports point to is that there were cracks in the unanimity and relief that greeted the arrival of George Hutchinson. These dissenting journalistic voices suggest Hutchinson's usefulness to police may have been transitory at best, and appear to refer to some level of official disillusionment with his value as a witness. Certainly, there is little to suggest he played a part in aiding their enquiries any later than the first few days after coming forward.

What he did manage to do was blunt the impact of Cox's suspect identification and overthrow its pre-eminence; a situation that has essentially gone undisturbed for 130 years. Given the prejudices of the times possibly, it may not have helped that she earned her living on the streets and was readily described as "a wretched looking specimen of East-end womanhood"[221]. On the other hand, modern students of the case who advocate in favour of Hutchinson's value as a witness can boast none other than Inspector Abberline in his corner at a critical moment in the preserved record: a vouchsafe caught in the crystal amber of that first evening, forever more maintaining its potential to transfix.

However, in 1903, the by then retired Abberline was interviewed by the *Pall Mall Gazette* about elements of the case and their intersection with wife poisoner George Chapman, also known as Seweryn Klosowski[222]. There was nothing reported in that interview to say Hutchinson's testimony *per se* had survived the test of time by way of Abberline's esteem, and sufficient hints to suggest otherwise*. It is much the same story, when looking at latter-day recollections and theories put forward by other officials who had been involved with the case back in 1888. Or, as Dew put it diplomatically when championing Cox's suspect to the exclusion of Hutchinson's, "I believe the man of the billycock hat... was the last person to enter Marie Kelly's room"[223].

---

* In the Pall Mall Gazette interview of 24 March 1903, Abberline references descriptions of Jack The Ripper wearing a "peaked cap", as described by witnesses Schwartz and Lawende, and the *limited* nature of the views caught of the killer by witnesses.

<u>End of Chapter 5 notes:</u>
Word about town...

In famous London City,
in eighteen eighty-eight,
Four beastly cruel murders have been done...
Some say it was old Nick himself,
Or else a Russian Jew.
Some say it was a "cannibal" from the
Isle of Kickaiboo.
Some say it must be the Bashi-Bazouks,
Or else it's the Chinese
Come over to Whitechapel to commit
Such crimes as these[224].

Contemporary jingle

I'm not a butcher, I'm not a Yid,
Nor yet a foreign Skipper,
But I'm your own light-hearted friend,
Yours truly, Jack The Ripper[225].

Anonymous

CHAPTER 6

THE LEATHER APRON SHUFFLE

'Leather Apron' by himself is quite an unpleasant character... he is a more ghoulish and devilish brute than can be found in all the pages of shocking fiction.

Star, 5 September 1888

By the time he finally came forward, George Hutchinson's contention that the man last seen with Kelly was a foreign Jew seems to have had little impact on the streets. The East End community's sense of horror at the crime itself had been overwhelming. It was directed foremost at the killer, an inhuman monster who had taken on an ultra-national mantle, and then authorities: "heedless and helpless... the police did nothing" railed the press[226][227]. Together with the fact that attention, in the first instance, had fallen on Cox's non-Jewish suspect, these realities helped to mitigate against a recurrence of the racial tensions on display in the heady days after Chapman's murder. As has already been seen, after that riot the police hierarchy had operated highly mindful of not inflaming community antagonisms, and by mid-November the Jewish crisis had been successfully brought off the boil, passing into what might be described as an anti-climactic phase. Possibly too, it was an early case of a media cycle having played itself out, in conjunction with the press having belatedly come to exhibit a higher degree of responsibility in its reporting. Though it may have taken a while to have effect, an early indication of such was the *Times'* editorial edict of 25 October, which refused further discussion on the blood libel. All indications are that Kelly's murder marked the moment at which the other newspapers followed suit. Effectively, it meant that the Jewish angle had become yesterday's news – something the killer could not have foreseen, though it would spur his frustration and ultimately help flush him out.

An indication of this changed environment can be seen by the scant attention paid to coverage of religiously inspired blood-lust stories that entered circulation after Kelly's murder. Only briefly did it raise its head, on 22 November with a short article out of Warsaw published by the *Daily News* and *St James's Gazette*: "Religious Fanaticism Among The Polish Jews" the headline read. The piece failed to gain traction, and quickly disappeared.

Yet, Hutchinson had managed to reinvigorate a degree of racial narrative at a crucial moment in the investigation itself. All well and good in the spirit of the cards falling where they may; if the murderer had been a Jew, and Hutchinson correct. But was something else going on?

Looking carefully at Hutchinson's police statement and his subsequent elaboration as reported in the press, there appear to be recurring references reminiscent of one of the big stories which had graced newspapers in September, that of "Hebrew menace" Leather Apron. Keen to do their jobs, while mindful of the potential to inflame passions, the authorities had quickly and carefully brought justice to bear and defused the issue, eliminating John Pizer as a suspect. Yet parts of what Hutchinson recounted seem to have been ripped out of the pages describing this old story. At times, the very language used is uncomfortably similar.

For example, it might be taken that his suspect's initial approach towards Kelly was relatively sudden, and she caught unawares. The man does not seem to initiate contact, for all that he is coming in a front-on direction, until he is close enough to tap her on the shoulder. A contemporary image in the *Illustrated Police News* displays Hutchinson's gentleman pivoting around to announce himself by gently grabbing Kelly as she walks past[228]. Similarly, Leather Apron is described as having the "uncanny peculiarity" of leaving victims unaware "of his presence until he is close by them".

Interestingly, the following week's edition of the *Illustrated Police News* featured an artist's impression of Hutchinson's villain as the front page centrepiece and in various scenes from the night's events, plus drawings of other "incidents in the case". In one of those, the unannounced tap on the shoulder Kelly receives, as described in Hutchinson's account, has become transposed onto a scene harking back to the Leather Apron saga, with a blurb underneath, "a man of villainous appearance seen accosting women in Whitechapel". It demonstrates that a muddled link between Hutchinson's man and Leather Apron had been made even at the time, at least on this occasion.

Closer analysis reveals that there are eight such points of parallel in total between Hutchinson's man and Leather Apron:

Leather Apron:

… the most singular characteristic of the man is the universal statement that in moving about he never makes any noise. What he wears on his feet the women do not know, but they agree that he moves noiselessly.

Hutchinson's suspect:

One thing I noticed, and that was that he walked very softly

Leather Apron:

… never by any chance attacks a man.

Hutchinson's suspect:

The man I saw did not look as though be would attack another one.

Leather Apron:

His expression is sinister.

Hutchinson's suspect:

… looked at me very sternly

Leather Apron:

His hair is black... He has a small black moustache.

Hutchinson's suspect:

… dark complexion, and dark moustache turned up at the ends[229]… dark eyes and eye lashes ("dark" deleted) slight moustache, curled up each end, and hair dark[230]

Leather Apron:

His lips are usually parted in a grin which is not only not reassuring, but excessively repellent

Hutchinson's suspect:

… very surly looking

Leather Apron:

… all are united in the belief that he is a Jew or of Jewish parentage, his face being of a marked Hebrew type

Hutchinson's suspect:

Jewish appearance

Leather Apron:

… always carries a leather knife

Hutchinson's suspect:

He carried a small parcel in his hand about eight inches long, and it had a strap round it. He had it tightly grasped in his left hand.

In light of this realisation alone, it is opportune to critically re-asses Hutchinson. There are those students of the case today who limit their suspicions of his witness statement to someone possibly looking to have his moment in the spotlight. The accusation is that he either exaggerated what he saw, or being an out-and-out charlatan, fabricated it. There are also those who see Hutchinson's motivation in a more sinister light.

As pointed out by reports published in the days and weeks after giving his witness statement, there remain legitimate questions when considering Hutchinson's evidence. Why for example, did he wait three days plus the business end of a fourth after the discovery of Kelly's body to come forward? In other words, why dally until the inquest into her murder had wrapped-up? In his media statement, Hutchinson goes some way to tackling this question by saying that he told a police officer on the street on the Sunday, but this is less than convincing. Why would a policeman at the height of the Ripper scare not act on the information? Such was the climate in the days following Kelly's murder that police were throwing all possible resources at tracking down any leads. From a contemporary press report:

> All the constables and detectives available were distributed throughout the district, and a house-to-house visitation was commenced, and all who knew the deceased woman were interrogated as to the persons last seen in her company.[231]

During the course of the investigation, police ran to ground every conceivable theory from travelling cowboys to Portuguese sailors, and would interview a cast of thousands. At least several hundred of those would be based on approaches from the public[232]. "No clue was turned down as too trivial for investigation," recounts Dew[233]. One of his senior colleagues said as much: "No stone was left unturned. We followed out the suggestions of the public"[234]. Inspector Abberline corroborated his fellow officers, telling the press of the role played in the investigation by potential clues supplied by members of the East End population, "all of them requiring to be recorded and searched into"[235]. Not surprising then, that the officer Hutchinson mentions has never been identified.

One reason that his modern-day doubters have suggested for his coming forward is that Sarah Lewis' inquest testimony compelled him to do so by placing him at the scene with a certain air of mystery, "looking up the court as if waiting for someone to come out"[236]. The following extract is an example[237] of early coverage from an edition published on the same day as the inquest, 12 November, though whether Hutchinson read about her testimony, heard it first hand as evidence was being tendered, or indirectly via the neighbourhood telegraph, is open to speculation:

MAN SEEN IN THE COURT

Sarah Lewis, of 24, Great Pearl-street, Spitalfields, stated that she worked at a laundry. On Friday morning witness was at No. 2 Room, Miller's-court, at half-past two o'clock. She went to call on a woman she knew - Mrs. Keyler. It was half-past two by Spitalfields' Church clock. She saw a man at the entrance to the court. He was not talking to anyone. (coroner) Was he tall? - Not very - a stout-looking man. I do not know whether he had dark clothes on. He seemed as if waiting for some one.[238]

There is a loose consensus within Ripperology today that Hutchinson was the man Lewis observed. Whether innocuously, as his statements assert, or menacingly, as some of his detractors argue, remains to be seen. Certainly, his own proffered chronology and movements dovetailed neatly with Lewis at the moment their respective statements meet up at 2.30am.

A detail that has helped fuel suspicion, was Hutchinson's contention that on at least one occasion during his vigil he "went up the court and stayed there a couple of minutes, but did not see any light in the house or hear any noise"[239] thus putting himself inside Miller's Court, outside Kelly's room; displaying knowledge of her domicile to boot.

In doing so he put himself in the potentially vulnerable position of being the last person identified at such close proximity to the victim. Why place himself in such an awkward spot? Was it maybe to pre-emptively stave off accusations if the need became necessary?

There are other things that don't gel, rendering his testimony internally inconsistent. He was able to furnish an eagle eye description of a suspect seen relatively briefly in poor light, including details of the man's eyelashes and a watch chain which boasted "a big seal, with a red stone hanging from it". It was the nature of the man's ostentatious attire replete with "thick gold chain" dangling from his waistcoat, which Hutchinson claimed piqued his curiosity. The man stood out. But how long would a man drawing such attention to himself* at two o'clock in the morning have lasted unmolested in some of the worst and darkest back streets of London's most notorious slum? Hutchinson's clear implication was that the gentleman was not a local. "My suspicions were aroused by seeing the man so well dressed," as he put it. But at the conclusion of his media interview he changed tack: "I believe that he lives in the neighbourhood, and I fancied that I saw him in Petticoat-lane on Sunday morning". It is quite a contradiction.

There is also the issue of how Kelly's gentleman managed to whisk her off Commercial Street and into Miller's Court under the nose of police and Vigilance Committee patrols who were on the lookout for unusually dressed passers-by[240][241]. Recounts Dew:

> Hundreds of police, in uniform, in plain-clothes and in all manner of disguises - some even dressed as women - patrolled every yard of every street in the 'danger zone' every few minutes. The most obscure corners were periodically visited. All suspicious characters were stopped and questioned.[242]

Or as more than one editorial observed, "few could have failed to notice them at that hour of the morning," given their contrasting appearances[243][244]. Yet only Hutchinson did, seemingly.

---

* A freshly disembarked colonial subject was robbed of £30 by two women in Spitalfields at about the same time; *Star*, 10 November 1888.

One of the key questions is what was Hutchinson doing in and around Miller's Court on his three-quarter hour-plus vigil in poor weather? It was a rainy night in late autumn, when temperatures got down to about 36 degrees Fahrenheit (2.5 degrees Celsius), and if he is to be believed he had just walked back to London from Romford, roughly 12 miles (20 kilometres).

A similar question applies to Kelly. Why would she have gone back out again in those conditions, the pressing need to pay for a roof over her head notwithstanding? Cox recounts her singing, as do others, ensconced at home not long after one o'clock after having seen her an hour or so earlier in a thoroughly intoxicated state, barely able to speak. Kelly's near neighbour from the first floor, Elizabeth Prater had arrived at the corner of Miller's Court and Dorset Street at about one o'clock and waited there fruitlessly near McCarthy's shop for her male companion. She eventually called it quits at about 1.30am. During that time "no one passed up the court (and) if they did I would have seen them" she told police[245]. In other words, Kelly must still have been home. As Prater turned in for the night and took the stairs, all was quiet in Kelly's room. She recalled not so much as a glimmer being seen, though she told the inquest she should have been able to observe any light[246]. In the time it took her to quickly fall asleep, Prater did not hear any noise to suggest Kelly went out again[247].

There are reports too of Kelly's socialising and drinking in local pubs. These point to a time frame considerably earlier in the evening. In conjunction with Prater and Cox's evidence, it suggests that Kelly had already settled in for the night by the time Hutchinson had her walking down Commercial Street. His 2am scenario would almost certainly have taken place in the rain, which interestingly is a detail he did not mention for all the minutiae he catalogued. But Cox did mention it. Twice. When she went in and out to warm and dry herself at about 1.00am[248]; and again at around 3am by which time she said it was "raining hard"[249].

All indications are that Cox was correct in describing a cold and wet night. The Lord Mayor of London's show got under way later that morning to less than upbeat weather conditions, in "muddy streets and drizzling rain" commented the *Pall Mall Gazette*. "During the preceding night heavy rain fell, and the morning dawned with a damp, drizzly atmosphere, the air being raw and cold," wrote the *Echo*[250]. There were many such reports that were consistent with the previous day's forecasts. The *St James's Gazette* of the 8th had predicted:

> The weather over the British isles this morning is in the most part entirely overcast. The forecast for London and south of England for the twenty-four hours ending at noon to-morrow (ie the 9th): - South-easterly and easterly winds increasing in force again, Snow-showers at time. Warning signals still up on all coasts.[251] (author's parentheses)

The *London Evening Standard* had provided an even grimmer prognostication[252]:

> London Weather forecast this day: Easterly and south-easterly winds, strong, a gale in places. Squally, some sleet or snow showers.

It is a feather in Cox's cap that her testimony is consistent with the weather conditions, which she is quick to refer to. On the other hand, such an obvious omission in Hutchinson's account rankles. He paints a highly detailed portrait, but it has all the air of a Sunday afternoon promenade. And not just because he omits reference to the cold and rain in those early morning hours of 9 November, 1888.

In the account of his 2am saunter, he claims that he and Kelly bumped into one another on Commercial Street, while he was travelling north toward Flower & Dean Street. They quickly parted company after she unsuccessfully tried to borrow money from the penniless labourer, and "she went away (south) towards Thrawl Street" leaving him presumably to resume his trajectory north. Yet he was supposedly within earshot, and more importantly facing in the right direction (i.e. south) to see her accosted by the suspicious gentleman. In Hutchinson's telling, a few flirtatious pleasantries are exchanged before Kelly turns around together with her new friend and they make their way north up Commercial Street towards Hutchinson. However, he seems to stay ahead of them, with all three now moving north, according to the internal dynamics of his account. Hutchinson must have kept tabs on the pair either by anticipating their moves, with the duo at his back, or alternatively walking back to front. Whichever the case, it appears to have been a successful manoeuvre because he next pops up strategically positioned under a lamp by the Queen's Head public house in time to see the couple come past. Here he gets a leering look under the gentleman's hat at his face, before Kelly takes her client across the road to Dorset Street. Hutchinson is in hot pursuit and spies them arrive at destination outside Miller's Court. But, for the prospective lovers it is a case of so close yet so far away. Cold and raining it may have been (not that Hutchinson mentions it), but despite appearances, what had transpired on Commercial Street between working girl and punter had failed to seal the deal. So the pair stop to flirt or negotiate for another three minutes, much of it within earshot of Hutchinson upon whom the snippets of captured dialogue make a profound impact, imprinting on his memory. Success finally achieved, it is poetically celebrated by the unfurling of a red handkerchief, gifted to Kelly by her late night admirer. At which point, and only then, Hutchinson recounts, they "both went up the court together".

Which begs the question why should a prostitute and her client grab Hutchinson's attention in such a way, a stone's throw from Christ Church Spitalfields, the soliciting epicentre of the neighbourhood? Especially given he must have known what Kelly did for a living and would later tell the media he harboured no suspicions that the man might be a murderer. Why go to such lengths based on nothing more than the questionable look of a gentleman's clothing, which he is unlikely to have had a particularly good view of until the subject of his curiosity walked past the Queen's Head? But according to both his police and media accounts, he had already well and truly committed himself to the task, having walked nearly 200 yards with the pair under some degree of observation.

It is by now apparent that the more Hutchinson's statements are scrutinised, the more difficult they are to reconcile, and the comedic undertow, harder to ignore. "I could swear to the man anywhere," then almost in the same breath, "I fancy that I saw him… but I was not certain". "I have spent all my money," he says, but is presumably able to pay for his lodgings when he enters the Victoria Home "as soon as it opened in the morning". He says he abandoned his vigil at 3am but Cox who came home at that time does not mention him. He says he was able to identify Kelly at Shoreditch mortuary, but the condition of the corpse was such that even her former partner Joseph Barnett could only do so with difficulty and on precarious grounds. The inconsistencies are everywhere. He describes an extraordinary act of foresight, vigilance and perseverance in following Kelly and her client on the night in question, but can't manage to get himself to a police station until many days afterwards, and then only at the behest of a fellow lodger.

And yet…

Tempting as it may be to throw the baby out with bath water, Hutchinson's account cannot just be laughed off. At a certain point, at 2.30am outside Miller's Court, it catches up with the reality of Sarah Lewis' inquest testimony. There is no denying the veracity of that element of the story. But once the realisation dawns that his account falls into two parts – one corroborated, the other an unsubstantiated fantasy – Hutchinson is undone and the two components cannot be put back together. Instead, a self-serving alibi can be seen for what it is: having been brought into the service of a tight spot. Method to madness, crazy as a fox, Hutchinson grafted a fictitious tale onto a genuine element staking it would provide his deliverance.

Illustrated Police News, 24 November 1888

Is Hutchinson channeling Leather Apron? *Illustrated Police News* front page, 24 November 1888

Passing pivot: *Illustrated Police News,* 17 November 1888

Victoria Home For Working Men (1902)

End of Chapter 6 notes:
A night at the Victoria Home

The Victoria Home For Working Men, where George Hutchinson usually stayed was situated on the corner of Commercial and Wentworth streets. It had clear and strict rules in place that covered all manner of practical considerations from hygiene to behaviour, including a system governing when residents were required to pay for their stay, as well as admittance times. According to a contemporary report:

> Tickets for beds are issued from five p.m. Until 12.30 midnight, and after that hour if a man wants to get in he must have a pass.[253]

For those with a more regular income, weekly tickets were available too. Not being in possession of one of the pre-arranged passes would explain why Hutchinson walked right past his lodgings, as he made his way up Commercial Street at 2am on his supposed return from Romford. But it begs the question what was he doing practically across the road from home, one and half hours after missing his last chance for a warm bed? He does not mention what his plans were prior to being waylaid by Kelly and her customer. It would be an interesting point to ponder but for the problem of taking his evidence at face value.

To wit, he told the press, and presumably the police, that after leaving Miller's Court and wandering about, "I came in as soon as it (the Victoria Home) opened in the morning". Which only brings up another question: how did he come upon the money to pay for his entry, given he told Kelly, "I am spent out"? Also, wouldn't he have had to wait until evening to be admitted?

Author Jack London seems to answer the last question in *The People Of The Abyss* (1903) when he almost certainly described the Victoria Home in part of his book discussing lodging houses. He summed up the expectations governing guests' routine generally as being "forced out of bed willy-nilly first thing in the morning" and at the Victoria Home specifically as "in the morning out you go"[254]. Consistent with this, is an undated leaflet sighted by the author during research, with the heading/s, "The Victoria Homes For Working Men - Instituted 1887 - Rules". Rule number 12 presents the span of time during which bedrooms were at the disposal of lodgers: from 7.00pm to no later than 9.00am[255].

As is the case with so much of Hutchinson's evidence, the more it is explored for validation, the greater the head scratching which ensues.

CHAPTER 7

MUDDY WATERS

… it would be just as well to keep a sharp eye upon Hutchinson himself. He may be a convenient person to have about at a critical stage of the investigation which is soon to follow. The man popularly known as "Jack the Ripper" is full of devices, and it would not be surprising if it were found necessary later to put Hutchinson in his turn on the defensive.

Washington Evening Star, 14 November 1888

Trying to establish a full understanding of what Hutchinson was hoping to achieve by coming forward with his account is not a straightforward task. There is no doubt that Sarah Lewis placed him in a compromising position by spotting him at 2.30am outside Miller's Court, nailing him to the scene. The flip side was that she had inadvertently provided him with an opportunity to attach a cover story in the form of the earlier, fantastic part of his tale. Is it possible that here, within this earlier time frame, lay something that particularly concerned him? Something so bad it required a caricature Jewish villain invested with the dual role of patsy, and importantly, pied piper to shift the focus away from Miller's Court.

The spell he has been able to cast over the case has proven seductive ever since. A practical effect of which has been to impose a wedge on the chronology and geography of the timeline with the benefit of affording himself a good degree of protection. Certainly, it relocated Kelly's last supposed movements away from Miller's Court and onto Commercial Street at what was a critical time. Conveniently, Hutchinson placed himself on the road from Romford in the lead-up, allowing himself a comfortable time span for an alibi, as perfect as it was next to unverifiable. Hutchinson's long march remains uncorroborated by direct evidence to this day.

Curious too, that Hutchinson's tale should find Kelly on Commercial Street at a time when all indications previously had pointed to her being ensconced at home in poor weather conditions after a night of hard drinking leaving her "very much intoxicated"[256] and barely able to speak[257]. Cox had heard Kelly for the last time just after 1am; and between the hours of 1am to 1.30am Prater had stood at the archway of Miller's Court, practically within view of Kelly's front door and saw nobody come past and heard nothing.

It is high time to put Hutchinson's testimony aside and ask whether something happened in Kelly's room in that critical blind spot between 1.30am when Prater retired, and 2.30am when the timeline joins up again in Miller's Court courtesy of Lewis, as well as Hutchinson's corroborating admission. According to Dr Bond, it did: Kelly was murdered. Qualified as his autopsy report may have been regarding the time of death, the medico was "pretty certain" one or two o'clock was "the probable time of the murder"[258]. It boils down to Dr Bond's professional opinion versus Hutchinson's word.

Granted, there is an early *Times* article which attributes to Dr Phillips a time of death several hours[259] after that quoted in Dr Bond's report. Unfortunately, an in-depth exploration of medical evidence as was expected at the inquest was left suspended. It leaves Dr Bond's report to Assistant Commissioner Robert Anderson as the sole official word extant covering what time Kelly was murdered from the medical standpoint.

What are the broader implications of Kelly lying dead in her bed at the same time that Hutchinson would otherwise have her walking down Commerical Street? For starters, Prater and Lewis' evidence of having heard a cry of "murder" a few hours later starts to rest on questionable ground. Realistically, *more* questionable ground.

It is true that both Lewis, "a little before four", and Prater "probably after four", told the inquest of hearing a single cry. But Prater had been less than certain about the time when police took down the original witness statements on the 9th, suggesting there was a half hour time frame in which it might have happened from 3.30am, and that she heard it two or three times.

Neither Prater nor Lewis felt it constituted grounds for alarm, given how common it was in the neighbourhood, and there was nothing in either's testimony to tie it definitively to Kelly or her room. Prater told police, "I did not take much notice of the cries as I frequently hear such cries from the back of the lodging house where the windows look into Millers Court". Might part of the explanation lie contained within this elaboration of Prater's? There is also her preamble of being woken shortly beforehand by Diddles the kitten, which contains almost a ring of poetic device, even cliché. In the Victorian era, cats were popularly considered to have supernatural sensibilities and able to portend bad tidings.

In Prater's case it is tempting to ask whether this aspect of her inquest evidence may not have reflected the high emotion of belatedly realising she had come so close to a great evil and the associated guilt of having heard nothing while an acquaintance close-by was being murdered. An interview she gave to the *Star* on the 10th suggests an element of what we might recognise today as 'survivor's guilt'. While describing her relationship with Kelly, the article refers to Prater breaking down and sobbing violently:

> "I'm a woman myself," she says, "and I've got to sleep in that place to-night right over where it happened." Mrs. Prater saw the dead and mutilated body through the window of Kelly's room, which it is to be remembered was on the ground floor. The pump stands just by there, and Mrs. Prater took advantage of a journey for some water to peep through the window for which, when the door was broken open, the curtains were torn down. She says, "I could not bear to look at it only for a second, but I can never forget the sight of it if I live to be a hundred."

As for Lewis, she was a visitor at Miller's Court. She may not have been the best placed to locate the direction of such a cry and she made no pretence to be able to recognise the sound of Kelly's voice. She told the police: "I did not know the deceased."

None of the other residents are reported to have heard it. Cox was adamant at the inquest that she had heard no cry, and of the three, she alone remained awake throughout[260]:

> I feel certain if there had been the cry of "Murder" in the place I should have heard it; there was not the least noise.

Another on the resident list of 'insomniacs' was Julia Ventury who told police, "I was awake all night and could not sleep". She lived in the room opposite Kelly's, at number one, and her window almost faced Kelly's door. Like Cox she testified that, "I heard no scream". Referring to another neighbour residing next to Ventury, at number three, the press reported that, "although his rooms face the scene of the murder, he heard nothing of it"[261].

Prater and Lewis may have been jumping to conclusions, or they may have had good cause, but it is noteworthy that almost immediately elements of the media seem to have settled on the belief that nothing had been heard. On the 10th the *Times* wrote that, "it appears clear that no noise of any kind was heard"; while as might be expected, the *Star* made the same point in a more polemic style:

> The desire to be interesting has had its effect on the people who live in the Dorset-street-court and lodging-houses, and for whoever cares to listen there are a HUNDRED HIGHLY CIRCUMSTANTIAL STORIES, which, when carefully sifted, prove to be totally devoid of truth. One woman... who lives in the court stated that at about two o'clock she heard a cry of "Murder." This story soon became popular, until at last half a dozen women were retailing it as their own personal experience. Each story contradicted the others with respect to the time at which the cry was heard. A *Star*

reporter who inquired into the matter extracted from one of the women the confession that the story was, as far as she was concerned, a fabrication; and he came to the conclusion that it was to be disregarded.[262]

Open-ended as the evidence for a scream having been heard remains, it rests in contradiction with Bond's autopsy report. Working back then, towards his estimate for Kelly's time of death between one and two o'clock, a key question becomes, what was Hutchinson doing looking up the court at 2.30am and demonstrating the amount of interest described by Lewis? If he had just butchered Kelly it is unlikely he would have been milling around in the open afterwards and he may have been quite messy from the task of mutilation. Based on the extensive nature of the wounds, it would have taken some considerable time, so the chronology alone suggests the scenario doesn't quite gel.

Is it possible that she was already lying dead on her bed, but as yet unmutilated? It makes for an interesting premise when teasing out the evidence. One side of Kelly's room was situated within the neck of the entrance passage opening into the court and very much exposed to the noise of passers-by coming and going by her door, as well as from the court onto which her windows faced. Prater for one is known to have made her way to her own room at about 1.30am. Might such nearby noise in conjunction with a defiant Kelly in the face of imminent death have startled the killer at a critical moment, acting as a hiatus to his bloody plans?

While not conclusive, there is a hint in the official medical record that Kelly may not have been taken totally unawares and made some attempt to defend herself. Dr Bond's autopsy notes that:

Both arms & forearms had extensive & jagged wounds... The right thumb showed a small superficial incision about 1 in(ch) long, with extravasation of blood in the skin & there were several abrasions on the back of the hand moreover showing the same condition.

This interrupted scenario would explain Hutchinson's vigil as observed: Kelly dead, he was left rattled, unsure whether her murder had gone off unnoticed. Cautiously, he made his way outside to see if anybody was the wiser and to survey the situation; a possible genesis of sorts for his account that he "went up the court and stayed there a couple of minutes". All appeared calm, but only time would tell. In the meantime, discretion was the better part of valour. He decided to evaluate the situation from a distance and bide his time, keeping Kelly's front door under careful observation. Such an outline has a degree of overlap with elements of the story from Berner Street, on the night of the double-event, when the killer managed to keep his cool despite things moving out of his control. Was his vigil on the open thoroughfare of Dorset Street a sign of his determination not to get trapped in another cul-de-sac as may have happened in Dutfield's Yard? Is the image of Hutchinson waiting in front of Miller's Court a real-time and ugly vision of a serial killer gaining in sophistication, mindful of the pitfalls around him? In this regard, the observation of one Dorset Street resident* is telling: "the murderer couldn't have come to a worse place for escaping than this court"[263].

Such a consideration might help to provide an expanded understanding of Lewis' evidence. What she saw at 2.30am was not someone watching the court intently as if waiting for someone to come out as she assumed, but Hutchinson waiting to observe anyone going into Kelly's room and satisfying himself the alarm had not been sounded. In which case, his strategy was to prove successful and eventually allow him to regain the initiative.

"As the clock struck three," is the time Hutchinson says he abandoned his vigil. There may have been an element of truth to it, an insight into a convoluted tale. It was also raining hard by then, an ideal incentive and the perfect cover to return indoors and resume his work. He had allowed sufficient passage of time since his scare to satisfy himself that the coast was clear. Now he could finish what he

---

* Thomas Bowyer, the man who found Mary Kelly's body.

had come to Miller's Court to do. As long as the rain poured, nobody would hear a thing, nobody was coming, and Kelly was beyond a care in this world.

Cox's testimony seems to provide a degree of support for such a scenario. By both her and Hutchinson's accounts there is every chance she should have bumped into him as he readied to depart the scene before he says he wandered off down Dorset Street. But he was nowhere to be seen. It is frightening to contemplate the notion that he was just ahead of her, moving in the same direction, not away from Miller's Court, but back indoors. As Cox made her way through the passageway, past Kelly's room and through the courtyard to her own, Jack The Ripper was settling himself in behind the door of number 13. ■

Liberated from the effects of Hutchinson's story on the earlier part of the evening, the evidence of Cox and other Miller's Court residents is free to re-assert itself. Indeed, prior to Hutchinson's muddying of the waters, the police had given focus to a timeline consistent with Dr Bond's estimated time of death between 1am and 2am, with suspicion resting on Cox's man with the billycock hat.

Cox testified that Kelly was the worse for drink when she was last seen, evidenced by her condition and her singing, the later fact corroborated by at least one other resident, Catherine Picket. In fact, Kelly had a well-established reputation for being partial to a tipple[264][265]. That the man last seen with her had been carrying a pot of beer adds a degree of consistency to the picture, enhanced by reports that Kelly had been seen drinking earlier the evening, an issue broadly confirmed by Dew's memoires[266].

Unofficial accounts printed in newspapers like the *Illustrated Police News* and the *Morning Post* placed her drunk at the Britannia public house on the corner of Dorset and Commercial streets around 11.00pm[267]. She was also supposedly seen, at the Horn Of Plenty between 10pm and 11pm in the company of friends. Neither report is without its problems, underscored by the fact they were not raised at the inquest, which is not to say they do not contain an element of truth. Even if they help paint but a general picture, it is enhanced by a more reliable statement given to the Press Association by a friend of Kelly's, Elizabeth Foster, who stated that she had been drinking with her at the Ten Bells on the corner of Commerical and Church streets until around 7pm[268].

A point worth noting is that Hutchinson's police statement originally had a lamppost outside this pub, as the setting for his leering observation of the villain allegedly spied in Kelly's company. This was deleted and replaced with the Queen's Head, which made more sense, situated as it was diagonally across the road from the junction of Dorset and Commercial streets. But it is worth considering whether his mention of the Ten Bells may have been a momentary slip in a tangled tale, perhaps revealing the how and where he had really spent some of his time while supposedly on the long road from Romford; a peek at how he had come to find himself in Kelly's company.

There is another element that deserves mention. John Douglas is a renowned pioneer and authority of the science of modern criminal profiling and co-author of the seminal work, *Mindhunter: inside the FBI elite serial crime unit*. In an FBI special report that presents a brief overview of the Ripper case, prepared in the centenary year of the murders, he opined that "prior to each homicide, the subject (Jack The Ripper) was in a local pub drinking and lowering his inhibitions"[269]. In 1896, upon retirement, Detective Inspector Edmund Reid, who was in charge of the Whitechapel Criminal Investigative Department during the murder spree, told the press much the same thing. It was his belief that Jack The Ripper had been a drinker who used the local public houses to pick up his victims[270]. Indeed, all the women who fell prey to him were either alcoholics or known to partake with gusto, and it is to be remembered that the man seen entering Kelly's room was carrying a pot of beer.

All told, it becomes clear why Cox's man was such a focus of attention prior to Hutchinson's arrival on the scene. Even after the passage of half a century, Dew had faith in the original timeline:

I believe that the man of the billycock hat and beard was the last person to enter Marie Kelly's room that night and was her killer.[271]

Which begs the question whether Hutchinson, demonstrating a breathtaking boldness, came forward not simply because of Lewis' testimony, but in light of Cox's too. No doubt, Lewis compromised his presence at the scene. The question is, did a consummate opportunist choose to make use of her 2.30am sighting for the corroborative value it earned him? Firstly, as a launchpad to undermine the real timeline of events, introducing a Jewish villain into the mix. And secondly, by way of a potential alibi in the event he was ever required to stave off Cox and her midnight observations. In this sense, he may have been counting on the two and half hours-plus between the women's sightings working to his advantage and against Cox, assuming she were able to provide a positive identification if push ever came to shove[272] – mindful too, of the unfavourable, dark and poorly lit conditions. Nothing exists, however, in the surviving official record or in media reports to suggest the investigation ever brought Cox and Hutchinson together. As a well-meaning witness who had volunteered to come forward, he was likely counting on forestalling both the possibility, and its outcome in the event.

A basic consideration, of the police-investigative kind and worth noting, is that the suspect observed by Cox has never been identified. Once Hutchinson presented his account, the man was 'off the hook' as it were – a not insignificant repercussion. Yet, he never did come forward, nor was he ever accounted for. In this respect, the *Illustrated Police News* made the obvious point:

> It is probable that the man with the "carroty" moustache seen in Kelly's company shortly before midnight will soon be found, and it is possible that he may come forward voluntarily now that *he has been to a great extent relieved of the suspicion which rested upon him*.[273](author's italics)

That the man observed by Cox was actually Hutchinson, may help make sense of the conundrum. It might also shed light on why he waited until those hours immediately after the inquest had concluded to come forward. Delaying, certainly mitigated against his chances of being in the same room as Cox, while earning himself the potential to impact directly on the investigation, free of the inquest's legal spotlight. Hiding in plain view in the guise of a concerned witness was the best way of not falling under suspicion; and so it proved. It was the most efficient way forward for each of the purposes of: pre-emptively providing himself with a guarded explanation for what he was doing at Miller's Court; attempting to steer the police timeline of events in a direction of his choosing; and most importantly of all, putting a Jew in the frame for Kelly's murder. All things, which to varying degrees of success, he managed to achieve.

Demonstrating a chilling audacity, it is reminiscent of another act of bravura: Jack The Ripper's actions on the night of the double-event, when having nearly come undone in Dutfield's Yard, he struck again and completed an evidence drop replete with anti-Semitic motif, police hot on his trail. The day after Kelly's murder, Dr Bond warned police that the person they were after was a man "of great coolness and daring"[274]. It is unlikely he was foreseeing the police themselves becoming victims, and so quickly.

Where there is sufficient information available, a degree of overlap in the identifications of the two men seen at Miller's Court comes into singular focus. Both women saw a man they described as "short" and "stout", wearing a "black hat"; Cox a "billycock", Lewis a "wideawake", though the latter's description of the suspect did not provide details of dress and headwear in the original police statement.

The proposition that the two men last observed within line of sight to Kelly's door were in fact the same person bears a good degree of continuity in the timeline, and a fair consistency when comparing the identifications proffered by Cox and Lewis. Importantly, it would have provided a multi-barrelled impetus for Hutchinson to come forward and wreak havoc on the investigation. Of such an effect, Dew was still mindful 50 years after the events, recounting in his memoirs how Hutchinson's belated evidence literally "shook the police reconstruction of the crime"[275]. According to reports in the media, the most practical repercussion was clear:

> … Hutchinson's statement has been thought to throw discredit upon the evidence given at the inquest by the woman Cox, and it is now believed that the murderer was the second man whom the victim took home upon the eve of her murder.[276]

End of Chapter 7 notes:

Cox and Lewis' witness descriptions from their police statements, and testimony as reproduced in the media either on the day of the inquest, or on subsequent days (the *Times* & the *Daily Telegraph*)

	Cox - shortly before midnight	Lewis - about 2.30am
height	short, stout, short and stout, 5ft5in	short, stout, stout-looking, not tall, not very tall
headwear	black felt hat, a hard billy cock, hat, black hat, round billycock hat	black hat, wideawake black hat
dress	shabbily dressed, shabby dark clothes, dark clothes,	
overclothes	dark overcoat, longish coat, black coat	
age	35 or 36	
facial hair	sandy whiskers and moustache, sandy whiskers and full moustache, full carrotty moustache, thick carroty moustache, heavy carrotty moustache	
chin	clean shaven, clean	
face	blotchy, fresh complexion	

A Short Stout Man.

Cox's man (and Lewis' ?): *Famous Crimes,* 1903

CHAPTER 8

OTHERING JACK THE RIPPER

TO THE EDITOR

Sir, - Having been long in India and, therefore, acquainted with the methods of Eastern criminals, it has struck me in reading the accounts of these Whitechapel murders that they have probably been committed by a Malay, or other low-class Asiatic... The mutilations, cutting off the nose and ears, ripping up the body, and cutting out certain organs - the heart, &c. - are all peculiarly Eastern methods and... when the villain is primed with his opium, or bang, or gin, and inspired with his lust for slaughter and blood, he would destroy his defenceless victim with the ferocity and cunning of the tiger.

Your obedient servant, NEMO.
Times, 4 October 1888

Courtesy of modern criminal profiling, serial killers who wade in to 'assist' police investigations into their own crimes are, today, a recognised species. Elaborating on this aspect of serial murder investigations, profiler John Douglas describes the archetype:

> … some killers – the more organized or premeditated type – sometimes even inject themselves into the police investigation to provide bogus information. They do it for different reasons. They may want to find out where the investigation is headed or look for cues that it's progressing along nicely because, naturally, they're concerned about that. They may go to the police in order to beat them to the punch, just in case someone may have seen them or provided

a description… This way, if their names pop up later, they can come back and say, "Oh, wait a minute, I went to you guys a month ago. I was cooperative."[277]

Apart from covering himself in just such a manner, Hutchinson had also provided grist to an illusory mill, that of the "dark foreign looking" Ripper theory referred to in the *Daily Telegraph* on 13 November. It came at the expense of an emerging and by then consistent suspect identification that pointed to one of the indigenous locals. In reality, until Hutchinson's intercession, there was little reason to point the finger at a Jewish suspect apart from Elizabeth Long's limited and problematic sighting on the morning of Chapman's murder[278]. Indeed, without Hutchinson, Long's evidence is left out in the cold, confirming police doubts about its value.

As Cox described her Miller's Court suspect, he gave the impression of being what might loosely be considered an Anglo-Saxon: sandy whiskers, carroty moustache, fresh complexion. There were also several eyewitness reports from the night of the double-event in September. None, noted a foreign accent or a suspect of Jewish appearance; on the contrary, they pointed to a British native.

Moreover, these sightings matched the physical attributes outlined by both Cox and Lewis, in particular a suspect with a stout frame who was not very tall. Returning then to events of that late September night and early morning; Israel Schwartz, who had seen Elizabeth Stride being assaulted at the entrance to Dutfield's Yard not long before her body was found there, gave police details of a man he described as: "age about 30, height 5ft.5in, complexion fair, small brown moustache, full face, broad shoulders". The *Star* quickly tracked Schwartz down and flushed out an addition detail: he was "rather stoutly built"[279].

It was raining fast shortly before eleven o'clock, when John Gardner and John Best entered the Bricklayers' Arms. The pub was only several minutes' walk from the eventual scene of Elizabeth Stride's demise in Berner Street, an event which was less than two hours away. In the doorway, they noticed a woman they would later identify at the mortuary as Elizabeth Stride. She was in the company of a man who was hugging and kissing her. It wasn't long before Gardner and Best engaged in a minor tiff with him, chiding him for his less than chivalrous behaviour and not inviting Stride into the bar. The man remained impassive at the doorway and "would look nobody in the face," says Best.

> If he had been a straight fellow he would have told us to mind our own business, or he would have gone away. I was so certain that there was something up…

The description Best gave of the suspect was corroborated by Gardner and their sighting published in the *Evening News*, on 1 October:

> The man was about 5ft. 5in. in height. He was well dressed in a black morning suit with a morning coat. He had rather weak eyes. I mean he had sore eyes without any eyelashes. I should know the man again amongst a hundred. He had a thick black moustache and no beard. He wore a black billycock hat rather tall, and had on a collar. I said to the woman "that's Leather Apron getting round you." The man was no foreigner; he was an Englishman right enough.

An important feature, corroborating the identification of the pair came courtesy of something Stride was wearing, as Gardner explained to the *Evening News* journalist:

> …before I got to the mortuary to-day I told you the woman had a flower in her jacket, and that she had a short jacket. Well, I have been to the mortuary, and there she was with the dahlias on the right side of her jacket. I could swear (s)he is the same woman I saw at the Bricklayers' Arms.

The amorous couple were next spotted in Berner Street 45 minutes later by a resident, William Marshall. He told the inquest into Stride's murder that he had seen the pair pass the International Working Men's Educational Club on their way south down the street, though he "did not take much notice of them". What little attention he paid them, was courtesy of their public canoodling:

> ...he was kissing her. I heard the man say to deceased, 'You would say anything but your prayers'.

Marshall's eyewitness testimony is mitigated by his admission that there "was no lamp near, and I did not see the face of the man", the latter point being one that he would return to before he was finished providing testimony. He felt on safer ground discussing information that was relevant to Stride, who he had positively identified at the mortuary, although he made a good effort in describing the man, who was "5ft6in and he was rather stout", and "seemed... to be middle-aged". From the little he saw of the man's face, Marshall thought he might not have any whiskers.

At about 12.30am, Police Constable William Smith's beat took him to Berner Street, entering from Commercial Road. Diagonally across the road from the club, he noticed a man with a woman who he would later identify as the murder victim: "I noticed the woman had a flower in her jacket". Like Marshall, he "did not see much of the man's face except that he had no whiskers". He "was about 5ft7in, as near as I could say," and "about 28".

While questioning the value of PC Smith's evidence against the benchmark of Schwartz's, a later police report prepared by Chief Inspector Swanson would add further details to the man Smith described at the inquest[280]. These particulars, a small, dark moustache and a complexion described as dark, fit less than harmoniously with Smith's sworn evidence before the coroner, but take nothing away from the police constable's valuable contribution to the timeline and provide a few broad brushstrokes to add to the suspect's general appearance.

James Brown, a resident of Fairclough Street, was on his way to fetch his supper from a chandler's shop on the corner of Berner and Fairclough streets at "about quarter to 1 on Sunday morning". As he approached the intersection, in an unlit spot standing by the Board School in Fairclough Street, he noticed a man and a woman:

> As I passed them I heard the woman say, "No, not tonight, some other night". That made me turn round, and I looked at them… I did not notice any flowers in her dress. The man had his arm up against the wall, and the woman had her back to the wall facing him… I should say the man was about 5ft7in in height. He appeared to be stoutish built.

What has tended to blunt the value of Brown's testimony is that at first glance it seems to coincide with Schwartz's. In his defence, Brown is admittedly vague in arriving at the time, and only provides general estimates. It was an age where personal timepieces were a luxury, and Brown was a humble dock labourer. As one chronological metric, his account relies on a reference to hearing the first shouts of "police" and "murder", which no doubt described the fracas as club members poured into the streets to get police help. From inquest testimony, it is known that this incident in the evening's events happened just after 1am. Brown estimates having heard this street commotion "about a quarter of an hour after I got (back) in" and by which time he had nearly finished his dinner. In this further attempt at figuring out the time, he was effectively saying he had already returned home soon after 12.45am. But it is essentially the same time that he originally estimated seeing the couple while on his way to collect his evening meal. According to the internal dynamics of his account against the immovable benchmark of the yelling from the street, he must have seen the couple earlier than his originally estimated time of about 12.45am; sometime around or before 12.40am being a safe assumption.

That Brown had sighted Stride, he was in no doubt. He told the coroner, "I am certain the woman was the deceased". But forthright to a fault, he also said that he "did not notice any flowers in her dress" which adds the blemish of authenticity to his testimony. "I saw nothing light in colour about them," he said describing the area they were standing in, which he recalled as being "rather dark".

It is clear that coroner Wynne Baxter took his evidence seriously and was at pains to reference it in his summation. What adds further weight to Brown's testimony is that the London Board School near where he sighted the couple was literally around the corner, a minute's walk away, from the general location where Police Constable Smith had seen the pair at 12.30am, and where Schwartz would see the opening stages of Stride's losing life-struggle at 12.45am.

Importantly, Brown's evidence also presents a transitional point in the nature of the rapport between Stride and her companion: between the almost patronising affection directed at her, as observed by Gardner and Best at 11pm, and Marshall at 11.45pm; and then the final assault witnessed by Schwartz at 12.45am. There is an air of menace in the suspect described by Brown, with his arm up against the wall, potentially constraining the woman's freedom while she refuses his entreaties. It is difficult to view the scene that Brown paints as anything other than the last step in a crescendo to the attack which was, by that late stage, just minutes away; a point of logic touched on by the coroner in summing up[281]. Brown's evidence also helps to explain why neither club patron, Morris Eagle or Joseph Lave came across anything untoward at the entrance to Dutfield's Yard in the critical time window spanning the minutes after PC Smith's sighting at 12.30am and before Schwartz's at 12.45am: Stride and her assailant were just around the corner[282].

It is noteworthy that Marshall, PC Smith and Brown all saw the couple lingering within relatively close proximity to the club over an elongated period of time that spanned the hour before her fateful assault there, as witnessed by Schwartz. Gardner and Best saw them not far from Berner Street about two hours before she was killed. In summarising the pair's movements, the coroner touched on a not dissimilar line of reasoning when considering that the murderer "must have spent much time and trouble to induce her to place herself in his diabolical clutches"[283]. This geographic anchoring of sightings lends itself to the conclusion that the couple were not just promenading back and forth aimlessly in front of a Jewish radical club, but rather that the killer was choosing an opportune moment to leave a bloodied corpse on its premises with calculated and premeditated intent*. By the time Schwartz witnessed her assault there, she had been by the club no less four times in the space of about an hour. What adds further weight to this geographically predetermined scenario is that Berner Street was no haunt for prostitutes, according to the evidence presented at the inquest by PC Smith[§], a point underscored in the coroner's summation[284].

To this end Schwartz's evidence outlining what he saw of the assault on Stride provides a tangible offering. While the police report describes the assailant throwing Stride out of the yard's entrance passage, onto the street, it is opportune to acknowledge the *Star* report, which details Stride being pushed into the yard itself, which is where her body was ultimately found[285]. While the weight of authority naturally rests with the police version, a definitive answer may lie lost in translation, and the non-English speaking Schwartz's reliance on the interpreting skills of a friend ('translator, traitor', an old Italian proverb goes). Whichever version is correct, it cannot be denied that the assault occurred at the entrance to the club.

Turning to the slight discrepancies in the descriptions of the suspect who was observed with Stride; these need be put into context. Witness descriptions can be notoriously imprecise at the best of times. These sightings occurred in poorly lit streets during the darkest hours. At times it was raining. Some of the witnesses (Marshall, PC Smith and Brown) were quick to admit they did not get a particularly good look at the man. On the other hand, there is much that is consistent to tie these descriptions of the courting couple to each other, even putting aside the well-synchronised chronology they outline. While less than uniform, all describe a male individual wearing dark clothes and a coat or jacket. Gardner and Best, Marshall and PC Smith

---

* That Stride had learned to speak Yiddish and often worked for Jewish employers, might also provide an expanded appreciation of Jack The Ripper's choice of victim in light of the inculpatory framework he sought to build around the early morning's events.
§ Corroborated by the inquest testimony of the club's founding secretary, William West (born Woolf Wess, in Lithuania).

describe a man who was decently presented to mildly respectable. It is in headwear where the descriptions vary, though even here some overlap can be observed: from a tall billycock (Gardner & Best), to a round cap with a small peak "like what a sailor would wear" (Marshall), to a "black cap with peak" (Schwartz), to a "hard felt deerstalker hat" (PC Smith), and "I could not say" (Brown).

A better convergence is established by the witnesses that mentioned his age. Schwartz's man was about 30, he told police, while PC Smith and Marshall, who both attached the caveat that they did not see much of his face, mention a 28-year-old and someone who "seemed to be… middle-aged" respectively. Most importantly, and with uncanny repetition, an outline of the suspect comes into sharp focus when the witnesses describe someone of limited height and particular frame: 5ft 5in of "broad shoulders" and "rather stoutly built" (Schwartz), 5ft 5in (Gardner & Best), "about 5ft 6in" and "rather stout" (Marshall), "about 5ft 7in" and "stoutish" (Brown), "about 5ft 7in" (PC Smith).

Most, but not all, were silent on the question of ethnicity, which is not to say a conclusion cannot be surmised. Marshall heard him speak in English and made no mention of an accent, a potential line of questioning subsequently left unpursued by the coroner and jury, suggesting that the suspect may have been understood to be a native. Schwartz described a man of fair complexion with a dark brown moustache and intimately familiar with Cockney street vernacular ("Lipski"). John Best, who arguably got the best view, was adamant that the "man was no foreigner; he was an Englishman right enough". Reasonable, then, to imagine that Stride's assailant was home grown.

There is nothing to undermine that conclusion when the suspect is next sighted. By that stage, it was 1.35am. He had made his way from Berner Street, and was spotted together with Catherine Eddowes near the southern end of the Great Synagogue, by the corner of Duke Street and Church Passage. A police report by Chief Inspector Swanson dated 19 October, nearly three weeks after the double-event, provides details of a suspect as briefly observed by Joseph

Lawende. He describes a man 5ft 7 or 8 inches tall, complexion fair, fair moustache, of medium build, wearing a loose jacket and grey cloth cap with a peak[286].

To be fair to Lawende, his inquest testimony, as well as another document in the police record, shows a witness at pains to make clear he did not get a good look at the man. "I doubt whether I should know him again," he told the coroner[287]. Even Swanson's 19 October report, in a tangential discussion, mentions the limitations of Lawende's sighting when he describes the "serious drawback to the value of the description of the man"; and in another, on 6 November, he writes that Lawende "could not identify the man"[288].

Lawende's friend Joseph Hyam Levy got an even more cursory look and estimated the man to be 5ft3in tall[289]. Consistent with Levy and Lawende, their companion at the time of the sighting, Harry Harris, told the *Evening News* that neither witness saw anything more than he did, which "was only the back of the man"[290].

Whatever its limitations, police considered Lawende's eyewitness sighting significant enough to withhold its finer points from the inquest, and therefore the media. Which is not to say that long before then, the press hadn't got wind of it and published a description, including some added and interesting details, for example that he was wearing a "red neckerchief", was aged "about thirty" and of "shabby appearance"[291]. Together with Levy's partial sighting, the best picture that might be painted of the Duke Street suspect was of a man somewhere between 5ft 3in to 5ft 7 or 8in tall, of medium build, and fair complexion, sporting a moustache and wearing clothes that matched some of the accounts of the attire worn by the suspect in Berner Street. Yet again and importantly, the supposed "foreign looking" Jewish Ripper was nowhere in sight.

Collectively, this witness evidence from the night of the double-event is another nail in the coffin for Hutchinson's suspect. It also does not bode well for him personally that these accounts converge with sightings from the night of Kelly's murder when a short, stout man was observed looking up Miller's Court, and a man of the same description was seen entering Kelly's room.

More to the point is the question of Hutchinson having come forward to describe a Jew at a time when the East End's shock was overwhelming, and neither the community nor the police investigation were so focused. As an aside, it is worth referencing the aforementioned 1988 FBI report prepared by John Douglas, in which he says that on those rare occasions serial murderers choose to make announcements about their crimes "they generally provide information relative to their motivation"[292]. Given that Jack The Ripper's only two reliable pieces of communication had been anti-Semitic in nature, it is hard to ignore that in coming forward, Hutchinson was reinvigorating a particular narrative by proposing a Jewish suspect. Was this due in part to his frustration at waiting pointlessly for nearly four days for the police and the people of the East End to understand that Kelly's murder conformed to tales of Jews ritually butchering women, as had appeared in the media in the lead-up? Had he not ensured that Mary Kelly had been "frightfully mutilated" and had her breasts cut off as per the reports arrived from Leskau but a fortnight earlier, and appearing as late as the same week in which she was killed? These are some of the considerations that may well have played on Hutchinson's mind, like an overture of frustration before he launched into his decision to come forward, triggered finally by Lewis' and Cox's inquest testimony. It is a rationale that inevitably brings the spotlight on Kelly.

While the other victims had been in their forties, laid low by years of hardship, alcohol abuse and living off the street, Mary Kelly continues to perplex students of the case because of her youth, attractiveness and comparatively recent arrival to the East End. She is the victim that does not quite fit. Walter Dew, who boasted of knowing her by sight could attest to her beauty, describing her as "a good looking and buxom young woman"[293], while another police official wrote of her "considerable personal attractions"[294]. Fellow Miller's Court resident, Elizabeth Prater said she was "tall and pretty and as fair as a lilly"[295]. This presents a scenario where Jack The Ripper did not just chance on a random target, but sought out an attractive, youthful victim because he was trying to mirror cues taken from the most recent media reports out of Vienna, as part of an effort to incriminate the Jews. The Leskau murder victim who had her breasts removed was a young woman of 19. At 24 or 25, Kelly was closer to her age than she was to any of Jack The Ripper's other victims. And like the Moravian sisters, who were reportedly "renowned for their beauty", she was seemingly an attractive, young woman herself, "a pretty, blue-eyed, youthful girl", as Detective Inspector Reid described her[296].

It would indicate that Mary Kelly was tracked down with forethought and for special reasons. Possibly too, the added luxury afforded by working indoors, allowing a more charged degree of carnage, so as to bring to mind bloody reports arriving from continental Europe. The level of mutilation, specifically to Kelly's face, is consistent in offender profiling with a victim who knew her assailant, and a Ripper who went looking for someone in particular. By his own admission, Hutchinson had known Mary Kelly for some years.

There are a few potential glimpses left in the witness record that may give added validity to this view. They come courtesy of two inquest witnesses – Thomas Bowyer, the man who discovered Kelly's body, and another Dorset Street resident, Caroline Maxwell. Although worthy in many respects, neither contribution is without problems. Tellingly, the sightings do provide a picture of a man by now fitting a recurring description in terms of his age, height and body frame. Once again, no hint of a Jewish Ripper is discernible.

The main focus of Bowyer's assistance to the police had been to provide information relevant to the how and why he came upon the mutilated remains in room number 13. For that important reason, he was the second witness in order of appearance at the inquest after Kelly's ex-partner, Joseph Barnett. There is, however, a suggestion he may have had other information of potential interest. He briefly told the inquest, "I last saw (the) deceased alive on Wednesday afternoon in the Court". That was at least a day and a half before

Kelly was last seen alive. Is it possible that the vagueness of the reference, its distance from more pressing events in the timeline, and the authorities' reliance on Bowyer as the witness who discovered Kelly's body, led to a potential evidentiary nugget being overlooked? Indeed, Bowyer's police statement did not even note this sighting which he later mentioned at the inquest. But the *London Evening Standard*, may well have been referring to the same event when it described Bowyer as having seen a man speaking to Kelly on Wednesday night: "He was about eight-and-twenty, had a dark moustache and somewhat peculiar eyes. In appearance he was rather smart"[297]. The report is either corroborated, or likely just repeated, with minor variance in the *Western Mail* edition of the same day. The fact that Bowyer mentioned the man's strange eyes is very interesting, keeping in mind Gardiner and Best's description of the man seen with Stride at the Bricklayers' Arms and his noticeably "sore / weak eyes".

However, the failure of Bowyer's sighting to have registered with clarity in a more official capacity leaves this tantalising piece of evidence with an understandable question mark hanging over it. A similar situation presents itself when considering Caroline Maxwell's sighting, but for different reasons. There has occasionally been a tendency to dismiss what she had to say, with the explanation that she most likely got the morning of her sighting confused, which is almost certainly true. What may have gone unappreciated is its value in spanning the very period covering the few days before Kelly's murder.

According to Maxwell, at about 8.30am on the same Friday morning that Kelly was found dead, the two women had a conversation at the corner to Miller's Court, with Kelly bemoaning the effects of a bender of several days duration and counting. About 20 minutes later, Maxwell spotted Kelly again, on the corner of Dorset and Commercial streets, outside the Britannia public house in the company of an unknown man she described as "about 30, height about 5ft5in, stout, dressed as a market porter". She told the inquest he "was not a tall man – he had on dark clothes and a sort of plaid coat". Though the sighting was at a distance, it bears the hallmarks of a familiar figure by now. Occasionally, Joe Barnett, Kelly's ex-partner, a market porter, is put forward as a possible match for the man Maxwell saw. But it cannot be the case. Maxwell made it clear to both the police and in her inquest testimony that she knew Barnett.

Her obvious confusion about the day of the sighting created a certain degree of controversy even at the time and was on display at the inquest. Coroner Roderick MacDonald seemed almost to be warning Maxwell when he said: "You must be very careful about your evidence, because it is different to other people's"[298]. Nevertheless, the witness held her ground, "positive" that she had spoken to Kelly. She said the pair's conversation had been conducted on a first name basis, giving the inquest and posterity reason to understand the Dorset Street neighbours were well enough acquainted. However much Maxwell may have been thrown by the date, there should be little doubt about the broader value of her evidence and that she was in earnest. As Dew put it:

> If Mrs Maxwell had been a sensation seeker – one of those women who live for the limelight – it would have been easy to discredit her story. She was not. She seemed a sane and sensible woman, and her reputation was excellent. In one way at least her version fitted into the facts as known. We knew that Marie had been drinking...[299]

That said, Dew was sure she had got the day wrong, if nothing else, based on the medical evidence. However, his memoirs go on to repeat how impressed he remained with her, noting the consistent and convincing nature of what she had to say. Not unreasonably, he concluded: "I know from my experience that many people, with the best of intentions, are often mistaken, not necessarily as to a person, but as to date and time... and I can see no other explanation".

Maxwell and Bowyer provide some evidence for the scenario that Kelly's murderer was keeping her under scrutiny in the lead-up, and that her murder was planned. It is worth considering whether the ending of Kelly and Barnett's relationship the previous week may not have been a case of the perfect opportunity landing in Jack The Ripper's lap.

Hutchinson had said he knew Kelly in his own right, but he may have had a secondary connection to her through Joseph Barnett's brother Daniel, according to some modern sources[300]. The first census that was taken after the 'Autumn of Terror', that of 1891, shows Daniel Barnett to have been a lodger at the Victoria Home For Working Men[301]. It would not be surprising if the two men knew each other, given their shared class and geography, and that they had at least one mutual acquaintance: Kelly.

Some researchers propose that Daniel may have taken a brotherly interest in the romantic drama affecting Joseph and Mary Jane at that moment[302], and the notion has some element of corroboration from reports in the press[303]. If Daniel Barnett knew George Hutchinson, did he nonchalantly discuss the particulars of his brother's romantic woes with him? Details that would confirm a wily predator on a course of action in the same days reports from Leskau were appearing in the newspapers? It would help make sense of one perplexing issue: why the killer took the apparent gamble of becoming trapped in a confined space during the lengthy task of mutilating Kelly. If he knew there would be nobody coming home to her, it would have been one mitigating factor against the risk.

The crude, approximate re-staging of key elements of the Leskau episode, so soon afterwards, in Miller's Court, offers an insight into Jack The Ripper's thinking: most notably his determination to make use of the blood libel for his own ugly ends and his anti-Semitic agenda. It also demonstrates that the murderer's ear was keenly attuned to the street and that he had a degree of malicious understanding of the psychological susceptibilities of his community. Importantly, he was an avid reader of newspaper reports.

It is evident in reading coverage of Kelly's murder that its news value was easily able to trump the fanfare which normally would have been given via post-media coverage to the Lord Mayor's Show. It reinforces the idea that Jack The Ripper had an instinctive knack for the dark arts of public relations, and that he wanted to garner maximum outrage and publicity to his cause. It was a point not entirely lost at the time:

> One word more. The murderer chose his time well. There is a theory – not an impossible one – that he is one of those diseased creatures who, drunk with an insane love of notoriety, are determined to be the sensation of the hour. So he decided to get up a counter-demonstration to the LORD MAYOR'S Show. If that was his intention he succeeded beyond all expectation. He got his sensation. While the well-stuffed calves of the City footmen were being paraded for the laughter of London, his victim was lying cold in a foul, dimly-lighted court in Whitechapel. Whitechapel is once more to the fore – a grim spectre at our shows and banquets.[304]

At this juncture, the red handkerchief that Hutchinson has his Jewish villain so dramatically unfurl at the entrance of Miller's Court can safely be attributed to its most immediate inspiration: a close reading of the newspapers. Press coverage of the double-event carried reports of Eddowes' "red silk handkerchief", Stride's "silk handkerchief", and even Lawende's partial sighting had featured references to a "red neckerchief". Whatever imprint this item of apparel may or may not have made on him on the night of the double-event itself, there is little question that a probably innocuous item of clothing was raised to the level of bloody motif by Hutchinson's subsequent perusal of media reports. If it is true that serial killers follow media coverage intently, as criminal profilers contend[305], then it is safe to say that Jack The Ripper was the very first in what would prove to be a long line of infamy.

That said, there may be another current running even deeper when looking at Hutchinson's Jewish rogue and this act of bequeathing Kelly a handkerchief. And it seems to cut down to Jack The Ripper's most basic narrative; potentially laying bare its inception and with it, its rationale. For a red coloured handkerchief has an even earlier media genesis, and has come up before in the pages of this study in another but important context. The 'End of Chapter 4 notes' detail episodes from the 'ritual murder' trial at Tisza-Eszlar; an example of what was want to appear in the British media throughout the 1880s as part of that case's reportage. A close perusal of which, will recall readers' attention to the Jewish raftsman Smilovics, who according to the article, was understood to be in league with the co-accused. It was he who had consigned a young woman's body to the river by way of disposal. But not before the "especial" task of dressing her in preparation. Smilovics completed his work by placing a handkerchief, coloured red and blue, into her hand, potentially leaving susceptible readers to assume it held some significance relative not just the corpse's substitution with Esther Solymosi's, but with Jewish funerary custom, or 'ritual murder' which ultimately frames the report.

It is even possible that Hutchinson's reference to a red handkerchief was meant to convey an easy, additional hint: that his gentlemanly Jew was a socialist – a quintessential era stereotype* – and keeping in mind, that Stride's body, on the morning of the double-event, had been found in the courtyard of a Jewish radical club after the conclusion of a public lecture entitled, "Why Jews Should Be Socialists". In which case, what might such considerations reveal about the witness himself? The following chapter explores that and other questions.

---

*There were still echoes of this bygone mindset discernible as late as 1948 when some in the West feared that a nascent state of Israel might effectively amount to the establishment of a communist state. To wit, in a Jerusalem correspondent's special report by a young Robert F. Kennedy, he refuted scuttlebutt about a 'socialist Israel' as, "fantastically absurd". 'Communism Not to Get a Foothold', 6 June 1948, *Boston Post*.

Louis Diemschutz discovers the body of Elizabeth Stride in the courtyard of the International Working Men's Educational Club. The larger of the two triangular roofed buildings in the background housed the printing presses of the club's Yiddish language newspaper, *Arbeter Fraint* (Worker's Friend).

The Great Synagogue, Duke Street. Catherine Eddowes was last spotted here, on the corner of Church Passage, which leads directly to Mitre Square. Her mutilated body was found there soon after. She was observed standing, approximately, underneath the lamp (bottom left) in the company of a man, almost certainly, her killer.

End of Chapter 8 notes:
Facial hair and characteristics

witness	moustache	other facial characteristic	complexion & other notes
Gardner & Best	thick black moustache	weak / sore eyes; no eyelashes	Englishman
Marshall		no whiskers (?)	
PC Smith	small, dark moustache (?)	no whiskers	dark (?)
Lawende	fair moustache		complexion fair
Schwartz	small, brown moustache	full face	complexion fair, hair dark
Bowyer (?)	dark moustache	peculiar eyes	
Cox	full carrotty moustache; brown moustache (?)	sandy whiskers; clean shaven chin; blotchy face	fresh complexion

Author's comment:

When looking at the suspect described on the night of the double-event and the man seen entering Mary Kelly's room in November, a degree of overlap in the witness descriptions has been observed, as outlined in preceding chapters. It comes into particularly sharp focus when noting the height (short), frame (stout), and possibly, age (about 30 +/-). The complexion and details pertaining to facial hair, as detailed in the table above, also offer a relatively consistent comparison to ponder.

The vagaries of relying on less than perfect witness recollection in conjunction with poor lighting has been noted, which is not to ignore that the police themselves may have been left frustrated on occasion. There is an article from the *Echo*, which appeared five days after Mary Ann Cox gave her original statement and two days after the inquest, suggesting there could have been an attempt to make a greater degree of sense of one aspect of her evidence:

> As time goes on fresh facts are elicited respecting the wretched criminal's description, and it is now thought that the witness at the inquest who spoke of the man's "carrotty" moustache was labouring under a mistake in thus describing it. His moustache is thought to be dark.

Echo, 14 November 1888

The first reaction on reading this information is that it may have been reflecting the recent impact of Hutchinson's suspect on the investigation; except that nowhere in the case or media record were the two descriptions ever considered other than in direct opposition. It was always a matter of a 'foreign' Ripper versus a more generic, everyday, native version – Hutchinson's account versus Cox's.

Moreover, by 14 November there was already some indication that Hutchinson's evidence was being treated with a certain degree of caution, the *Echo* itself having reported on such suspicions the preceding day, dedicating column space accordingly. It was telling too, that in concluding, the article of the 13th had affirmed the dichotomy which existed between Hutchinson's and Cox's suspects:

> The most remarkable thing in regard to the latest statement (Hutchinson's) is, that no one else can be found to say that a man of that description given was seen with the deceased, while, of course, there is the direct testimony of the witnesses at the inquest, that the person seen with the deceased at midnight was of quite a different appearance.

(author's parentheses)
Echo, 13 November 1888

CHAPTER 9

RIPPER CENTRAL

> … them furriners… they'll go to hell… hundreds of carpenters are out of work now, men who've been foremen. Jews and foreigners do jobs so cheap he hasn't a chance.
>
> *Out Of Work* (published London, 1888)
> novelist, Margaret Harkness

In preceding chapters, the scant evidence that may have existed for a Jewish suspect has been laid bare, overwhelmed by much evidence to the contrary. The only potential lifeline that afforded such a hypothesis had arrived with George Hutchinson's demonstrably tainted sighting. It is interesting to note, that in doing so, he tied together notions of race and class in describing a well-to-do, swarthy Jew in Kelly's company. It exposed a window into perceptions carried by many of the British-born working class and confirmed Hutchinson's own membership. He was also remaining on-script with a political narrative that had featured strongly in the Ripper story from its inception and in many of the twists and turns along the way. His anti-Jewish fixation is a theme which cannot be escaped, and is closely tied to local geography.

A good example is on display thanks to an important difference between Hutchinson's police and media statements. In his police statement, he outrightly fingered a Jewish suspect. His media version, however, contained the more politic euphemism of "foreigner", almost certainly an imposed journalistic nicety[*]. Besides the

___

[*]By that stage, also, a possible police-inspired preventative; *The Complete Jack The Ripper A to Z*, Begg, Fido, & Skinner (John Blake Publishing 2010) p.212

inlaid references to the 'Hebrew' bogeyman, Leather Apron, it is interesting to note how Hutchinson managed to piggyback his anti-Jewish message and get it out anyway. As his media statement neared its conclusion, he said, "I believe that he lives in the neighbourhood, and I fancied that I saw him in Petticoat-lane on Sunday morning."

Petticoat Lane, or Middlesex Street as it was officially called, was the beating heart of Jewish East London, or as the London-born author Israel Zangwill commented in *Children Of The Ghetto: A Study Of A Peculiar People* (1892): "The Lane – such was its affectionate sobriquet – was the stronghold of hard-shell Judaism"[306]. What Hutchinson was giving his audience to understand, not all too subtly, was that his "foreigner" was a Jew, almost breathtakingly creating another opportunity to underscore his message.

George Arkell's map of *Jewish East London* of 1899 shows both Petticoat Lane and Wentworth Street and their surrounding blocks with a high density of Jewish residents, predominantly in the 95-100% dark blue category, the remainder in the 75-95% bracket. The immediate neighbourhood had historically been home to a notable Jewish presence, particularly those engaged in the garment trade from which Petticoat Lane had received its name. That demographic reality had become notably extenuated in more recent times.

Near its junction with Wentworth Street, Petticoat Lane was renowned for its market, a version of which remains popular today. By the end of the 1800s, it was also known as "the Jews' market"[307]. Open six days a week in its various guises, this open-air marketplace only shut on Saturdays, the Jewish Sabbath, at which point Petticoat Lane was "completely emptied... not a soul in sight"[308].

On 27 July 1888, Superintendent Thomas Arnold, Head of H (Whitechapel) Division appeared before the House of Commons Select Committee on Emigration & Immigration (Foreigners). He went into some detail in describing this junction, allowing posterity to build a better picture of its very Jewish nature.

Sir John Colomb:	Is Wentworth-street in your division?
Thomas Arnold:	Yes.
Sir John Colomb:	You have frequently, I suppose, attended the market there on Fridays?
Thomas Arnold:	Yes.
Sir John Colomb:	Is it the case that the whole of that street is taken up by costermongers's carts and hawkers' carts, principally owned by foreigners there?
Thomas Arnold:	Yes; in Wentworth-street and the upper end of Goulston-street, and a portion of Middlesex-street just in that immediate locality.
Sir John Colomb:	On Friday is that part very crowded?
Thomas Arnold:	Very crowded indeed.
Sir John Colomb:	Does the English language, or do foreign languages, predominate?
Thomas Arnold:	Foreign languages.[309]

The future editor of the *Jewish Chronicle*, Simon Gelberg put it more poetically when describing much the same thing, writing at the turn of the century: "the alien with his Yiddish holds the field.... (and) kosher butcher shops are clustered in thick bunches... seven of them at the junction of Middlesex Street and Wentworth Street"[310].

It will be recalled that committee deliberations had previously touched on similar evidence, courtesy of another witness, Henry Dejonge. Wentworth Street in particular had seen some drastic demographic changes to its make-up over the past eight years and was much "altered" or "foreign", according to Dejonge, himself Jewish:

Chairman:	There are a great many stalls in those streets, too ?
Dejonge:	A great many.
Chairman:	They are chiefly foreign?
Dejonge:	Yes

Chairman:	Not English?
Dejonge:	Not English; I counted last Tuesday 90 per cent foreign.
Chairman:	In what particular street was that?
Dejonge:	That was in Wentworth-street... out of 85 shops, there were 48 in the hands of Polish and Russian Jews.[311]

Zangwill's *Children Of The Ghetto* provides an intimate look at these streets. The following is one of a number of scenes that capture its everyday life. It forms the beginning of that chapter which in many editions is entitled, 'Petticoat Lane':

THE Sunday Fair, so long associated with Petticoat Lane, is dying hard, and is still vigorous; its glories were in full swing on the dull, grey morning when Moses Ansell took his way through the Ghetto. It was near eleven o' clock, and the throng was thickening momently. The vendors cried their wares in stentorian tones, and the babble of the buyers was like the confused roar of a stormy sea. The dead walls and hoardings were placarded with bills from which the life of the inhabitants could be constructed. Many were in Yiddish, the most shamelessly corrupt and hybrid jargon ever evolved. Even when the language was English the letters were Hebrew. Whitechapel, Public Meeting, Board School, Sermon, Police, and other modern banalities, glared at the passer-by in the sacred guise of the Tongue associated with miracles and prophecies, palm-trees and cedars and seraphs, lions and shepherds and harpists. Moses stopped to read these hybrid posters... He turned aimlessly into Wentworth Street and studied a placard that hung in a bootmaker's window. This was the announcement it made in jargon:

Riveters, Clickers, Lasters, Finishers, Wanted.
BARUCH EMANUEL, Cobbler.
Makes and Repairs Boots.
Every Bit as Cheaply
as
Mordechai Schwartz,
of 12 Goulston Street.[312]

In the same year as *Children Of The Ghetto* was published, a presumably real life Mrs Brewer told *Sunday Magazine* of her experience walking down the same streets as Moses Ansell. Effectively retracing the fictional character's steps, she covers the view from a gentile perspective. Her consternation at hearing English overthrown by Yiddish and seeing advertising in Hebrew underscores the two accounts, which are remarkably similar. Any divergence between them reflects the two subjects rather than the landscape. Whereas Moses is portrayed in his element, Mrs Brewer compares Whitechapel with "some far-off country... the people in the streets not of our type":

...in its courts, streets and alleys, are to be found the dwellings of the poor Jews, special streets and lanes being dear to their hearts... Such are Wentworth Street, Petticoat Lane, and Old Montagu Street. The density in and about there is fearful... Wentworth Street in full swing, as it is called, is a sight worth seeing. It is difficult to make one's way. Its shops are crowded, barrows with their wares of every kind fill the road, and are surrounded with busy, picturesque groups... In Wentworth Street I first saw meat... bearing the word "Kosher"... Old Montagu Street is almost entirely occupied by Polish and Russian Jew tailors... [313]

Is it surprising at this point that Hutchinson should have told the media he spotted his suspect in Petticoat Lane? He may as well have claimed the man was wearing a *yarmulke*, the traditional Jewish skullcap. Indeed, Zangwill commented that if the Jewish community's "religious life converged on the Great Synagogue, then their social life focused on Petticoat Lane"*[314].

Turn it this way or that, Hutchinson's message remained determinedly the same: *'he was a Jew'* ("Jewish appearance"), *'he was a Jew'* (Leather Apron references), *'he was a Jew'* (sighted in Petticoat Lane), *'he was a Jew'* (lives locally), *'he was a Jew'* (red hanky touting socialist). But there may have been yet another racially accusatory layer which he wove into the alleged weekend sighting of his gentleman in this locale. He said that he had seen him on the Sunday morning. Was he trying to imply that this was the first opportunity for the man to go about his business as normal following the events at Miller's Court throughout Friday, and given Petticoat Lane was deserted on Saturdays? Was Hutchinson trying to make some kind of garbled insinuation that the man was not just a Jew but an observant one, re-emerging post-Sabbath? It is a speculative point, but one worth considering. Another intriguing prospect, is that in describing an ostentatiously wealthy Jew, Hutchinson may have given away a telling insight into his own twisted perceptions and, in fact, have provided a sketch in stereotype of his imagined class enemy.

Even if resorting to nods and winks by way of reinforcing his message, there can be little doubt Hutchinson knew what he was talking about when it came to this neighbourhood. It will be recalled, he resided a few minutes walk from Petticoat Lane down Wentworth Street, at the Victoria Home For Working Men on the corner of Commercial Street.

Given political, class and social factors as they applied to the East End at the time, it comes as no great surprise that a casual labourer like Hutchinson harboured anti-Jewish sentiments. What is more

---

*Activists from the International Working Men's Club were keen to enlist potential converts to the socialist cause, parading along Petticoat Lane on Sunday mornings to sell copies of the *Arbeter Fraint*, and as a consequence, being "very badly illused there" by their co-religionists. See, *Commonweal*, 15 September, 1888. Is it possible that Hutchinson noted the activists' presence and the ensuing fracas in those weeks leading up to the double-event, and drew new depths of inspiration for his future intrigues given Petticoat Lane's and the radical club's upcoming roles in the story? Were the radicals and the Arbeter Fraint at that moment publicising the upcoming lecture to be held at the club, 'Why Jews Should Be Socialists'?

consequential, is that circumstances should have led him to reside right in the middle of the most Jewish part of the Jewish East End. Using George Arkell's map of *Jewish East London,* by 1899 the epicentre of that demographic shift had become entrenched at the junction of Wentworth and Commercial streets. It is noteworthy that Hutchinson and East End Judaism were forced to share the same address.

Whole blocks to the immediate north, east and west of this crossroads were made up almost exclusively of Jewish inhabitants. To give a brief snapshot, the Jewish & East London Model Lodging House Association (1862) and the Jews' Infant School (since 1858) covered its north-western corner. The former consisted of 30 dwellings and six shops. Just off the south-western corner, at 42 Old Castle Street, stood the Shalom v'Emess synagogue (1870)[315].

Crossing Commercial Street, on the eastern side of Wentworth Street, was the Rothschild Building (1885) opened to tenants in 1887 to help alleviate the housing shortage among poor Jews, though according to Superintendent Arnold's testimony before the select committee, by mid-1888 this particular building was already bursting at the seams.

Overcrowding had two main effects, according to the senior policeman's evidence, one demographic, the other practical: "the places which were inhabited by the English working classes are now inhabited by foreigners"[316], and secondly, the new tenants tended to congregate on the pavements near their lodgings[317]. Where families were large and houses small, the street became a communal leisure resource[318]. Arnold's evidence spoke of this being prevalent, "judging by the numbers we find sitting about... outside the houses, I should say they were overcrowded"[319], "they stand about the street gossiping with each other"[320], and he pinpointed the narrow streets leading from Commercial Street "and in that locality" as among the more problematic[321].

Not all would be so diplomatic in making the point. A letter writer to the *Jewish Chronicle* on 19 October 1888, indirectly confirms the accuracy of Arnold's testimony while complaining that 300 yards either side of the junction of Wentworth and Commercial streets, from Petticoat Lane, east to Osborne Street (and Brick Lane), could be particularly notorious:

> As one who lives in the district of Whitechapel, I am surprised to find every Saturday hundreds of foreigners, our co-religionists, standing in groups of 5, 10, and as many as 20, in the public footpaths to the annoyance of passers by... I do not know for what purpose they loiter in this particular spot, and have often heard very obnoxious remarks made by passers by. I should not at all be surprised that one Saturday they will be stringently interfered with. I must give police in the neighbourhood great credit for their forbearance. They try all means in their power to remedy the evil, but so soon as the police move them from one spot they collect at another... The feeling against this class of people, I am sorry to say, is not of a very friendly nature, and by making themselves conspicuous they may bring trouble to themselves and others.[322]

The mere thought that this little scene of neighbourhood life may have captured an anonymous George Hutchinson, one of any number of such passers-by, cursing his Jewish neighbours as he came and went from his lodgings, brings this old anecdote to life with a jolt.

If English Jews were complaining about such public displays by their foreign brethren spilling into the streets, how much worse must have been the response elicited in the likes of the underemployed Hutchinson, seeing his neighbourhood transformed to his real or imagined detriment and blaming the newcomers for his woes? In fact, the select committee's deliberations go some way towards answering that question and providing an insight into the grumblings that were going on in the minds of many English workers in Hutchinson's situation:

Chairman:	I understand that you have been in that district for 13½ years; do you consider during those 13½ years there has been a very considerable change in the constitution of the population *as regards the substitution of foreign for British workmen*?
Arnold:	Yes, there has been.[323] (author's italics)

In a subsequent appearances before the select committee, Arnold's questioners would hone in on this working class antagonism as it played out against the newcomers:

Committee:	Are whole districts of the town now occupied by foreigners which some years ago when you went there were occupied by the English working class?
Arnold:	Yes, and the area seems to me to be spreading...
Committee:	Do they often come into collision with British workmen or British workwomen?
Arnold:	Not to a very great extent, and I have noticed myself that it is often brought about by British workmen setting upon them first.
Committee:	Then there is bad blood existing between British workmen and Continental workmen?
Arnold:	Yes, amongst those of the lower class.
Committee:	And that results in quarrels and fights?
Arnold:	Yes.
Committee:	Do you think that there is a good deal of common talk amongst the working classes as to the large number of foreigners in the East-end?
Arnold:	Yes.
Committee:	And you think it is a source of irritation?
Arnold:	Yes, I think it is.
Committee:	And that leads to this bad blood of which you were speaking?

Arnold:	Yes, at different times they have rows, but we can only interfere with them when they are passing through the streets. It is whilst the foreigners are passing that the roughs interfere with them.
Committee:	Because the foreigners, we have been told, run away, and they interfere with them then.
Arnold:	Yes…
Committee:	You mentioned just now that there was bad blood between the British workmen and the foreigners; is there a mutual quarrel, or is it on one side?
Arnold:	It is on one side principally. I do not think that the foreigners entertain much bad blood to other people, on the score of working.
Committee:	But they are interfered with by the British workmen?
Arnold:	More frequently than otherwise by the lower order of British roughs.[324]

As Head of the Whitechapel Division, Superintendent Arnold's ability to provide geographic context when describing this socio-economic dislocation and its effects at street level provides invaluable depth to elements of the Ripper story. Indirectly, it helps build a better picture of Hutchinson's material surroundings, with their impact on his morale and view of the world, easy enough to imagine.

It is fair to say Hutchinson's life must have been a dreary one, living day to day with limited prospects. Inspector Abberline described Hutchinson as being in "no regular employment". The press elaborated by adding that he was of "military bearing", a member of "the labouring classes" and "formerly a groom, now a labourer". His own statements to police and the media are testament to the fact that he was next to penniless at the time, and his residence at the Victoria Home reinforces these impressions. Hutchinson's personal situation resonates in the depiction of the central character in *The*

Enemy In Our Midst (1906). This is from a contemporary review (see also appendix iii):

> The story begins with the experiences of an Englishman in "Alienland". These experiences are given to us in the person of John Steel, a strong British working man, who has no special trade because he has served his time as a soldier, and finds no opening for his untrained energies except in "casual labour," for which, however, he is well fitted. Yet he can get no work in the capital of his native land, all possible positions being occupied by aliens, who gladly work for starvation wages. Steel applies mainly for work at the docks, where he sees shiploads of these people constantly entering. He tries every other opening, but finds no place.[325]

For working men struggling to make ends meet, the Victoria Home provided good but basic accommodation, run on philanthropic, 'model' principles. While it provided somewhere for hundreds of workmen to lay their weary heads every night, it was no bed of roses and it wasn't free. In Jack London's, *The People Of The Abyss* (1903) detailed reference is made to what is understood to be the Victoria Home*, one of "the bigger and better ones not far from Middlesex Street"[326]. The author was quick to dispel any romantic misapprehensions, while acknowledging that it provided something better than the "unmitigated horrors" experienced in many of the privately run 'doss-houses'. For all of the Victoria Home's more enlightened style, it remained a soul-crushing experience that was common to time spent in any such establishment. London referred to their "uninhabitableness", even in the case of these better-run examples:

---

* Long suspected to have been a depiction of the Victoria Home. Almost certainly confirmed as such by the author upon locating the Victoria Home (VH) file in Nov. 2016, and matching the surviving plans of the basement floor with Jack London's written description appearing in *The People Of The Abyss*; particularly, the basement kitchen and the open space on descending the steps located adjacent to the side-walk entrance. See VH file, Salvation Army Heritage Centre (William Booth College, London).

I do not mean that the roofs leak or the walls are draughty; but what I do mean is that life in them is degrading and unwholesome. 'The poor man's hotel,' they are often called, but the phrase is caricature. Not to possess a room to one's self, in which sometimes to sit alone; to be forced out of bed willy-nilly, the first thing in the morning; to engage and pay anew for a bed each night; and never to have any privacy, surely is a mode of existence quite different from that of hotel life.

He uses the metaphor of the descent into hell* as a poetic device when singling out the Victoria Home:

The entrance was by way of a flight of steps descending from the sidewalk to what was properly the cellar of the building. Here were two large and gloomily lighted rooms, in which men cooked and ate. I had intended to do some cooking myself, but the smell of the place stole away my appetite, or, rather, wrested it from me... In the whole room there was hardly a note of conversation. A feeling of gloom pervaded the ill-lighted place. Many... sat and brooded over the crumbs of their repast, and made me wonder... what evil they had done that they should be punished so.

Whatever its limitations, the Victoria Home was situated on prime real estate as far as the bloody events of 1888 were concerned. In that sense, the corners of Wentworth and Commercial streets formed a veritable Ripper Central, with the murder sites fanning out in all directions from this point: east, west, north, north-east and south-east, as did the lodging houses and pubs which the victims were known to frequent. It was a point not lost on Detective Inspector Edmund Reid, Head of the Whitechapel Criminal Investigative Department, as he explained in post-retirement interviews in 1896 and 1912[327].

---

* There are recurring poetic references to the East End being akin to hell in *The People Of The Abyss*. Note the title, for example, and there are chapters entitled, "The Descent", "Suicide", and "... Inferno" - Jack London introduces his experiences as, "going down into the under-world of London" and "sinking... down into the East End of London".

In an exercise akin to an early form of geographic profiling, he pinpointed one pub in particular as being at the epicentre of any such considerations: the Princess Alice. In so doing he provided a telling marker: the pub was located directly across the road from the Victoria Home, on the south-eastern junction of Commercial and Wentworth streets. There would have been times, presumably, when Hutchinson could have seen the Princess Alice from his dormitory or cubicle window.

A minute or so's walk away was the White House, a lodging house situated at 56 Flower and Dean Street, where Mary Ann Nichols resided during the last week of her life. Prior to that she lived practically on the same block as the White House, at number 18 Thrawl Street.

From about May 1888, Annie Chapman resided at Crossingham's lodging house at 35 Dorset Street, about three minute's walk from the Victoria Home; Elizabeth Stride was a regular at a lodging house at 32 Flower and Dean Street (one minute's walk); Catherine Eddowes, Cooney's lodging house, 55 Flower and Dean (one minute's); Mary Kelly, 13 Miller's Court in Dorset Street (three minutes').

The women were all noticeably the worse for drink on the nights they met their ends with the possible exception of Elisabeth Stride, who was nonetheless seen drinking at the Bricklayers' Arms. That pub was on the corner of Settle and Fordham streets, ten minutes' walk from the Victoria Home. One of the last sightings of Mary Ann Nichols was as she left the Frying Pan public house on the corner of Thrawl Street and Brick Lane (two minutes' walk); Mary Kelly was variously spotted at the Horn Of Plenty (on the corner of Dorset & Crispin streets – three minutes'), the Britannia (on the corner of Dorset & Commercial streets – three minutes') and the Ten Bells (on the corner of Commercial & Church streets – four minutes'). Catherine Eddowes and Annie Chapman were both observed significantly under the influence of alcohol in the lead-up to their murders. It is not known which establishments served them, if any, though their immediate movements remained locally confined.

Taken together, the proximity of these locations to the Princess Alice and the intersection on which it was located lends credence to Reid's belief that it held a notable geographic importance. It might be safely assumed that George Hutchison was a familiar face around this neighbourhood, with all its potential to lower the guard of women in his company, even during this time of heightened peril. In his FBI report, profiler John Douglas noted that Jack The Ripper did "not look out of the ordinary"[328]. Given both victimology and geography, there is a good likelihood that just as he knew Kelly, Hutchinson was no stranger to the other victims and gave off external reassurances of posing no threat. Like Douglas, Dr Bond had opined that the "murderer, in external appearance is quite likely to be a quiet, inoffensive looking man"[329].

In addition, the site of the Goulston Street graffito was practically around the corner from Hutchison's lodgings. It brings an added perspective to the events immediately following the murder of Catherine Eddowes in Mitre Square and subsequent discovery of the graffito and bloody apron piece at the entrance to the Wentworth Model Dwellings. The evidence drop lay in a direct path to Hutchinson's lodgings, on the most obvious side of Goulston Street for such an escape route.

However, things are not as straightforward as they seem, even in making such an obvious point, for the Wentworth Model Dwellings were also on the most logical side of the street for a reverse approach from the Victoria Home. It begs the question whether Hutchinson could have gone home and made a lightning foray out again, maybe after cleaning himself up and hiding his knife. Audacious as it may seem, there is evidence that he did.

A quick recap. Eddowes was murdered at about 1.45am and Goulston Street was only five minutes' walk distant. Yet at 2.20am when PC Long's beat took him past where he would later find the apron piece, he said that it "was not there"[330], nor did he notice any graffito. His evidence is corroborated by Detective Constable Daniel Halse of the City force, who came down Goulston Street at about the same time and "passed over the spot where the piece of apron was found, but did not notice anything then"[331]. It would not be until PC Long's next swing by Goulston Street at 2.55am that he would discover the important evidence. It leaves open two possibilities. Either the killer was lingering out in the open for anywhere between half an hour to an hour amid the clamour of two constabularies trying to run him to ground; or alternatively, he made directly for his bolthole from Mitre Square and later ventured out for the very specific purpose of an evidence drop near a building "occupied almost exclusively by Jews"[332]. That the Victoria Home was one block away to the east along Wentworth Street, a minute or two's walk from Goulston Street, is a reminder of what a ripper location it enjoyed in that respect.

To this end, it could be significant that at its rear, the Victoria Home eventually backed onto a tiny passageway by the name of Castle Court. This lane merged into Old Castle Street, which ran off Wentworth Street. Might Hutchinson have found some sort of access via the backyard area of the Victoria Home, providing himself an all-important luxury: anonymity of movement? Further, if the rear of the premises contained auxiliary structures such as outhouses, he may even have been afforded an extra degree of privacy, although a drain and a source of water would have sufficed.

Legal correspondence from 1918, tracked down during research, provides a glimpse of the property at the start of the lease in 1887 and 1888. It makes reference to there being an "External back... washing room" on site; also, of toilets in the backyard area, under a section headed, "Yard and W.Cs."[333]. (Though the letter was written on the cusp of the home being wound down, decades after the events of 1888, it is nevertheless interesting to read the following 'make-good' notice: "Basement... doors to yard have jammed and do not close. Restore missing bolts to door.")

Also worth noting, is that the Victoria Home operated over two contiguous plots, both being the sites of ready-converted, former warehouses owned by Miss Amelia Levy. The lease for the property at number 41 was signed in 1887, when the home first opened its doors. The lease for number 39 was signed on 19 June 1888. A thought worth considering, is whether the institution's newly expanded operation may have played a crucial role in events, by becoming available to a greater intake of lodgers, and in turn to Jack The Ripper, just as the 'Autumn of Terror' was about to get under way.

This was the lay of the land; and in its totality, the geographic evidence places Hutchinson in an awkward spot: right in the middle of it.

A room with a view: looking out across Commercial Street to the former Princess Alice pub on the corner of Wentworth Street. Detective Inspector Reid believed the geography represented by this pub played a central role in the case. The modern view afforded here is comparable to George Hutchinson's in 1888 gazing out from one of the upper floor windows of the Victoria Home.

End of Chapter 9 notes:
Close-call in Wentworth Street?

The following point is conjecture. It comes courtesy of one aspect of Detective Constable Halse's testimony at Catherine Eddowes' inquest, and triggers curiosity. His involvement with the early morning's events began when he was on patrol with colleagues from the City force, near Aldgate Church. When, at about 2am, they heard that a woman had been murdered in Mitre Square they made their way there. On arrival at destination, and taking in the situation, Halse quickly gave instructions that the neighbourhood be searched and the officers fanned out. He proceeded east and made his way to Middlesex Street then Wentworth Street, where he stopped two men who, to his mind, gave satisfactory accounts of themselves. He kept going and proceeded down Goulston Street, past the Wentworth Model Dwellings, noticing nothing untoward as he went by at about 2.20am.

Almost certainly, Hutchinson was out and about, mischievously intent on capping-off his night's work armed with part of Eddowes' apron and a piece of chalk, but did he observe this scene? Or, almost shocking to conceive, was he one of the men questioned? Was his guile such, that he used the opportunity, to step into the relative safety of the Detective Constable's wake as Halse made his way down Goulston Street? It could offer an explanation as to how the graffito and apron popped-up in that particular location so soon after, in a general area brimming with police activity.

The scenario should not be ruled out. As one of many contemporary editorials put it when describing Jack The Ripper's audacity[334],"he lays his plots with devilish ingenuity, and carries them out with unsurpassed cunning"[335].

CHAPTER 10

WHERE IN THE WORLD IS GEORGE HUTCHINSON?

> The biggest and worst East End shelter (during the Blitz) was the Tilbury goods depot on Gower's Walk, off Commercial Road... Shelterers could be heard muttering about the Jews; how this was a Jews' war, how the bombs were chasing the Jews, whose abundance in the East End was making the area a popular target. Every action in the shelter by a Jew was magnified and singled out for complaint. The prams which Jewish mothers were bringing in were not protecting a baby but valuables, many claimed. The prams of all Jewish women were searched. There was a baby in all but one.
>
> Ed Glinert
> *East End Chronicles* (2005)

Having wandered into Commercial Street police station after the close of the inquest into Mary Kelly's murder, George Hutchinson seems to have vanished from the face of the earth not long thereafter. He remains one of the story's most enigmatic players.

Researchers have spent decades diving into mouldy archives, scouring yellowing newspaper articles, and been left scratching their heads. Post-contemporary reports pick up an alleged trail roughly a century later, involving a son's recollections of his father, George William Topping Hutchinson, successful career plumber and accomplished violinist. But many students of the case were, and remain, unconvinced by the purported breakthrough, presented as it was within a context of Royal-masonic conspiracy featuring the supposed involvement of Lord Randolph Churchill[336]; and as part of a work referencing the so-called "Abberline Diaries", where the famous detective got an important biographical detail wrong: his own name.

Also cited against the two Hutchinsons being one and the same is the opinion of the renowned Sue Iremonger, a member of the World Association of Document Examiners, who opined that George William Topping Hutchinson's signature was unlikely to be that of the 1888 witness[337]. (Indeed, even a layperson's casual perusal might be enough to confirm some marked stylistic differences).

Age too may have mitigated against G.W.T. Hutchinson being the underemployed labourer who in 1888 was doing his best to keep his head above water. Where modern literature ventures an opinion, it puts the police witness at about 28 years of age at the time, whereas G.W.T Hutchinson was 22. Critics also question the latter's association with the East End during the crucial period in question, and point to the fact that the police witness only ever appeared in contemporary police and media reports as plain old George Hutchinson, no middle names or initials. Ultimately, it needs to be remembered that the son's proposed identification of his father as the Miller's Court witness, is hearsay, presented more than half a century after G.W.T. Hutchinson's death*.

There, the issue of the witness' disappearance from the record, or otherwise, has rested; essentially unresolved. However, new information has recently come to light, opening up evidence of a fresh trail§.

Forbes. Colony of New South Wales. In 1896 it was already a *former* gold rush town, transitioning to agriculture as its mainstay. Located 250 miles beyond the Great Dividing Range west of Sydney, Forbes had seen better days, its population having dwindled from a peak of over 40,000 a few decades earlier. Not quite the end of the earth,

---

* For a broader discussion, see the author's letter as published in edition n.156 of *Ripperologist*, June 2017 and his article in n.160, Feb/Mar 2018.

§ Early findings published by the author in edition n.146 of *Ripperologist*, October 2015.

but some might have thought it viewable from there, especially if they were an Englishman looking to disappear. However, staying beyond the grasp of British justice required laying low, even in the colonies.

No such luck. On Tuesday, 1 December, his Honor Judge Docker presided over a trial in a case of indecent exposure. In earlier phases of the legal process, media reports had described the charge as "indecently assaulting two boys", confirmed as such in the official *New South Wales Police Gazette*[338]. The victims were aged 11 and 8.

Over the course of three editions, spanning late October to early December, the *Forbes & Parkes Gazette* had provided details of the proceedings, culminating in the following account[339]:

> His Honor summed up very strongly against prisoner who had no defence whatever to offer, and the jury after a retirement of only five minutes, returned into Court with a verdict of guilty.

Judge Docker then delivered sentence:

> I am sorry that owing to the charge which is laid against you and of which you have been found guilty, I am unable to order that you be whipped, were I able I certainly should give it you. The sentence of the Court is that you be imprisoned for two years with hard labor in Bathurst gaol.

Consistent with that, the facts of the case had been considered too shocking for proceedings to go on as normal in earlier phases of the court process. The reporter had described them "of a most revolting nature and totally unfit for publication".

> After hearing evidence - which was of such a nature that the Bench decided to hear it with closed doors - the prisoner was committed to stand his trial at the next Court of Quarter Sessions to be holden at Forbes on 1st December next.

The man in the dock was George Hutchinson a "stranger" or foreigner, no initials. He would plead not guilty, be placed on remand, and court room events play out in the manner described.

Corresponding documentation from Bathurst gaol refers to him as prisoner 1166, born in England, who arrived on board the RMS Ormuz in 1889[340]. The ship had sailed from the port of London and deposited George Hutchinson in the colony of New South Wales on 29 October, aged 29[341].

The relevant Sydney port authority document has him down as "British" and one of the "crew". However, there is no other listing of this "crew" member at hand in the nautical record. This is consistent with information from the prison file, which refers to his arrival in the colony with a single entry, 1889. He does not appear in Australian documents for any of the Ormuz's other readily verifiable arrival dates into Sydney, despite trawling over records covering 5 years between July 1887 and July 1892, or 11 other voyages[342]. Even when casting the net beyond the silhouette of the Ormuz there are no matches, suggesting the trip was a one-off. There are other reasons for suspecting as much. The following discussion might serve to broaden the horizon.

Nowhere in the extant record was witness Hutchinson known to be a sailor, although in Tom Cullen's *Autumn Of Terror* (1965) he is referred to as a night watchman. In the maritime record, covering the Ormuz's arrival into Sydney, Hutchinson's station is listed as "A.B." or able seaman, meaning an unlicensed member of the deck department, often working in relatively menial roles like watch-stander, simple workman or other general maintenance duties.

A maritime career seems somewhat incongruous with the Bathurst gaol record of 1897, which lists his occupation prior to conviction as "tinsmith", and information recorded by the court reporter in Forbes in 1896, who described him as a "labourer". This was corroborated in a later *New South Wales Police Gazette* that also listed him as a "labourer"[343]. These jobs are consistent, however, with the employment details of George Hutchinson, the witness from 1888. How to make sense of this nautical intermezzo?

It will be recalled, that Inspector Abberline had described his witness in an official document as being "at present in no regular employment", while media reports in 1888 referred to him as a "labourer" and "a member of the labouring classes". What seems consistent from both Australian and British sides was a professional record encompassing the lesser-skilled end of the spectrum, and the work of labourer specifically. Normally, London's unskilled and semi-skilled urban poor had few means to travel the world. A working passage would have offered one opportunity, but the port of London and its docks were a closed shop. However, during late-August to early-September 1889, at the same time that the Ormuz was making preparations for departure to Australia, the Great London Dock Strike was at its height, and "blackleg" labour was being encouraged onto ships to replace unionised elements[344]. Might this provide context?

By 22 August, the whole of the dock system had been closed down. Just six days later, it was estimated 130,000 men were on strike from stevedores to seamen, firemen, lightermen, watermen, dockmen, bargemen, plus other tradesmen and women in solidarity[345].

It is known from contemporary Australian and British media reports covering the strike that the Ormuz was the subject of international controversy at that moment, "having shipped blackleg crews of seamen and firemen"[346]. Another headline, referencing the "Orient liner Ormuz" reads, "Boycotting Vessels Manned By Blacklegs"[347]. Specifically, these reports referred to the journey the vessel was in the process of undertaking with George Hutchinson on board.

In the very days the ship was making ready to leave for the Australian colonies, a manifesto had been cabled from the Seamen and Fireman's Union in Britain to their brethren at the Wharf Labourers' Union, an Australian organisation that had played a crucial role in supporting the industrial action in London. The cry across the ocean was clear: *'brothers, do not load or unload the Ormuz!'* [348]. Or to put it in the Australian vernacular, the crew are *bodgie*[*]. This might explain why the passenger list described Hutchinson's station as able seaman. There would have been no means or desire to write the alternative, as might otherwise have jumped out of the technical manual of organised labour: *scab*. Consistent with this, the official Australian record only ever lists him henceforth as either "labourer" or "tinsmith". Nowhere has the able seaman, so-called, resurfaced.

The strike wasn't just news of international importance, its immediacy reached right into the heart of the East End. The London port system had an integral relationship with the area's workforce. Indeed, the "East End casual worker"[349] formed its most basic industrial component. In 1886, Tilbury dock was opened as the port's newest and easternmost expression 20 miles downstream, and would soon come to handle roughly half the Thames' tonnage. It is where the Ormuz moored when in port[350].

The London, Tilbury & Southend Railway connected these two ends of the system – labour force and dock. The Cheap Trains Act of 1883 ensured that workers travelled at reduced rates before 8am and after 6pm[351], and the journey sped passengers to and fro in about 40 minutes[352]. One writer had only high praise:

> Considering that it is practically only a suburban line, its train services are admirable. Southend (35¾ miles from Fenchurch Street) is within 50 minutes run; Tilbury (22½ miles) is only 42... Results like these are given by scarcely any other line in the neighbourhood of London. But perhaps even more praiseworthy than the excellence of this fast and frequent service is its punctuality.[353]

The railway's main depot, which would come to be known colloquially as "the Tilbury depot", was situated practically in the heart of Whitechapel, between Leman Street and Commercial Road,

---

[*] Bodgie, also bodgy: in Australian and some British regional vernaculars, means inferior, false, or counterfeit.

and allowed for the speedy delivery of goods as these were newly unloaded from arriving ships[354][355]. The equating of Tilbury with the East End came up incidentally in evidence before the House of Commons Select Committee on Emigration & Immigration (Foreigners) in 1888, when Tilbury dock and Leman Street railway station were mentioned together in the context of unloading newly arrived migrants:

Chairman:	Last Friday there was an arrival?
Dejonge:	Yes, rather better than 200 arrived.
Chairman:	Where did they arrive?
Dejonge:	At Tilbury.
Chairman:	What boat did they come by?
Dejonge:	I did not inquire.
Chairman:	Did you see them arrive?
Dejonge:	I saw them arrive at Leman-street by rail.

During the height of the strike, it was in the streets of the East End, as much as the docks themselves, where much of the industrial action played itself out. A good example of this was the strikers' daily midday procession in August and September that made its way west into Whitechapel along Commercial Road, led by one of its union leaders, John Burns. This is a colourful contemporary eyewitness account:

There were burly stevedores, lightermen, ship painters, sailors and firemen, riggers, scrapers, engineers, shipwrights, permanent men got up respectably, preferables cleaned up to look like permanents, and unmistakable casuals with vari-coloured patches on their faded greenish garments; Foresters and Sons of the Phoenix in gaudy scarves; Dogget's prize winners, a stalwart battalion of watermen marching proudly in long scarlet coats, pink stockings, and velvet caps, with huge pewter badges on their breast, like decorated amphibious huntsmen; coalies in wagons fishing aggressively for coppers with bags tied to the end of poles…

Skiffs mounted on wheels manned by stolid watermen; ballast heavers laboriously winding and tipping an empty basket.[356]

The industrial action was noted for its high level of organisation and discipline. To boot, the Jewish community was marshalled in solidarity[*]. By most accounts, the strike was conducted with dignity, and violence was largely avoided. Thousands of picketers were organised to effect in an effort to convince the blacklegs to support the cause[357].

Inevitably, the Ormuz got caught up in the protests, one practical effect being that its departure was held up. The ship had been due to leave on the evening of Friday 13 September, but the strike had made keeping to schedule almost impossible[358]. In desperation, 16 clerks from the Orient Line's Fenchurch Avenue city office, plus a bit of hired muscle, had to be brought in to act as stevedores under the taunts of picketers. With only the odd accident and a relatively negligible delay "the pseudo dockmen"[359], as they were described in the media, managed to get the Ormuz loaded and she steamed out of port in the early hours of the next day, Saturday the 14th. At the very moment the Ormuz was making its last preparations to cast-off, the final details were being put to an agreement to bring the Great London Dock Strike to a close after five weeks[360]. In the end, it had taken the intercession of none other than the Archbishop of Westminster, Cardinal Manning, hailed a hero by dockers and seamen for evermore[361]. Their demands met, the strikers began to return to work on Monday, 16 September[362].

For George Hutchinson, casual labourer come union-buster, the end of the Great London Dock Strike amounted to a sentence of exile, as it must have for many non-specialists caught up without professional credentials to fall back on. Blackleg elements caught in an Australian port in the aftermath would have found themselves

---

* A not dissimilar dynamic to the famous 'Battle of Cable Street' in 1936, when the broader East End Left, including the Jewish community, stood united against Mosley's Black Shirts; see 'Cardinal Manning and the Great Dock Strike 1889', *Independent Catholic News*, 12 Sept. 2014

in a particularly unenviable position, given the militant role that the Australian harbourside had played in support of the industrial action. Effectively, they were stranded.

With an accord in place, those seen as 'scabs' must have dreaded the settling of accounts. While technically the industrial peace agreement sought to afford blacklegs some protection, the following report from the *Guardian* makes clear it was a mere fig leaf, allowing unionised labour and employers to get back to business. To all intents and purposes, the former union-busters were cut loose, as the man who had led the daily midday processions through the East End, John Burns, made clear:

> It was after seven o'clock on Saturday evening when the Strike Committee drove down to the West India Dock gates to announce the agreement arrived at. First of all Mr. John Burns stated that they had that day received another mark of expression of goodwill from Australia in the shape of 1,500*l*. When he read the condition that other workmen should be unmolested an uproar arose, and men jumped about, shouting "Never." The speaker quietly said, "We'll see." As soon as the disturbance had somewhat subsided Mr. Burns said the masters would save them the trouble of clearing out the blacklegs by doing it themselves in their own interest. There was not a single blackleg in the docks worth his salt, besides his money. Did they think the masters were going to give men not worth twopence the preference? In their own selfish interests they would get these men to go quicker than they the labourers could. Putting the agreement into plain and simple language, what did it mean? A *Voice* – "That the directors did not care."[363]

This too argues against George Hutchinson the professional mariner. Whereas a career sailor would at least have had a qualification to call on, hired muscle was expendable. That he was still working in Australia as a labourer in 1896 suggests he was no professional seaman but a man whose prospects had been raised for a month or so in 1889, courtesy of the strike. The dynamics of George Hutchinson's Australian odyssey and how they played out seem clear. It is hard to conceive that he did not see that jumping on board the Ormuz was an immediate term option only, as indeed it proved. It speaks ultimately of a decision that is consistent with a casual labourer's desperation to get out of London.

That said, there may have been more to it, or a secondary layer of context. One analysis of East End voting patterns juxtaposed against economic realities suggests that there was a disproportionate spike in the Conservative vote which should not, realistically, have been there for most of the two decades beginning in 1886[364]. Simply put, working class, nativist elements did not automatically gravitate to the Liberals, as they might have been expected to, and did elsewhere. It is argued, that this was owing to political and social antagonisms as directed at their Jewish neighbours. The desperate newcomers were often perceived as making up a ready-made, leftist constituency against which the British workers saw themselves pitted[365]. It was this 'downward envy', this 'displaced intergroup competition', which the socialist newspaper, the *Commonweal*, alluded to when in May 1888 it asked rhetorically whether there was, " ...nothing grimly grotesque in this national hypocrisy; in the desperate Jew-baiting as a last attempt to blind the native workers against the real causes of their misery?". It is hard to ignore the notion that this political state of affairs, as it played out on the ground locally, could explain much about George Hutchinson's story, even and particularly, his decision to commit himself to the cause of capital during the strike. (It might also help place the murder of Elizabeth Stride, at the door of a Jewish socialist club and newspaper, within its proper context).

Union-busting exploits aside, there were other ways to get on board, short of paying: "The cheapest way of travelling on the Ormuz was as a stowaway, who once discovered were usually put to work as a member of the crew"[366]. The evidence, however, suggests there was no need to go down that route on this occasion when the strike afforded a more lucrative option – and apparently, a politically palatable one.

Press-ganged stowaways as some of the crew may have been from time to time, the Ormuz's greater claim to fame was its touted status as "the fastest ship in world", as described in 1887 in the *Melbourne Daily Telegraph*[367]. Built in Glasgow and launched in 1886, the Ormuz serviced the London to Melbourne and Sydney run. Boasting a top speed of 18 knots, it managed to place the great "metropolis of the world", London, "within twenty-seven days six hours of its antipodes". The Ormuz could steam from London to Sydney in 30 days; 42 with passengers on board.

Which begs the question: what might have prompted George Hutchinson at that moment to gain passage on the "fastest ship in the world" and flee to the ends of the earth?

THE ORIENT LINE STEAM-SHIP ORMUZ.

RMS Ormuz: *Illustrated London News*, 14 May 1887

End of Chapter 10 notes:

Will the real George Hutchinson please stand up...

It is interesting to note that there is another George Hutchinson, an Englishman, that appears in the nautical record at about this time, but he is not the same George Hutchinson who arrived in Sydney on the Ormuz in 1889[368]:

- The shipping document from the British end of his journey describes him as 28 in 1894. He arrived in Sydney on the RMS Ophir on 3 November 1894, but no age is given for him in the corresponding Australian record.

- The British record describes him as a "farmer". There is no reference to his occupation in the Australian version.

- The shipping document available in the New South Wales government archives confirm the English record of him travelling as a normal passenger, which suggests that this George Hutchinson could afford the price of passage.

There is a third-class passenger, a T. Hutchinson, no age or nationality given, listed on the Ormuz's arrival into Sydney in early March 1890. To be sure the initial "T" could not have been mistaken for a capital "G" during transcription, it was compared by this author to examples of that initial and even the lowercase letter "g" that appeared in other parts of the original document[369]. There is no question that the letter is a "T" both as transcribed and in the original. The issue is put beyond doubt when considering:

- The corresponding British record lists a passenger by the name of Tom Hutchinson departing London for Sydney in January 1890 on board the Ormuz. He is recorded as being single, an English male of 25 years of age. Almost certainly, he is the T. Hutchinson that appears in the corresponding Australian maritime record.

There is a G. Heukhison as transcribed (in error for Hutchinson) who appears once in the New South Wales record. On that occasion he was 28 years of age in October 1886, a ship's trimmer. The role was one of keeping the ship's furnaces stoked. His vessel was the Elamang of Sydney with a tonnage of less than a third of the Ormuz's, and seems to have limited its runs exclusively up the coast between the colonial capitals of Melbourne and Sydney. But for a few northern Europeans, the crew were all "British", as colonial subject then were. There were no "Australians" until 1901 when the six colonies formed the Commonwealth of Australia. There is no evidence of him having travelled beyond Australian waters. While George was a popular name at the time, the record shows him only as a "G".

This form to be carefully folded in six parts.

88

No. *1166*   Name   *George Hutchinson*

Bathurst

Date when Portrait was taken........ *4 3. 97*

Native place *England*
Year of birth *1867*
Arrived in Ship *Ormuz*
Colony Year *1889*
Trade or occupation previous to conviction *Gunsmith*
Religion *C of England*
Education, degree of *R & W*
Height, without shoes, *5* feet *5½* inches
Weight in ℔. On committal *54*
On discharge
Colour of hair *Brown*
Colour of eyes *Blue*
Marks or special features
Nose has been broken
little finger right
hand broken
also right eye
broken scar
on left breast   No. of previous Portrait.............................).

CONVICTIONS.

Where and When.			Offence.	Sentence.
Forbes QS	*Dec 1*	*96*	*Indec Exposure*	*2 years H*

George Hutchinson, prisoner 1166: Bathurst gaol record, 4 March 1897

CHAPTER 11

SHORT LEASH

It is the opinion of this crime analyst that there were other attacks in the Whitechapel area that either went unreported or for some reason were not considered by authorities to be crimes of Jack The Ripper.

SUBJECT: Jack The Ripper
FBI profiler, John Douglas
6 July, 1988

Since November and the close of autumn, when Mary Kelly's murder had shocked London, a winter and spring had come and gone uneventfully. Not that there hadn't been a few scares along the way, but by the summer of 1889 Jack The Ripper was nowhere in sight. It was a greater normality which greeted a soon to be fêted special guest when he arrived in London on the first of July, his majesty the Shah of Persia. The image of that exotic eastern potentate being received at Windsor Castle by her royal highness Queen Victoria made a nicer cover to the *Illustrated London News* than some of the bloody front-page headlines of the previous year[370]. As for the monster himself, he was either lying low or had disappeared, possibly forever. Whatever bitter feelings of unfulfilled justice such a possibility elicited, it also held out some positive prospects. True, there had been no breakthroughs in the case, but London's East End had just about managed to drift back into a more normal pattern of life.

It wasn't to last. The Shah had only just left London for Scotland a few days prior, after a sumptuous send-off at the Crystal Palace. It was Wednesday, 17 July, and the city was about to wake to frightful news. "Jack The Ripper At It Again – Another Whitechapel Tragedy

– A Woman Murdered And Mutilated"[371]. Snapping his fingers, the serial killer had magically reappeared and taken another life as though part of a macabre routine.

This time the victim was Alice McKenzie, a 40-year-old prostitute and alcoholic[372]. Her throat had been cut and she was found with her clothes pulled up to her chest, exposing her genitals and mutilated abdomen[373]. Her body was discovered in Castle Alley, practically around the corner from George Hutchinson's last known address at the Victoria Home. It would be ascertained that she had been drinking earlier in the evening.

The wound to the left side of her neck was sufficiently severe that H Division police surgeon Dr George Bagster Phillips who attended the scene, believed death was probably "instantaneous"[374]. The *Times* edition of 19 July reported:

> The wound in the neck was 4 inches long, reaching from the back part of the muscles, which were almost entirely divided. It reached to the fore part of the neck to a point 4 inches below the chin. There was a second incision, which must have commenced from behind and immediately below the first. The cause of death was syncope, arising from the loss of blood through the divided carotid vessels.

The conclusions of his colleague Dr Thomas Bond are worth quoting (below). It will be recalled he had conducted the postmortem on Mary Kelly. At the request of Assistant Commissioner Robert Anderson in October he had prepared a report that pooled all the medical and inquest testimony on the canonical victims prior to Kelly, confirming they were all victims of the same hand. In the intervening period, Dr Bond's discerning judgement was brought to bear when he examined the body of Rose Mylett in December 1888 and dismissed the proposition that she had been murdered by Jack The Ripper.

Upon conducting a medical investigation of the injuries suffered by Alice McKenzie with Dr Phillips present, Dr Bond reported:

I see in this murder evidence of similar design to the former Whitechapel Murders, viz: sudden onslaught on the prostrate woman, the throat skillfully & resolutely cut with subsequent mutilation, each mutilation indicating sexual thoughts & a desire to mutilate the abdomen and sexual organs. I am of opinion that the murder was performed by the same person who committed the former series of Whitechapel Murders.

On arriving at the scene of the crime, the new Metropolitan Police Commissioner James Monro, had formed a similar view which he reported to the Home Office: "... the murderer ...I am inclined to believe is identical with the notorious 'Jack the Ripper' of last year'"[*375].

Alice McKenzie walked along grey streets in the East End and inhabits a parallel grey area after death. She is not counted as a canonical victim of Jack The Ripper, though some Ripperologists dissent. This mirrors differing official opinions in 1889. Dr Bond and Commissioner Monro's assessment was not shared by important elements of the police hierarchy. That it was not, is in considerable part due to the opinion of Dr Phillips who concluded that:

I cannot satisfy myself, on purely anatomical & professional grounds that the perpetrator of all the 'Wh Ch. murders' is our man. I am on the contrary impelled to a contrary conclusion...[376]

There are good reasons why Dr Phillips' view won out. By July 1889 he was a veteran well versed in the case, having participated in post-mortems on four of the five canonical victims. Understandably, his opinion carried weight. But it is also true that the higher echelons of the police bureaucracy carried bitter memories of their failure from

---

* Controversially, Assistant Commissioner Robert Anderson claimed in his memoirs in 1910 that Monro had investigated Alice McKenzie's murder "on the spot", which is true, but concluded that she was *not* a victim of Jack The Ripper - this is in contrast to Monro's opinion, as stated in his own words in the official record, as well as his subsequent actions, such as bringing in additional plain-clothes officers to help survey the streets. Unlike Monro, Anderson was not in London at the time of the killing. Almost unbelievably, Anderson described McKenzie's slaying as, "an ordinary murder".

the previous year. The often vitriolic and ongoing press campaign directed against the police had not only fanned the flames of public panic but directed much odium at them. Many of the newspaper reports that followed Alice McKenzie's murder were unrestrained in their criticism: "… excuses and explanations do not satisfy the town", editorialised the *Daily News* in one such instance[377]. The constabulary's perceived incompetence had become the stuff of the most biting satire:

> Of course, when she had once been killed, and the murderer was well out of sight or hearing, the greatest activity was displayed by the police. Whistles were blown, and constables came hurrying up, and every avenue of escape was closed, and if the man had returned to the scene of his crime he would infallibly have been apprehended.[378]

Monro's predecessor, Sir Charles Warren, had resigned nine months earlier, on the same day that Mary Kelly's body was found. Still occasionally assumed to have been a political victim of Jack the Ripper, in reality he had resigned on a technicality: for penning an unauthorised article responding to broader media criticisms of the police, though it is also true that the Ripper scare had not done him any favours. Far from it.

Such was the charged political environment, and it was still fresh. Under the circumstances, Dr Phillips' post-mortem report must have fallen into the police's lap with a good measure of relief, though the ever hounding media appear to have sniffed the breeze. One accusing headline read, "England Is Not Surprised: Jack The Ripper's Latest Murder Accepted as a Matter of Course":

> London, July 18 - The fact is, people have all along settled down to the conviction that the murderer was only taking a holiday and no one is surprised at the discovery that he has again appeared to indulge in his pastime of murder. Then, too, the understanding that the police are impotent to solve the dread mystery serves to render the people callous, as the excitement of the chase after the perpetrator of the crime is entirely missing.[379]

In its late edition on the day of the murder, the *Pall Mall Gazette* introduced the story with a cutting introductory blurb, "Mr Anderson of Scotland-yard, has gone abroad – for a holiday, I suppose"[380].

The killing of Alice McKenzie had stirred the pot again, and in a manner unseen since the bitter days after the Miller's Court outrage. Commissioner Munro, having formed his own opinion that her murder was part of the earlier series, pressed an extra 42 plain-clothes policemen onto the streets of Whitechapel for the duration of the next two months. The pressure on the drafted officers to chase down leads was palpable. This much is clear on reading plaintive memos from Monro to his political superiors. He was seeking approval for better conditions to be paid to the officers brought in from other divisions. They were engaged in 15-hour days making enquiries, patrolling, and doing their best to gain information[381]. As Monro put it:

> … this work is specially irksome and unpleasant and makes considerable demand on the endurance of the men. They have continuous night duty and are practically doing the work of permanent patrols.[382]

Was the pressure starting to tell on George Hutchinson as well? Had he struck too close to home this time and slipped up? Is it possible that someone had decided to walk the five or so minute journey from where Alice McKenzie was last seen alive at the eastern end of Flower and Dean Street, to where she was killed in Castle Alley, and noticed that the easiest route led past the Victoria Home? Had Hutchinson, belatedly, made the same realisation himself?

Once again, the victim's abode, a lodging house close by the junction of Gun and Artillery streets, was not far from where he lived, no more than five minutes' walk. She had been there as recently as the last evening of her life. The site of the murder itself was about two minutes' walk from the Victoria Home via the most conventional route. However, as discussed in chapter 9, the warren-like lanes and alleys running off Old Castle Street and behind Castle Alley may have offered the murderer a quicker and safer route: to the rear of the

Victoria Home. If Dutfield's Yard and Miller's Court had sensitised him to the dangers inherent in a cul-de-sac, then Castle Alley would provide him with the very antithesis. The media were certainly aware of the opportunity afforded by geography, with more than one of them making points along those lines (see also, appendix iv):

> The murderer, on account of the narrowness and intricacy of the surrounding thoroughfares, would have no difficulty in getting away unobserved; and if, as is believed, he is residing in one of the dozens of common lodging houses or small houses almost within a stone's throw of the spot where the deed was committed, he would have no trouble in concealing his identity after making his escape.[383]

There is another reason for suspicion to rest on this other escape path. The thoroughfare made up of Old Castle Street and Castle Alley was always heavily patrolled. Detective Inspector Reid told the coroner that: "Two constables are continually passing through the alley all night, it is hardly ever left alone for more than five minutes"[384]. No fewer than three police officers had passed through it in the 20 minutes leading to the discovery of McKenzie's body, and owing to the Ripper-scare, there was one permanently positioned at the southern entrance to Castle Alley, on Whitechapel High Street[385].

Approximately half way down the thoroughfare at the dog-leg bend, where Old Castle Street met Castle Alley, the paths of two of those officers, Police Sergeant Edward Badham* and Police Constable Walter Andrews, met at 12.48 am. "All right," said PS Badham who was checking on patrolling constables. "All right" came the customary all-clear from PC Andrews. The senior officer moved off to the north toward the Wentworth Street exit. His subordinate continued south into Castle Alley, in the direction of the exit on Whitechapel High Street. He had only walked a few dozen yards, performing the odd

---

* Interestingly, it was PS Badham who had taken George Hutchinson's original statement on the evening of 12 November 1888, prior to Inspector Abberline being called.

cursory check along the way, when he came upon the prone form of Alice McKenzie close by a street lamp and a few carts...

When he heard PC Andrews' distress whistle, PS Badham had only just exited Old Castle Street. He came charging back down the way he came, throwing off his cape as he went. For the killer, it meant the Wentworth Street end became an impossible route of escape almost immediately. It would not be long before other policemen would arrive on the scene, and that northern exit sealed via police cordon. By the time Detective Inspector Reid arrived some time before 1.10am, he could attest to the other end being blocked as well. The murderer's disappearance was a point that baffled the press:

> All the murders have been audacious. The murderer has in each case taken chances which would have frightened any ordinary assassin from his purpose. But yesterday's murder beats them all in this respect. The police were in front of him, behind him and all round him... VANISHED.[386]

It was a point aired in report after report:

> It would appear almost a marvel how the murderer could have escaped, as no less than four policemen were on beats at the different exits to Castle-alley... and when the alarm whistle blew every constable who was about closed in and blocked all the openings.[387]

A thorough search of the area was conducted immediately but produced no results. The streets themselves that evening were practically deserted[388]. The only belated interloper on this scene was a local resident Isaac Jacob, plate in hand, going to get his dinner. Neither PC Andrews or anyone else, including nearby residents, had seen or heard anything suspicious. Yet by all accounts, the fatal assault on Alice McKenzie must have only just been committed when PC Andrews approached. The body was "quite warm" when the constable came upon it and blood was flowing from the fatal neck wound and a gash in the abdomen[389]. It was still running into the gutter when Detective Inspector Reid arrived[390]. One press report among many making the same point, read:

> ... he (PC Andrews) must have been quite near the place when the murderer was actually at work... hacking at his victim less than a minute or two previous to the discovery of the body.[391] (author's parentheses)

There is another reason to suspect the killer had only just struck. PS Badham's official report does not make clear which direction he had come from when he first caught up with PC Andrews at 12.48am. However, media coverage from the inquest indicates that it was from the Whitechapel High Street end. In other words, the two officers had crossed over, which stands to reason. From the *Times*:

> It is a remarkable fact that the assassin was not captured red-handed, for within six minutes of the time the body was found by the officer Andrews another constable had passed through the alley.[392]

Lloyd's Weekly made the same point but allowed for a slightly wider window of opportunity: "... the sergeant on duty in Wentworth-street and the vicinity passed the very spot only 10 minutes before"[393]. The autopsy revealed that McKenzie had been killed around 12.45am, consistent with PS Badham having just passed by and the *Times'* tighter six minute timeframe.

The victim's body had not been there at 12.25am when another of the beat constables, PC Joseph Allen stood near the very spot to take a quick break and a snack. He resumed his beat in a northerly direction. As he took the bend that led from Castle Alley to Old Castle Street, he noticed the publican from the Three Crowns, Myer Jacobs, closing up[394]. Its location, which was diagonally across from the murder site, recalls Detective Inspector Reid's belief that Jack The Ripper used the local pubs to pick-up his victims and that their closing times might have played a crucial role.

One newspaper report put forward the not unreasonable supposition that the killer had the patrols under observation: "they must have been watched"[395]. The journalist who penned the piece may have been closer to the mark than he realised. Paradoxically, it led to the murderer committing a blunder, though it was not of his making, nor did it take anything away from his cunning.

When he saw PC Allen disappear past the bend into Old Castle Street at 12.30am, and the back of PS Badham as he did the same some 15 minutes later, he likely thought he had some time up his sleeve in which to act, maybe as much time again until the next patrol. Instead, what transpired only several minutes later, was the appearance of PS Andrews emerging unexpectedly from the same bend. The probable cause of his miscalculation was in thinking PS Badham was a normal beat policeman. He was, in fact, on a roving commission to check-in on constables under his orders, without a beat of his own. It is likely that PS Badham proved the fly in the killer's ointment, as much as PC Andrews was the one to actually scuttle his plans. The scenario adds one more layer of understanding to events, and together with the medical evidence, helps to explain why the press were so convinced that the murderer had been interrupted. As the *Times* pointed out:

> Although the mutilation was not committed so savagely as in the other cases, it is thought that the murderer would have served this, his latest victim, in similar manner but that he was disturbed…[396]

Likewise, the media was convinced that the killer was an intimate of the neighbourhood, even proposing the rationale behind what may have proved to be the killer's fall-back strategy:

> If, as is probable, the murderer was acquainted with the locality he would know that the beat constable would pass along this narrow way, up along the flagstones of which heavy police boots would make a noise admirably adapted to the purposes of an alarm.[397]

It is true that the immediate area was a particular one. It was not just the press to understand the part it had played in the crime and the killer's subsequent disappearance. At least some among the police were inclined to thoughts along similar lines. Detective Inspector Reid's inquest testimony is worth noting:

> Coroner: Would any stranger be likely to find Castle Alley unless he knew the locality?
>
> Reid: It is approached by a narrow covered passage from (Whitechapel) High Street. I don't think a stranger would go down the alley unless he was taken... Although it is called an alley, it is a narrow court leading into a broad turning, with two narrow exits. Any person looking upon it from the Wentworth-street end would regard it as a blind street. No stranger would think he could pass through it, and none but foot passengers can.[398]

His testimony might help put into context an interview published a few days later by the *Evening News* with an unnamed "Chief of the Criminal Investigation Department"[399]. Some students of the case suggest the source may well have been Detective Inspector Reid[400]. Given his attested focus on geography in post-retirement interviews, the assumption would stand to reason. Whoever the insider was, he had this to say about Jack The Ripper within a week of Alice McKenzie's slaying: "He lives in Whitechapel, of that I am confident. His knowledge of the locality is astonishing"[401].

If local geography had played its part in helping make good his escape, it had been a close call all the same. The most practical effect of which had been to limit the time that was available to mutilate his victim. The relatively contained nature of those injuries would, in turn, create the case's greatest sticking point, ultimately excluding McKenzie from the list of Jack The Ripper's canonical victims. While Dr Phillips' opinion, already quoted, would underpin such an interpretation, what is often ignored is the caveat he attached to the end of his autopsy report:

> I do not here enter into the comparison of the cases *neither do I take into account what I admit may be almost conclusive evidence in favour of the one man* (ie. same perpetrator) *theory if all the surrounding circumstances & other evidence are considered.* (author's italics & parentheses)

There is a suggestion, courtesy of a media report, that he may well have momentarily entertained a more holistic perspective when first confronted by the crime scene:

> The discovery was made known at once at Commercial-street police-station, and Drs. Phillips and Brown were communicated with. Immediately on their arrival they examined the wounds, and informed the police that the murder must have been done by same person or persons who committed the previous murders in Whitechapel and Spitalfields[402].

One aspect that would have been difficult to dismiss, and mitigates for McKenzie's murder to be included among the previous year's, was the severity of the fatal neck wound. Dr Phillips noted that it had been deep enough to have hit down to the bone. Though he did not state it, this was a telltale sign of Jack The Ripper's involvement. Dr Phillips' post-mortem report described the wound as "the division of the Common Carotid... *down to the traverse processes of the Cervical Vertebrae*" (author's italics). Reporting inquest testimony, the media's lay version, put it: "the carotid vessels...were entirely severed down to the vertebrae of the spinal column"[403][404]. This important piece of minutiae speaks for itself. So too, the throat having been cut from left to right, a detail that McKenzie shared with each of the other victims. Tellingly, the mutilations had been attempted post-mortem and there was no evidence of sexual activity, other details shared with the canonical victims. Among some modern students of the case, McKenzie's lesser mutilations are often dismissed as 'scratches' by way of questioning her candidacy. However, the autopsy report makes clear that these particular cuts "were caused through the endeavour to pass the obstruction caused by the clothing". In fact, it is difficult not to see the issue of McKenzie's mutilations as part of a broader discussion: the interrupted nature of the attack. Indeed, if the murderer had wanted proof that his decision to head indoors, back in November at Miller's Court, had been correct, then Castle Alley provided him with the confirmation: it was now riskier and more difficult than ever to operate out in the open.

It has been discussed earlier in the chapter why Dr Bond, unlike his colleague, saw Jack The Ripper's clear handiwork on display and McKenzie's link to the rest of the series. Ultimately, Dr Bond had been brought into the investigation to compare the medical evidence spanning the cases[405]. He was arguably better placed to make the call in respect McKenzie than anyone else, even without going into non-medical details such as geography, victimology, seasonality, and the crime's execution during early morning hours – what even Dr Phillips conceded was the, "almost conclusive... surrounding circumstances & other evidence"*.

There are more grounds besides which support the dissenters, a list that seems to have included Inspectors Reid and Moore among them[406]. The *East London Observer* noted that Castle Alley and surrounds were "principally occupied by foreign Jews and the frequenters of common lodging-houses,"[407] painting by now a consistent picture of the immediate neighbourhood and the story's rationale. Another report noted:

JACK THE RIPPER'S HUNTING GROUND. (From Our London Correspondent.) London, July 19

---

* Modern-day speculation that McKenzie may have been the victim of an unspecified, copycat killer ultimately rests on the argument that another, equally bold and just as able, Jack The Ripper-like murderer was active in that very neighbourhood, at that same moment, and displaying all the original killer's *modi operandi*.

HEBREW INHABITANTS OF THE QUARTER. An observant and philosophical reporter on the London Star, visited the scene of Tuesday's murder with a view to studying the people amongst whom Jack the Ripper commits his mysterious crimes. He says: "It is a strangely quiet and indifferent crowd which peers at the splashes of blood underneath the lamp-post in Castle yard... It is a Jew crowd, for the two Castle streets are almost purely Jewish quarters. Little Jew boys, with big beady eyes and sallow faces, sit on the steps of the big barrack-like Board school hard by towering high above the ramshackle hovel of Castle street. Sallow, sickly little creatures are they, but shrewd and self-possessed. The women stand about in knots, huge, stayless women, with breasts hanging down. Then there is the Jew young man, with his cigarette, there, consumptive-looking, but wiry... comely daughters of Judah... There are Jew names everywhere. At the coffee-shop there is an inscription in Hebrew, and they are selling Kosher rum round the corner at the big bar in Whitechapel High street, where the proprietor is probably clearing his £IO,OOO a year. IT RAINS CHILDREN. Isaacs, and Jacobs, and Levis, and Abrahams are the common names, and there is a gabble of "Yiddish" among the children. What heaps of them there are![408]

Importantly, Castle Alley slotted in perfectly with the case's bigger narrative. The spot where McKenzie's body was found was almost adjacent to the prototype Jewish Board School, run along increasingly religious lines from 1874 by principal, Abraham Levy, a pioneer of Jewish education[409][410]. Castle Alley's continuation, Old Castle Street, was home to the Shalom v'Emess (Peace & Truth) synagogue, literally around the corner and on the same block as George Hutchinson's lodgings. As was the Bikhur Cholim Sons Of Lodz synagogue (1887), in New Castle Street, directly behind Castle Alley. Immediately parallel, to the east, was Commercial Street, where the Victoria Home was situated at numbers 39-41. The first street parallel to the west of Castle Alley was Goulston Street, where the inflammatory graffito and Catherine Eddowes' bloody apron piece were found. One street across again was Middlesex Street (Petticoat Lane), where Hutchinson claimed to have spotted his sinister Jewish gentleman a few days after Kelly's murder. It was the same street that marked the boundary between the City and Metropolitan Police. On that score, Middlesex Street had featured during the night of the double-event, as Jack The Ripper led his pursuers on a merry chase, changing jurisdictions as he skipped back and forth over that political dividing line.

It almost seems as though Castle Alley was bound to feature in proceedings sooner or later – not so much if, as when. It is often proposed that increased police and vigilance patrols after the double-event may have played a part in conspiring to set Kelly's murder indoors. In turn, the attack in Miller's Court led to an even greater degree of street surveillance. It is reasonable to assume that together with the onset of winter, a hiatus of some kind was always going to be the outcome of such a heavy police presence, while the killer waited it out. Indeed, internal police correspondence and media reports covering McKenzie's murder are testament to the extra police surveillance having tapered off "just preceding the recent crime"[411]. This argues in favour of Jack The Ripper being forced to lay low and a closing net interpretation, marked by exponentially increasing times between attacks, and their taking place ever closer to the safety of home.

Between the murders of Nichols and Chapman, 8 days went by; 22, between Chapman and Stride/Eddowes; 40 between the double-event and Kelly; and 250 between Kelly and McKenzie. The increasing delay between attacks was met with an inverse trend when observing distance from the Victoria Home. Bucks Row (Nichols) was 12 minutes away; Hanbury Street (Chapman) was 8 minutes; Berner Street (Stride), 8 minutes and Mitre Square (Eddowes) 8 minutes; Miller's Court (Kelly), 3 minutes; Castle Alley (McKenzie), 2 minutes via a conventional route, or even less via a hypothetical back alley approach. FBI profiler John Douglas noted something similar to this geographic consideration in his 1988 report[412]: he explained a subtle shift of comfort zones, relative to the locations of Jack The Ripper's crimes due to a "heating up" of the investigation.

It is not surprising then that the dragnet elicited by McKenzie's murder focused on surrounding lodging houses. At one point, the keeper of the Victoria Home became embroiled. He was called upon to vouch for one of its residents, later identified as a John Larkin Mills, arrested for loitering at the scene some hours after the morning's dramatic events[413].

If the ever closing net provided George Hutchinson with evidence that things were getting too close for comfort, then the Great London Dock Strike provided him with the perfect opportunity to get out. The eight weeks between McKenzie's slaying and the Ormuz's departure certainly left him in no doubt about what he was up against: "the streets and alleys of the district fairly bustle with policemen, some in uniform and others in plain clothes," one report read the day before the Ormuz was due to cast-off[414]. There is other evidence that the period was marked by Whitechapel being "overrun" with policemen, uniformed and plain-clothed, and with police informants. In late August 1889, it was arranged for a visiting American journalist to be given a tour of the area by Inspector Moore who had taken over from Inspector Abberline when the latter had moved on to other cases:

We walked on in silence for half a block, and then I suggested that he was using amateur as well as professional detectives in his search for the murderer. "About sixty," he replied laconically. The inspector was non communicative, but I could see and hear for myself, and a dozen times during our tour women in rags, lodging-house keepers, proprietors of public-houses, and idle young men, dressed like all the other idle young men of the district, but with a straight bearing that told of discipline, and with the regulation shoe with which Scotland yard marks its men, whispered a half sentence as we passed, to which sometimes the inspector replied or to which he sometimes appeared utterly unconscious. From what he said later I learned that all Whitechapel is peopled with these spies. Sometimes they are only "plain clothes" men, but besides these he has half a hundred and at times 200 unattached detectives, who pursue their respectable or otherwise callings while they keep an alert eye and ear for the faintest clue that may lead to the discovery of the invisible murderer.[415]

It may not only have come down to the near-run thing Castle Alley proved to be, or a shortening ring of comfort curtailing future exploits, or even that Hutchinson had brought police literally to his doorstep. He likely realised that there was little prospect of success in reigniting the narrative attributing the murders to the Jews. There had been no more riots as after the Chapman murder. Police had intervened to stifle the Goulston Street graffito from having its intended effect, and while the torrent of outrage after Miller's Court had been intense, it had jumped its intended anti-Semitic spillway. Now, the law of diminishing returns had well and truly kicked in. To put it another way: his campaign had become yesterday's news and was teetering on the verge of collapse. Though promising in its opening stages, it had veered off the mark. Intensified practical policing, not pogroms, had been its main response – in tandem with editorial responsibility in reporting (however belatedly) and the astute leadership of a culturally aware police force which almost belies the times.

Weighing up his options, it must have been with a sense of pique as much as self-preservation that George Hutchinson contemplated whether he could afford to miss his boat when the opportunity sailed onto the horizon.

End of Chapter 11 notes:
Bricklayer or watchmaker, butcher or horse slaughterer?

Post-retirement, two men at the centre of the investigation, inspectors Abberline and Reid, seem to have locked horns over differing views of the killer's possible anatomical knowledge and medical understanding.

In an interview that Reid gave in 1903, he dismissed the notion that the killer possessed any sophisticated understanding of the human body[416]. In part, Reid had been prompted to respond to Abberline, who was publicly entertaining a new theory pertaining to wife poisoner Seweryn Klosowski (a.k.a. George Chapman). Abberline had drawn Reid's ire by describing Jack The Ripper's work as that of "an expert surgeon", likely bent on organ procurement[417]. For all that Abberline's main tussle by then could only have been with posterity, rather than Jack The Ripper, his reported comments made for quite a statement, and Reid was incredulous:

> I think I know that gentleman (Abberline) better than to think he could have said that the series of murders was the work of an expert surgeon, when he knew that it was nothing more than a number of slashes all over the bodies of the victims... to compare his work with that of Chapman is like comparing the work of a bricklayer with that of a watchmaker.[418] (author's parentheses)

Reid was, in fact, not offering anything new in his rebuttal. He had long been on record, and his opinion had remained steadfast. A few years previously, he had said:

> The Ripper was a man with no skilled knowledge – not even the skill of a novice in butchery. In every instance the mutilation was clumsy in the extreme – (it) was the hacking and tearing of a man in a frenzy, increasing in intensity as his work proceeded.[419]

As far back as his retirement in 1896, he'd been publicly saying the same thing:

> "The idea that the murderer was a mad surgeon, or a man with any knowledge of the anatomy of the human frame," said Mr Reid, "was a most ridiculously inaccurate one. He was a vulgar man; that is, he was no scientist or medical man – not even a butcher – I should say, from the same clumsiness displayed in his frenzied work in each case. He was simply seized with a frenzy the moment he was alone with the women, hacked and tore at them in his frenzy, with no intent but the satisfaction of a horrible passion for destruction."[420]

His view echoed Dr Bond's, as can be seen in the latter's landmark 1888 report, which provided an overview of the medical evidence. It will be remembered, Dr Bond had also conducted the autopsy on the most mutilated victim, Mary Kelly.

> In each case the mutilation was inflicted by a person who had no scientific nor anatomical knowledge. In my opinion he does not even possess the technical knowledge of a butcher or horse slaughterer or any person accustomed to cut up dead animals.

But Bond's belief was not always in sync with his colleagues whose work and very opinions he had effectively been asked to assess. These ranged from Dr Llewellyn, who had examined the body of the first canonical victim, Polly Nichols, and seen signs of "rough anatomical knowledge", to Dr Phillips, who believed that the mutilations inflicted on the second victim, Annie Chapman, were "the work of an expert – or one, at least, who had such knowledge of anatomical or pathological examinations as to be enabled to secure the pelvic organs with one sweep of the knife".

To some degree, Dr Phillips was supported by Dr Brown, who found it particularly difficult to ignore the implied understanding of anatomy that was required to extract Eddowes' kidney. But Doctors

Saunders and Sequeira, who also examined Eddowes' body, were less sure. "He was not possessed of any great anatomical skill," opined the latter[421].

Dr Clark had assisted Dr Phillips at Alice McKenzie's postmortem and taken over his practice on the latter's retirement. Interviewed by the *East London Observer* in 1910, he was reported to have maintained a guarded interest in the case, even after the passage of so many years and was said to be in possession of a photograph of the mutilated remains of Mary Kelly. Dr Clark was of the opinion that there was nothing of a professional character about the wounds, "the bodies were simply slashed about from head to foot"[422].

The issue had been a live one for the police from relatively early on. Dr Bond had been brought in because they believed they had "*no reliable opinion... as to the amount of surgical skill and anatomical knowledge*" possessed by the murder[423] (author's italics). Dr Bond had essentially been asked to adjudicate both the matter, and indirectly, the evaluations of his colleagues given the diverging breadth of their opinions. Despite this, Bond's judgement would not prove to be the final word, and healthy discussion on the question continues to this day among students of the case.

Is it possible that the differing points of view might be reconciled by considering that Jack The Ripper was confident, in so far as he knew what he wanted to do, but not necessarily in how to achieve it? Were the doctors, perhaps all to varying degrees of accuracy, describing the actions of an untrained hand reaching beyond its grasp but purpose driven nonetheless? Might the wide gamut of medical opinion be explained by the mutilations having been inflicted by someone *staging* a mock ethno-religious ritual for dramatic effect, as brazenly contrived as it was callous: a media-monster taking his cues from the hype he had been reading in the newspapers?

Gaining a better understanding of the case may well lie caught up with the dynamics of those two notorious, continental causes célèbres of the 1880s, and their impact upon the public imagination. As early as

1882 the British media had reported in detail on the blood libel case from Cracow of Moses Ritter. According to the calumny engaged by the prosecution, the accused had been motivated by 'Jewish superstition' to cleanse himself of a sexual liaison with a Christian woman that had resulted in pregnancy. Ritter's 'atonement' allegedly rested on her murder, the dissection of the body and the distribution of her remains in various hiding places[424].

The main keystones of the Ritter story were sexual, and specifically reproductive. Might such news items, repeated in various forms as late as the 'Autumn of Terror', have given the killer both the focus and general outline for the kind of attacks he was to pursue: mutilating abdomen, womb and sexual organs, and stealing away with parts of the victims' reproductive anatomy, notably all of Chapman's and part of Eddowes' uterus (never to be found)? It would certainly go a long way towards explaining some of the peculiarities and the kind of injuries visited upon the victims, and demonstrate a determination to wield the knife mindful of accomplishing a set task. That the mutilations were carried out, effectively post-mortem, or after lightning death blows to the throat, tends to reinforce such an interpretation if only by ruling out simple sadism as the motivating factor, and focusing on the question of 'why?' were they performed. That Jack The Ripper's victims were all sex workers might also help frame such a consideration within the set parameters of the fallacious storyline that he may well have been trying to impart.

Similarly and importantly, the central point at issue in the Tisza-Eszlar case was the alleged ritual throat cutting of Esther Solymosi[425426]. The main tenet of the fanciful charges that faced the innocent men accused of murdering her was that while pinning her down inside the synagogue, a shochet or ritual butcher performed the task, approximating a beheading in its severity[427]. A number of those standing trial were widely reported to have been shochets. It is worth noting that one resilient point of contemporary (and occasionally, modern-day) speculation revolved around whether the bloody mayhem on the streets of Whitechapel was the work of a shochet run amok. Might this have been a roundabout but accurate reflection of Jack The Ripper's mischievous and malicious intent? Certainly, the hallmarks of the East End attacks and mutilations bear a conspicuous degree of overlap with reports of these two infamous contemporary cases from Austria-Hungary.

It raises the question of whether, on the night of the double-event, the killer felt compelled to make his point via anti-Semitic graffito, literally spelling things out, owing to his slip-up in Berner Street, which precluded the possibility of mutilating his victim and the very important message this component of his crimes was meant to convey. In turn, it raises the prospect of gaining a further degree of understanding when considering the choice of location of Catherine Eddowes' murder behind the Great Synagogue and the heightened level of mutilation inflicted on her.

An almost obvious question demands to be asked at this point, and it could be central to gaining a clearer perspective of the case: were Jack The Ripper's actions in Mitre Square and Goulston Street part of a frantic attempt to overcompensate? If he was worried that Stride's relatively straightforward murder, absent mutilation, might scuttle his narrative, it would help explain why he felt compelled to kill a second time during a single outing. Later events, as they were to play out in November at Miller's Court, might then be seen as tracing at least some of their roots back to that original and calculated decision to deliver the message in increasingly shrill tones: an escalation, triggered defensively by events in Berner Street, and motivated by the desire to publicise a very precise and malevolent, false accusation.

While the intensifying level of violence suffered by the victims has always been assumed to have been the result of a bloodthirsty killer losing himself in the mania of his demented work, an alternative explanation beckons: it was an organic development, born of circumstance, and delivered with calculated, political effect.

CHAPTER 12

MUNDANE MAN

> Investigators would have interviewed him during the course of the investigation and he was probably talked to by police on several occasions. Unfortunately at the time, there was no way to correlate this type of information; therefore, he was overlooked. Investigators and citizens in the community had a preconceived idea or picture of what Jack The Ripper would look like. Because of their belief that he would appear odd or ghoulish in appearance, he was overlooked and/or eliminated as a potential suspect.
>
> SUBJECT: *Jack The Ripper*
> FBI profiler John Douglas
> 6 July, 1988

Jack The Ripper's reign of terror over the East End had barely settled into its own burgeoning legend, when in February 1891 there was one last scare. A young woman, Frances Coles, was found by a beat policeman lying in a dark passageway not too far from the story's main setting. Her throat had been slashed three times and though still alive, she was beyond help. Authorities were sure they had her murderer when they charged her partner James Sadler, and remained so inclined even after the case against him fell apart. Whatever Sadler's involvement, if any, there were some decidedly non-Ripper facets to Coles' murder, particularly the absence of mutilation and its location at the outer periphery of the serial killer's usual haunts. Modern students of the case are broadly in agreement that Jack The Ripper was not involved. This reflects unanimous medical opinion at the time, and in that respect they were correct. The murderer's violent spree had long drawn to a close: in 1889, on the eve of George Hutchinson's departure for New South Wales.

The media and Jack The Ripper's police pursuers may have found themselves at loggerheads on many things during the course of the investigation, but in one thing there was no dispute: their subject was a man of unsurpassed daring when finding himself in a tight spot. A proactive strategy to his post-McKenzie predicament would have been in keeping with form, as when he had come forward after Mary Kelly's murder in the guise of a helpful witness. A rolling stone gathers no moss.

A flight to the furthest colonies on board the RMS Ormuz in September 1889 dovetails with events, and importantly, the dates under investigation. A 29-year-old Englishman named George Hutchinson is recorded as arriving in Australia on a ship from London within a year of Mary Kelly's murder and a few months after Alice McKenzie's. A violent rampage came to a close in the East End. George Hutchinson, the witness, disappeared from the record during the same period, never to be heard of again, until now. In fact, there is much to link the three facades of the man to a single individual: George Hutchinson the witness, George Hutchinson prisoner 1166, and Jack The Ripper. The Australian records have more to offer in this respect, and in perusing them a particular person of interest from 1888 soon comes into view.

Prisoner 1166's details from Bathurst gaol bring to mind that well recognised figure described by eyewitnesses: the short, stout* man most often and consistently described as about 5'5" or 5'6"§. Going over his photo and accompanying particulars, they recall in almost uncanny detail the assailant that Schwartz described attacking Stride, the man with the "full face, broad shoulders", "rather stoutly built", of "fair complexion", "dark hair", "brown moustache" and 5'5". George Hutchinson's Bathurst gaol record describes his height as 5'5½" and weighing 154 lbs, which puts him in the stocky range. His hair colour is recorded as brown, eyes blue, which suggest the fresh or fair complexion described by several eyewitnesses# and possibly, the

---

* Gardner & Best, Schwartz, Marshall, Brown, Cox, Lewis, and Maxwell.
§ Gardner & Best, Schwartz, Marshall, Cox, and Maxwell.
# Cox, Schwartz, and Lawende.

"Englishman" described by Gardner and Best[428]. It is not known for sure whether the witness from 1888, George Hutchinson, was born in England, though he did reside in its capital and both his Christian and surname suggest a quintessentially English provenance. George Hutchinson, prisoner 1166, certainly was English, and his religion was recorded as Church Of England.

Another noteworthy detail is that prisoner 1166 appears to be slightly cross-eyed or strabismic. Whatever the reason, his eyes draw attention. Whether from misalignment or simply seeming a little odd, they recall the evidence of Gardner and Best ("rather weak eyes") and Thomas Bowyer ("somewhat peculiar eyes").

Prisoner 1166 arrived in Sydney in October 1889 aged 29, according to the shipping master's records. In other words, he was born in 1859 or 1860. This sits well, but less than perfectly with the date of birth cited in his prison paperwork, 1861, which cross-references said details from the shipping records. There is no question they refer to the same individual, as does the official *New South Wales Police Gazette*, which added another year of birth to the mix, 1862, upon his release from gaol. Frustratingly, these discrepancies contradict *and* support one another simultaneously. Be that as it may, they manage to cast a consistent net around prisoner 1166's age. At the time of Mary Kelly's murder, he would have been no younger than 25 and no older than 29.

When looking at the issue of Jack The Ripper's possible age, profiler John Douglas had this to say:

> The age of onset for these types of homicides is generally between the mid to late 20s. Based upon the high degree of psychopathology exhibited at the scene, the ability of the subject to converse with the victim until a suitable location is found, and the ability to avoid detection, (it) places him between the age bracket of 28 to 36 years of age.[429]

There is a vein of modern Ripper lore that places witness George

Hutchinson's age at the time of Mary Kelly's murder at 28. It may or may not be accurate, which has not stopped it being repeated authoritatively in some of the modern literature. It seems to stem from the recollections of two trailblazing Hutchinson critics, Brian Marriner, deceased, and author Bob Hinton. According to Hinton, both independently recalled sighting a contemporary media report to that effect, but unfortunately, the original source material could not be tracked down after the event[430]. While it would tend to give some indirect support to the thesis that Hutchinson was born in 1859 or 1860, realistically, there is nothing tangible or precise from the Victorian era sources. What comes closest is courtesy of Walter Dew's memoires which refer to Hutchinson as "a young man"[431].

The only other possible help falls into the category of a thumbnail sketch, not figuratively but literally. Thanks to the *Illustrated Police News* edition of 24 November 1888, Hutchinson is depicted in one of the very scenes he described to the police and media, as part of a montage of events surrounding Kelly's murder. He is shown spying on her in the company of her villainous customer. Given the intricate level of nuance on display in the depiction of the suspect, it is quite possible that the newspaper's illustrator consulted with Hutchinson to flush out as much detail as possible, in turn suggesting it is a genuine representation of the witness himself. It would seem reasonable enough to imagine as much from a publication whose recent editions boasted that it, "faithfully pictures... this sensational story and fully describes all the details connected with these Diabolical Crimes".

A closer look, reveals the background figure of Hutchinson, portrayed as someone of broad chest and shoulders, and of quite stocky frame. He is represented as a young to middle-aged looking man with a moustache. The chin, jowl and eyes appear remarkably similar to those of prisoner 1166, as does the face, more generally. But it is the nose which might just about give the game away for George Hutchinson – as much as any signature. The prison record accompanying the photo notes a "broken nose" as one of his "marks or special features", and it appears the same could be true of the nose of the background figure depicted in the *Illustrated Police News*. Both comparative images show a slightly bulbous schnoz with a bump on the bridge, high up the nose, and a clearly defined dip at the tip – the latter characteristic being more prominent in the *Illustrated Police News,* but ultimately confirmed to be just as pronounced by the additional side-on view provided by the second gaol photo. Without dwelling overly on the similarities, it might be worth asking why the illustrator would have given such a distinctive nose – what might otherwise have been pencilled in as a generic feature – to a background figure no less, unless he was drawing a distinct person? Why *that* nose unless it was a real one? It is a fundamental question. And the answer suggests, that this is a real life drawing of George Hutchinson from 1888.

Broadly consistent with the newspaper artwork, is illustrator Ferdinand Fermo Fissi's take, which appeared in *Famous Crimes Past & Present* (edited Harold Furniss, 1903). As an interesting aside, an eminent Ripperologist made a memorable remark to this author on first being shown the image of prisoner 1166: "it actually looks like Hutchinson!"[*]. Another cognoscente of the case, on reading the preliminary report in which the gaol photos were first presented, said that he experienced, "an almost visceral reaction"[§]. As the author nearly did on realising that the *Illustrated Police News* sketch shows Hutchinson in a billycock hat in the very weeks after the Miller's Court atrocity. While it was a popular enough item of attire, it is worth recalling that the man seen by Cox, entering Kelly's room, was wearing a billycock.

What seems hard to ignore, is that eyewitnesses from 1888 describe a person of interest sporting a moustache (Gardner & Best, Schwartz, Lawende, Cox, Bowyer). They put his age at "about 30" (Schwartz, Lawende, Maxwell), with outer markers on either side: 28 (PC Smith, Bowyer) and 35 to "middle-aged" (Cox, Marshall). Using these broad brushstrokes to paint a picture of Jack The Ripper's age, nothing

---

[*] September 2015.

[§] Relevant correspondence, August 2017, reproduced with permission: "When I saw the photo of his mug shot I had an almost visceral reaction. He fits the most credible witness descriptions – even the broad face, broad shoulders, height, moustache – even the 'weak/strange' eyes.

in the Australian record is out of frame. To the contrary, there is a corroborating degree of overlap, especially keeping in mind the issue of his limited height and the notably stout build recalled by nearly all the eyewitnesses.

Quite possibly, in keeping with his labouring and class background, prisoner 1166 was carrying a few scars and injuries, which were recorded in the first months of his spell at Bathurst gaol as identifying marks or special features: a broken nose, a broken little finger on his right hand, a broken right knee, and a scar on his left breast. As noted, the witness George Hutchinson too was described as being a member of the labouring class.

Jack The Ripper's intimate association with Whitechapel implies he was a native local, at a time when being from the East End and working class might have been taken as synonymous. His use of a then-current Cockney epithet "Lipski" adds to the suspicion, particularly when considering that not a single witness described hearing a suspect with a foreign, or in any way distinctive, accent. Detective Constable Halse described the Goulston Street graffito as having been written in "a good schoolboy hand"[432]. It also contained a spelling error, "Juwes" (for "Jews"). The two observations suggest literacy but not much besides, consistent with a limited education. Also noteworthy, the message's double negative, a standard pattern of Cockney speech. All points, taken together, that indicate an author from a local, working class background.

"He lives or works in the Whitechapel area," opined the FBI profiler Douglas[433]; while at least some elements of the investigative team of 1888-9 were in no doubt about that aspect of Jack The Ripper's personal story. Witness George Hutchinson and prisoner 1166 can both claim a similarly close relationship with Whitechapel. The former's residence was situated right in the middle of events, while the latter's association relates to Tilbury dock's intimate connection with the East End, as discussed in chapter 10. A further point on the subject may be worth considering. At the turn of the century, 70% of casual dock labourers were London-born[434][435]. Keeping in mind that the riverside was dependent on the East End casual labourer to staff its industry, it may well offer a glimpse of prisoner 1166's antecedents and his presence on the waterfront, culminating in employment on board the Ormuz during a moment of crisis. This statistic is an interesting one when discussing someone whose Australian record refers to twice as a labourer, and could mean his relationship to London was familial, as well as professional.

Prisoner 1166's record states that he was able to read and write. This is consistent with both Jack The Ripper, author of the graffito, reader of newspapers, and witness George Hutchinson, who was able to sign the three pages of his police statement.

When laid out, a comparison table of the three faces of Jack The Ripper presents a picture that is in harmony in its essential detail:

	Jack The Ripper	Prisoner 1166; George Hutchinson	1888 witness; George Hutchinson
Connection to the East End	✓	Likely	✓
Englishman	Likely	✓	Likely
Frame	Stout	Stout	"stout"*
Height	5'5" to 5'6"	5'5½"	"short, not tall"*
Fair to average complexion	✓	✓	?
Moustache	✓	✓	✓§
Anti-Semite	✓	Blackleg	✓
Working class	Likely	✓	✓
Labourer	?	✓	✓
Literate	✓	✓	✓
Violent offender	✓	✓	?
Age in November 1888	30 +/-	28 +/-	28 (?)

* According to Sarah Lewis' account of the man staring up Miller's Court at 2.30am, who was undoubtedly Hutchinson, by his own admission.

§ According to the front page depiction from the *Illustrated Police News*, 24 November 1888, George Hutchinson had a moustache.

Among many present-day students of the case, a point that resonates against witness George Hutchinson's candidacy as a suspect is the implied criticism of Inspector Abberline. It is inconceivable, the argument goes, that Abberline could have committed such a blunder as allowing Jack The Ripper to slip through his fingers. But even putting George Hutchinson aside, it is only stating the obvious to say that the killer eluded Abberline's best efforts and the case went unsolved. It was a point his colleague, the retired Chief Inspector Moore, was only too aware of when critiquing his own failure at the serial killer's hands in a 1913 interview looking back over his career[436].

This is not to suggest Abberline was anything less than a fine detective, as able an officer as the police force of 1888 was able to put into the field against a new phenomenon: the first modern serial killer. Abberline's defeat at the hands of Jack The Ripper notwithstanding, there are no grounds for reproaching his dedication, conduct and knowledge of his métier as applied to the locale in which it was put into practice. It is a shame then, that he would have one final cross to bear: that of becoming a fatherly Victorian infallible among many aficionados of the case. This state of affairs conveniently ignores that Abberline was flesh and blood, a man brought to the brink of exhaustion by his dogged efforts in pursuing the killer.

Inspector Moore was the detective who took up Abberline's lead role in early 1889. He well knew the strains that the job and Jack The Ripper placed on his time and well-being:

> It is not an easy piece of work, I assure you. I work seventeen and eighteen hours a day. If I get into bed I think maybe he is at it now, and I grow restless, and I finally get up and tramp the courts and alleys till morning.[437]

Abberline would concede as much himself. Discussing the case with *Cassell's Saturday Journal* in 1892, the weekly newspaper noted[438]:

> …the number of statements made – all of them requiring to be recorded and searched into – was so great that the officer

almost broke down under the pressure… his anxiety to bring the murderer to justice led him, after occupying the whole day in directing his staff, to pass his time in the streets until early morning, driving home fagged and weary at 5am. And it happened frequently, too, that just as he was going to bed, he would be summoned back to the East End by a telegraph, there to interrogate some lunatic or suspected person whom the inspector in charge would not take the responsibility of questioning.[439]

Maybe this provides some degree of context as to how he came to give George Hutchinson a free pass. A man whose admitted involvement with the critical events of the early morning of 9 November 1888 placed him at their epicentre, and whose only alibi for the hours either side seems to have been wandering the streets. The sense of unease the realisation elicits is compounded when considering that Abberline's report which gave Hutchinson the green light could only have been written a few hours after interrogating him, if that. It begs the obvious question – how did Abberline manage to pin down Hutchinson's nebulous explanation of his whereabouts in the lead-up and aftermath in such a short span of time and considering the wide geography it spanned?

An alternative question, and one that has earned its right to be asked is, whether a sly killer flew in under Abberline's radar? Overworked, under pressure, an inconclusive inquest having just concluded, and absent a smoking gun, it is certainly understandable how Abberline could have made an error of judgement, just when his guard must have been at its lowest. Like the street-smart women whose murders he was investigating, Abberline made the mistake of looking right past the innocuous looking labourer, fixing instead on the opportunity he came bearing. Such was the false bargain all the victims made by taking George Hutchinson at face value. It was a disarmingly bland calling card that introduced an ugly and audacious Jack The Ripper.

Hutchinson spies the scene: *Illustrated Police News,* 24 November 1888

Fissi's vignette: *Famous Crimes,* 1903

Composite: proportions and portions and hats

End of Chapter 12 notes:
Martha Tabram, also known as Turner...

Martha Tabram was 39 years old and got by, by resorting to prostitution. A contemporary once described her, colourfully, as preferring a glass of ale to a cup of tea[440].

On the early morning after Bank Holiday Monday, on 7 August 1888, she was found in a pool of blood on a first floor landing of a building in George Yard. Tabram had been killed some time between 2.30am and 2.45am, although nobody had heard anything, and her corpse went unnoticed as such, until hours afterwards. Her clothes were disarranged, and she had died in a frenzied hail of knife blows. The stab marks were all over the body, 39 in total, including wounds to the abdomen and groin. Some reports suggest no less than nine were inflicted to the throat[441]. According to the postmortem, one stab wound on its own, that to the heart, could have proven fatal, though she was alive during the whole ordeal: "all of them were caused during life"[442]. Death was due to loss of blood[443].

Interestingly for the purposes of this study, she was discovered in a building located on the next block along from the Victoria Home, a few minutes walk away. She had been living in a lodging house in George Street, also only several minutes walk from the Victoria home. Her common-law husband, Henry Turner, from whom she had separated in preceding weeks, was himself a resident of the Victoria Home, raising the prospect of an acquaintance with George Hutchinson[444][445]. There is a faint hint of elements of the Kelly case in that respect: the possibility of a second degree of personal connection to the Victoria Home (through Dan Barnett / Henry Turner), and the recent termination of a domestic relationship (Joseph Barnett / Henry Turner). Media coverage from 1888 describes the location as "a squalid block of buildings", and the tenants, "people of the poorest description", also reminiscent of Miller's Court (see the end of chapter 13 notes)[446][447].

There is much about the timing, location, geography, nature of the attack and victimology to suggest Tabram was an early victim of Jack

The Ripper's, though she is officially a non-canonical one. Part of the reason for her failing to make the list may be owing to a quirk of fate, a decision whose reason is no longer clear: when Dr Bond was brought in to survey the medical evidence in the investigation in late October, Martha Tabram's case was not among those he was asked to evaluate. There may have been good reason for that. There were no signs of mutilation per se, though given the nature of her murder it might be considered a moot point. Also, Dr Killeen who performed the autopsy, thought he saw evidence suggesting one of her wounds may have been delivered by a dagger or bayonet. The importance of this would become caught up with Tabram having last been seen in the company of a soldier. Though extensive enquiry was made pursuing this martial angle, it ultimately bore no fruit. Officially, her violent death went unexplained and the inquest verdict of wilful murder by person or persons unknown would reverberate throughout the series.

Inspector Abberline only came on board to head the investigative team afterwards, from September. Nevertheless, looking back, he considered Tabram to have fallen prey to Jack The Ripper[448]. Walter Dew, who was already on the case, was clear in his memoires:

> … there can be no doubt that the August Bank Holiday murder, which took place in George Yard Buildings… was the handiwork of the dread Ripper.[449]

The connection to the Victoria Home, courtesy of Tabram's estranged partner, one point among many, is certainly a tantalising one to ponder. So too are the dramatic hallmarks of the violence, by now recognisable to readers. These are best summed up by Deputy Coroner, George Collier, who presided over the inquest:

> It was one of the most dreadful murders any one could imagine. *The man must have been a perfect savage* to inflict such a number of wounds on a defenceless woman in such a way.[450] (author's italics)

The question is, whether the murderer was counting on his work being seen in just such a light?

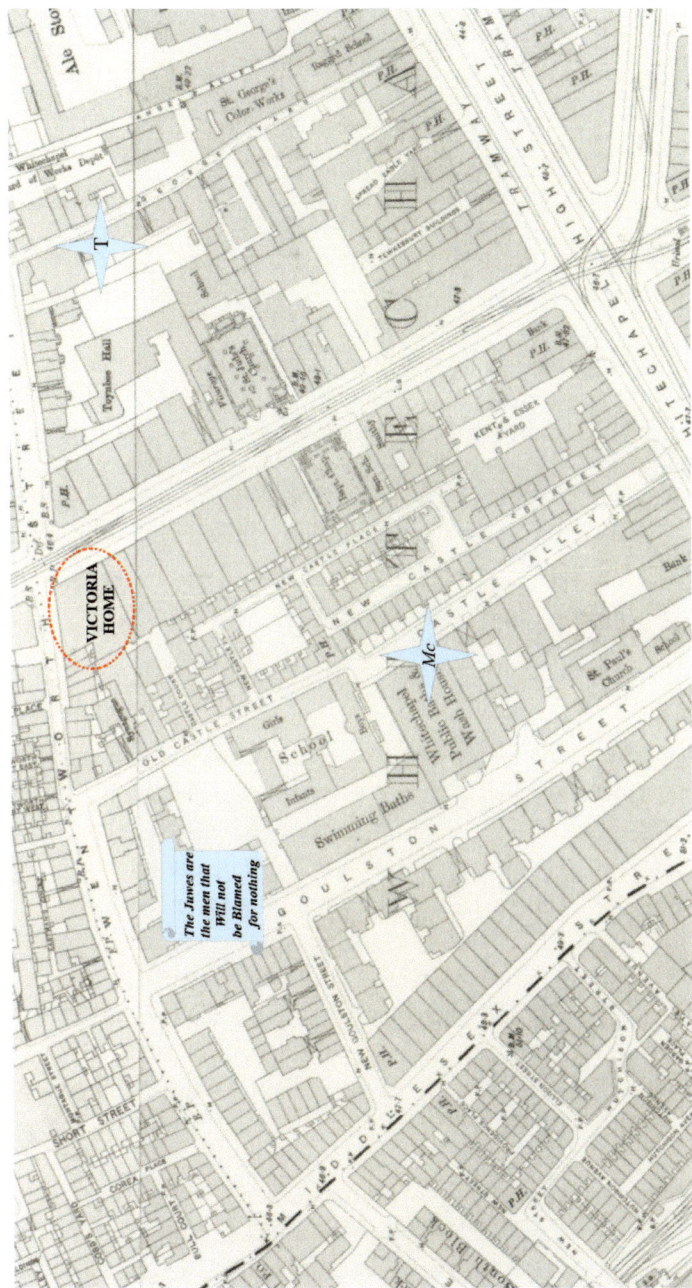

The Victoria Home relative the Goulston Street graffito, McKenzie and Tabram murder sites.

CHAPTER 13

INTO THE EAST

> Many persons have been suspected of being Jack The Ripper, including Queen Victoria's grandson, the Duke of Clarence; James Fitzjames Stephen's son, J.K. Stephen; Druitt, a barrister who later committed suicide; a group of masonic conspirators that included a leading doctor... I cannot, unfortunately, offer a solution. It is clear, however, that most of the voluminous Ripper literature has neglected to place the murders in the context of the then-growing anti-Semitism in England and the possibility that someone was trying to place the responsibility for the murders on the Jews.
>
> Martin L. Friedland, *The Trials Of Israel Lipski* (1984)

It is not a straightforward exercise determining exactly when George Hutchinson ducked into the convenient slipstream offered by the Jewish ritual murder libel as a means of giving vent to his anti-Semitism and capacity for violence. Did he even believe it to be true? Implicitly, his own murderous actions can only suggest he put little store in it. It would not be surprising were that the case. Even a young Adolf Hitler, himself a resident of a model lodging house in another imperial capital a generation later, is recorded by a contemporary as not believing it[451]; which did not stop Nazi propaganda making extensive use of the blood libel during his reign of terror in Germany and occupied Europe.

Did Hutchinson simply slip into its convenient wake midstream, playing it for all it was worth as his murder spree picked-up momentum, or did he set out with preordained malice on a public relations exercise to tarnish the Jewish community? Was he making it up as he went along, consummately exploiting racial tensions as these broke surface, or was he committed to a plan, perversely and personally motivated by the same angsts that pervaded across significant sections of the East End? These are considerations that cut to the heart of the story.

By way of tackling the question, it is hard to ignore the significance of key milestones that relate to the creation and reporting of two parliamentary select committees looking into the 'Jewish question', keeping in mind that East End street sentiment had played an important part in bringing them to life. As one local workman told the *British Weekly* while the select committees' initial deliberations took place during the spring of 1888:

> If we broke the heads of fifty Jews down here in Whitechapel something would be done to prevent this immigration. While we content ourselves with singing 'England for the English,' Government will say that these foreigners are a blessing to us.[452]

A parallel strategic thinking, no doubt, fuelled the actions of the bombastic nationalist, Arnold White: he had been caught out, cynically trying to stage-manage and manipulate deliberations before the committees, in at least one instance, going so far as to fabricate evidence[453]. George Hutchinson's approach was of a not entirely dissimilar vein to these examples. The first murders were his opening salvo in response to dashed hopes that the select committees would quickly recommend an end to Jewish immigration when they brought down their much anticipated reports in late July.

Given expectations in certain quarters, these initial documents could only have been met with disappointment, as would happen when subsequent and final ones were delivered in the following years[454]. In the case of the Lords committee's final report in 1890, it resulted in preparations for strike action[455]. In fact, the industrial response paled in significance compared to the dramatic internal ructions within the committee itself as it prepared to deliver its final report. On that eve, the anti-alienist Earl of Dunraven severed ties to the very committee that had colloquially taken his name over the two years he had served as its spearhead and chairman. He cited as one of his reasons, the need to stop "the introduction of foreigners, who compete so largely with the home workmen in the trades in which sweating is most prevalent"[456]. Whereas, the official report of his colleagues would conclude with a diametrically opposed finding: "undue stress has been laid on the injurious effect on wages caused by foreign immigration"[457].

The Earl of Dunraven (and for better or worse, even White) had counted on working within the system to desired effect, and been left smarting. The workman quoted above in the *British Weekly* on the other hand, and others of his class, were as sceptical as they were seething from the outset of the process. Media coverage, such as the following from the *Standard*'s edition of 4 August 1888, makes clear some of the early cynicism elicited by the effective postponement of recommendations, referring to the initial report from the Lords committee as "a brief and guarded document", a commentary repeated by others newspapers[458]:

> The Select Committee do not, for the present, offer any suggestions for the remedy of the evils they have been inquiring into. All that they have done, and all that they pretend to do for some time to come, is to collect facts, and, so to speak, to diagnose the malady...[459]

To add insult to injury, the select committee advised of its intention to abandon the local focus that had constituted part of its very terms of reference. Crucially for the purposes of the story's bigger picture, the media reported: "... so far as the East-end of London is concerned, it is believed that a few weeks of the Autumn Session will suffice to exhaust all the evidence to be obtained in that quarter"[460]. That determination would prove a lightning rod to someone in Whitechapel who had his own thoughts about such presumption. As long as the select committees continued to gather evidence and take soundings, the spotlight was on. Mutilated corpses were the result and the 'Autumn of Terror' would become its name.

In a roundabout way, an acknowledgement of just such a link, between the murders and the very particular political, social and industrial conditions on the ground, was in evidence as early as the 13 October edition of the *Commonweal*: "The method of life adopted by Annie Chapman and her fellow-victims is the alternative one to slow murder for sweaters' pay". A front page editorial in the *Star*, in the days after Mary Kelly's murder, dwelt on the connection in some detail:

> There is no precedent for these deeds... They have sprung upon us like a thief in the night. They are as unfamiliar to ordinary experience as the wildest of nightmares. One thing, however, we can do, and that is, tell the truth about them, and admit that truth to our own consciences. Could the murder-fiend, looking the wide world over, find a choicer field of operations than Whitechapel? We hear of missionary efforts in the East-end... Let us look to Whitechapel and the sweating system, and content ourselves with no solution of labour questions which does not solve them. There lies our crux; there lies our duty, and if we do it, our hope of better things than the horrors which fill our minds to-day.[461]

The Commons committee on immigration resumed taking direct evidence over the spring and summer of 1889 and the proceedings were often referenced in newspapers reports. Serendipitous it may have been, but it is worth noting that Alice McKenzie was killed at 12.45am on the 17 July 1889 and the select committee had deliberated over the previous two days, with Superintendent Thomas Arnold having been recalled for his second appearance on 15 July 1889.

A few weeks later, on 8 August 1889, the final report of the Commons committee was ready and ordered to be published. Its official pronouncement recommended against placing restrictions on immigration. Details were carried widely in the media, and it is hard to imagine the news did not play its part in George Hutchinson's decision to leave England, coming as it did smack-bang within the short window between Alice McKenzie's murder and his departure on the Ormuz. Effectively, the date marked the moment when his xenophobic and macabre scheme was officially defeated. Jewish migrants would continue to arrive in London, essentially unrestricted, until 1905 when tighter controls on immigration were enacted as part of a legislative reform. For nearly 130 years, George Hutchinson would be the only person to be aware of the date's significance, but the 8th of August 1889 marked VJTR Day. Victory against Jack The Ripper. ■

Looking back to possible antecedents, there is evidence to suggest there may have been at least one earlier assault, on 28 March 1888, and it roughly coincided with the establishment of the Commons select committee on immigration on 20 March.

In the early morning hours, Ada Wilson, a 39-year-old dressmaker was attacked in her home by a man who, according to her version, presented himself at the door of her room and demanded money. He stabbed the half-dressed woman viciously in the throat twice. Confronted by her screams and the attention of a neighbour, he ran away. Wilson's situation at this point was desperate. Bleeding profusely from the gash in her neck, police were summoned. A local doctor was soon on hand to administer first aid and the victim rushed to hospital. Expert opinion thought it impossible that the injured woman could recover, such was the severity of the wound, but she surprised her doctors and survived[462].

A young Jewish neighbour, Rose Biermann, who resided in the same house, gave a somewhat different account of the events and their background. During their acquaintance, Wilson had told Biermann she was married. Though the Jewish woman had never seen Wilson's husband, she was aware that Wilson "often had visitors to see her"[463]. This was one such occasion and Biermann had actually seen her neighbour come home with the assailant[464]. She also provided the added detail that Wilson was due to be evicted – a precarious living arrangement not dissimilar to that of canonical victim, Mary Kelly who was behind with her rent. Importantly, she realised the man seemed to know his way out of the building, "as if he had been accustomed to do so before"[465]. The various facets of Biermann's account, and the victim's for that matter, suggest Wilson may have been making ends meet by working from home as a prostitute and was attacked by a client.

This potential precursor attack was of a lesser nature to the seemingly so un-English murders that were to come later, though the signature attack to the throat was present and the media referred to it as "a desperate attempt to murder"[466]. If profilers are correct and killers like Jack The Ripper don't just materialise as fully developed serial murderers[467], it might hint at an unsophisticated perpetrator feeling his way; a tentative and clumsy first bid perhaps. There are other reasons to ponder such a possibility.

The composite description of Wilson's attacker was of a "young fair man", aged about 30, with a fair moustache and 5'6" in height. Certainly the victimology, (non-winter) seasonality, early hours of the morning attack and witness descriptions are hard to ignore, so too the savage nature of the injury to the throat. But a word of caution comes courtesy of the geography, which places the event in a part of the East End, Maidman Street, Bow (Mile End), further to the east than Whitechapel.

There may be some degree of explanation for this less than perfect geographic fit, if that it is, and local political meetings in the lead-up may offer perspective. On 24 March, there had been a mass meeting of Conservatives at Mile End where grievances were aired against foreigners undermining the conditions of British workers[468]. Ten days earlier, Lord Rosebery, a former Liberal cabinet minister and future prime minister, had spoken out against pauper immigrants at the Bow and Bromley Reform Club in Bow Road in a speech reported widely in the press[469]. He described the desperate newcomers arriving on British shores as "the rubbish of the world... shot on our favoured islands," eliciting cheers and laughter from his East End audience[470].

Today, most politicians understand that their words need to be used carefully and can be the cause of unintended incitement to violence when not. Might something along these lines have played their part in sparking events in this instance? The attack on Wilson seems to betray the shadowy outlines of a plan in miniature as would take full form in the autumn. It is worthwhile considering whether her attempted murder was a botched bid by George Hutchinson to engage the two select committees' attention just as they were beginning their work. Under this scenario, the practicalities of failure saw him cast aside the plot, maybe in conjunction with other issues. It was only later, after the committees announced that they would keep going with their deliberations without having arrived at a resolution that Hutchinson's impetus revived, propelling him onto a resumption of his plan, invigorated perhaps by the time afforded to restore his confidence. That one of the select committees should have announced plans to limit its remaining focus on the East End, specifically to the autumn, may also have played a re-incentivising role.

It is worth noting that the location of the attack, Maidman Street, shared some notable geographic particularities with the site of the canonical first murder in Buck's Row. Both streets were one back and parallel to Whitechapel Road and its continuation, Mile End Road, and though both sites fell outside the main area of Jewish settlement, they were both around the corner, a few minutes' walk from Jewish cemeteries (see the end of chapter 13 notes and map). ■

When Jack The Ripper set down to his work in the autumn, the popular conviction that "no Englishman" could have committed such crimes soon became currency. That the connection between the atrocities and the blood libel had been publicly understood is clear from the "wilds of Hungary" report in the *Pall Mall Gazette* on 8 September, the same day that the second canonical victim Annie Chapman was killed, eight days after the first canonical victim, Polly Nichols. This and other more guarded reports show that it had registered early in the series, mindful of there being potential time lags for such street talk and racist rumour to have shown up in the press.

Media references to the "Hebrew menace" Leather Apron as early as 4 September in the first days after Nichols' demise, and to Tisza-

Eszlar and the Ritter cases from the early to mid 1880s and through to 1888 provide added grounds to think that Hutchinson was not simply flying by the seat of his pants, taking his breaks as they presented. Indeed, if the continental blood libel cases were able to pick up media momentum during the 'Autumn of Terror', it was largely in consequence of Jack The Ripper's campaign treading an already established, and almost certainly, well-scouted track.

In response to the two earliest canonical murders, it was well enough understood by a susceptible indigenous population that these were attributable to the Jews by the very nature of the atrocities, as the Leather Apron saga implies and the anti-Jewish riots of 8 September attest. That Hutchinson later decided to stoke the fires with an increasingly horrific level of mutilation, leaving clues implicating the Jews, either outrightly or via his choice of murder locations, suggests that he was motivated by a desire to ram home the point, doubling-down on his success. While the police were able to see past the theatrical ruses cast on the night of the double-event, an example of the kind of response he must have been seeking from officialdom was on display in the opinion of a Whitehall bureaucrat, Godfrey Lushington, Permanent Under-Secretary at the Home Office. In the Goulston Street graffito, this official saw the hand of a boasting Jew, and in the use of "Lipski" more evidence of Jewish involvement[471]. Naively but intuitively, the general East End population had taken the bait long before then.

It is notable too that aspects of the double-event should mirror Hutchinson's involvement with the Kelly episode so closely. In the former instance, he ventured back out into the lion's den, into streets crawling with police looking to run him to ground, for the purpose of an anti-Semitic evidence drop after he had already made it to safety. This is a not entirely different scenario to the high risk he took by volunteering his 'eyewitness' account, placing himself at Miller's Court and then accusing a Jew. The template in both instances was breathtakingly brazen, but more to the point, the same: deed > escape > safety > re-emergence in police midst > accusation against Jews.

Given the tinderbox social tensions in Whitechapel, the accompanying demographic shift under way in the East End, rising Judeophobia and the "un-English" nature of the crimes, it is difficult to see the campaign as discussed in preceding chapters outside the framework of a maniac's attempt to target the standing of the Jewish community at a critical political juncture. The collective eyes and ears of two parliamentary special committees were then investigating the East End and issues arising there from Jewish immigration. It was not simply a case of throwing his "pursuers on a wrong track while showing hostility to the Jews in the vicinity," as Whitechapel MP Samuel Montagu had put it, instinctively understanding the general gist of what was going on. Directing hostility towards the Jews was the very point of the exercise.

While the intensifying level of mutilation visited on the victims would suggest that Jack The Ripper was also satiating a deranged bloodlust, this author is not convinced that this aspect served other than a secondary consideration, important though it may have been to him at some level. More crucial, was George Hutchinson's desire to hype the level of outrage, presenting the very particular savagery on display as evidence of the ultimate price of Jewish settlement in East London. It was nothing short of a not so humble labourer making the best of his immediate surroundings as a real-life stage for a bloody, anti-Semitic, public relations campaign. In its very conception it dwarfed the supposed Ripper correspondence. No amount of letter writing could have compared to the scale of George Hutchinson's design, even if he had deigned to put pen to paper and signed himself Jacob Ripperwitz or Johan Von Ripper.

The fact that the murders stopped, never to be repeated, is an indication that they were intricately intertwined with time, place, and importantly, political purpose. Australian conditions could not replicate them. The colony of New South Wales was not just distant in miles travelled, but in socio-historical setting.

That is why the 1897 gothic classic *Dracula* provides such an interesting analysis. Bram Stoker, the novel's Irish author, lived in London from 1878 to 1912. He began writing it in the years immediately after the murders in Whitechapel. *Dracula* is set in large part, in and around London in 1893 and focuses on events after the count's relocation to England from his Transylvanian castle home near Bistritz, "in the extreme east of the country... in the midsts of the Carpathian mountains; one of the wildest and least known portions of Europe"[472]. The region was then part of the Kingdom of Hungary, which together with the Kingdom of Austria formed the dual parts of the Hapsburg Empire. Each of the gruesome cases that had featured in the British press, Tisza-Eszlar (Hungary), Ritter (Cracow, Galicia) and Leskau (Moravia), had taken place in this Danubian realm. In fact, together with Bistritz, the four locations form an easterly-orientated arc that roughly spanned points north, east and south along the dual monarchy's borders. In the popular imagination of the day, this eastern frontier marked the outer limits of where the last vestiges of enlightened Europe succumbed to the thrall of an untamed Orient. "The impression I had was that we were leaving the West and entering the East," Stoker's narrator tells the reader during the outward journey to meet the count.

There are numerous hints in the novel that suggest a degree of poetic transposition between the East End and Count Dracula's exotic provenance in the Carpathian mountains. If some Victorians and social reformers viewed the East End as a metaphor for the edge of empire, then here was the eastern boundary of European civilisation itself. One of the novel's protagonists, Jonathan Harker, makes his way through Dracula's homeland, literally the wilds of Hungary, by relying on his broken German; to this author, a subtextual reference to Yiddish: "I found my *smattering of German* very useful here; indeed, I don't know how I should be able to get on without it". It recalls Mrs Brewer's visit among the Jews of Petticoat Lane (see chapters 1 and 9):

> ...when I addressed them in English the majority of them shook their heads. This being so I tried German, which succeeded up to a certain point.[473]

A few years before *Dracula* was published, Zangwill's *Children Of The Ghetto: A Study Of A Peculiar People* had introduced the Jewish East End with a flourish as "a world of dreams, fantastic and poetic as the mirage of the Orient where they were woven, of superstitions grotesque as the cathedral gargoyles of the Dark Ages in which they had birth". While Zangwill's work explored this English offshoot, Stoker sends Harker back to its imagined source on a visit to the ultimate gargoyle: "every known superstition in the world is gathered into the horseshoe of the Carpathians, as if it were the centre of some sort of imaginative whirlpool". The demonic creature himself is portrayed with recognisable markers of Jewish stereotype, what Stoker referred to as a "very marked physiognomy"[474]. For late-19th century racial hygienists, it must have been the stuff of nightmares:

> His face was a strong – a very strong – aquiline, with high bridge of the thin nose and *peculiarly* arched nostrils; with lofty domed forehead, and hair growing scantily round the temples but profusely elsewhere. His eyebrows were very massive, almost meeting over the nose, and with bushy hair that seemed to curl in its own profusion.[475] (author's italics: note discussion later in chapter).

In her critical reading of the novel, the academic, Sara Libby Robinson proposes not only that Count Dracula is symbolically presented as a stereotype for Judaism, but particularly that:

> The fundamental connection between Jews and vampires is blood, specifically blood libels… Aside from the attacks on the two heroines, Lucy and Mina, Stoker's vampires are only shown attacking children. Gentile (non-Jewish) children were nearly always the victims featured in blood libels, from the time of William of Norwich in 1144.[476]

At least one authority on vampire literature has proposed an interesting case for Stoker having drawn inspiration for his work from the Ripper crimes[477]. In fact, there are direct references in the novel to the East End, and Dracula's English residence, Carfax, is established at Purfleet on the London, Tilbury & Southend Railway line. In the 1901 Icelandic edition of *Dracula*, Stoker references Jack The Ripper in the introduction[478]. Whatever degree of influence the murder spree may have played on his imagination, Stoker had something else, at least equally as interesting to impart in this introduction: "The strange and eerie tragedy which is portrayed here is completely true as far as all external circumstances are concerned". Certainly, there were similar societal factors that propelled the two stories, one told by Stoker, and the one driven by Hutchinson.

Were contemporary proof of such a close relationship required, it would be difficult to go past the following example from the *East London Advertiser*, published on 6 October 1888, in the same week as the double-event. It is nothing short of a lucid convergence between the Whitechapel murders and the broader vampire legend (complete with an inferred reference to the blood libel, in author's italics) at that very moment when the *Dracula* tale must have been revealing its outlines to Stoker's poetic vision:

A THIRST FOR BLOOD.

The two fresh murders which have been committed in Whitechapel have aroused the indignation and excited the imagination of London to a degree without parallel. Men feel that they are face to face with some awful and extraordinary freak of nature. So inexplicable and ghastly are the circumstances surrounding the crimes that people are affected by them in the same way as children are by the recital of a weird and terrible story of the supernatural. It is so impossible to account, on any ordinary hypothesis, for these revolting acts of blood that the mind turns as it were instinctively to some theory of occult force, and the *myths of the Dark Ages rise* before the imagination. Ghouls, vampires, bloodsuckers, and all the ghastly array of fables which have been accumulated throughout the course of centuries take form, and seize hold of the excited fancy. Yet the most morbid imagination can conceive nothing worse than this terrible reality; for what can be more appalling than the thought that there is a being in human shape stealthily moving about a great city, burning with the thirst for human blood, and endowed with such diabolical astuteness, as to enable him to gratify his fiendish lust with absolute impunity?

Though it would be remembered primarily as a gothic classic, the novel also fell under the umbrella of a genre known as 'invasion literature'. As the term implies, its main premise rested on the notion that Britain was in peril, which in itself reflected a psychological angst among segments of the population: "We've given a welcome to every bit of foreign scum that's too filthy to be kept in his own country," exclaims the protagonist, John Steel, in *The Enemy In Our Midst* (1906) considered a classic of the genre. In her analysis of *Dracula*, Sara Libby Robinson goes further, proposing that the immigration issue was at least in part related to:

> ... Britain's anti-Semitic anxieties during the end of the nineteenth century... In a larger cultural sense, *Dracula* serves as a metaphor for the dangers immigrant Jews posed to Britain during this tumultuous period.[479]

The premise of the anti-alienists who wished to close the door to Jewish immigration was that England was in great danger, specifically, from "foreigners... successfully colonising Great Britain under the nose of Her Majesty's Government"[480]. In the novel, Count Dracula does that literally when he clandestinely ships the native Transylvanian soil so necessary for his survival in 50 crates to his new estate on London's eastern periphery. One box even makes its way to the East End, to Chicksand Street, in the heart of Whitechapel.

Stoker also seems to have been tapping into a bigger, age-old narrative: the 'diabolisation', literally the demonisation, of Jews. Accusatory and racist slurs of Jews being vampires, parasites, leeches and worse were part of an anti-Semitic lexicon, particularly rife across continental Europe in the late-19th century[481]. Britain was far from immune. Readers will recall the "Rothschild leeches... blood-sucking crew" commentary from the *Labour Leader* in the opening chapter as one example cited. As another, it is timely to mention the "vampires" and "crucifying gypsies" accusation echoed so manipulatively in the instance of the Primrose League meeting in Goulston Street in July 1888. Stoker makes a not dissimilar poetic corollary by assigning the "Szgany gipsies" to Count Dracula as vassals, tapping into then common references to Jews as 'wandering Gypsies'. The demonic nobleman himself may have objected to such brightness, but the subtext in the following excerpt makes it clear as day that Stoker took artistic license and substituted two stateless people of eastern provenance, one for the other, Gypsies for Jews. Note, the parasitic allusions; the Diaspora reference; and the use of the adjective "peculiar", often employed during the Victorian era in specific relation to the Jewish people[*][482], and which Stoker weaves into the fabric of the text to describe both Count Dracula, and in this instance, his Gypsy underlings:

> A band of Szgany have come to the castle, and are encamped in the courtyard… They are peculiar to this part of the world, though allied to the ordinary gipsies all the world over. There are thousands of them in Hungary and Transylvania, who are almost outside all law. They attach themselves as a rule to some great noble or boyar, and call themselves by his name. They are fearless and without religion, save superstition.[483]

Standard anti-Semitic fare attached all manner of superstition to the practice of Judaism, while more clerical varieties painted the religion itself as superstition. No surprise then that Count Dracula should abhor Christianity's most potent symbol, the crucifix. It is hard to ignore that his revulsion at the sight of the sacred icon was being relayed to a readership mindful of Christian doctrine, which lay collective guilt for Christ's crucifixion on the heads of all Jews. Not until the 1960s and the Second Vatican Council was the historic charge of deicide finally repudiated.

---

* There was even a London newspaper started in April 1888 dedicated to Christian mission work among the Jews, called *The Peculiar People*.

It is by now obvious what the author was alluding to in the pages of *Dracula*. Consider, that of all the places Stoker might have set Castle Dracula, he chose Bistritz, a closely assonant, near-anagram of Tisza-Eszlar of blood libel notoriety. That both towns were located in the very eastern reaches of the dual monarchy's borders, 'the wilds of Hungary', stands as further evidence that a masked reference to 'Jewish ritual murder' constitutes the essential theme of the novel.

It was the same font of bloody inspiration that had stirred Hutchinson onto a course of action only a few years previously. The two authors, one of a grizzly series of murders, the other of a sanguinary gothic classic, were intuitively in agreement about the common currents swirling around them. In that sense, both men reflected what was a moment in time and place and the foul zeitgeist of the age*. A certain amount of cross-referencing in the later oeuvre would remain as testament of this shared space and that Jack The Ripper, the original, real-life item, had been the first to stake his wretched claim.

In 1955, Anglican authorities dismantled the shrine in Lincoln Cathedral of 'Little Saint Hugh'. The blood libel, the ugly lie, had come full circle and it was acknowledged by the Church Of England that the fantasy of 'ritual murder' had cost the lives of many Jews[484]. In that column of innocents might rightly be added the lives of seven gentile women from London's East End, killed during 1888 and 1889 as part of one man's cynical, macabre and ultimately failed, public relations stunt.

---

* What in his 1898 treatise, *J'Accuse*, Emile Zola famously denounced as, "the scourge of our time", nothing short of an "obsession": anti-Semitism.

Ada Wilson's attack - *Illustrated Police News*

Satirical portrayal of police, *Punch* 22 September 1888. Note racist imagery and inference, and the early date *ie* even before the double-event.

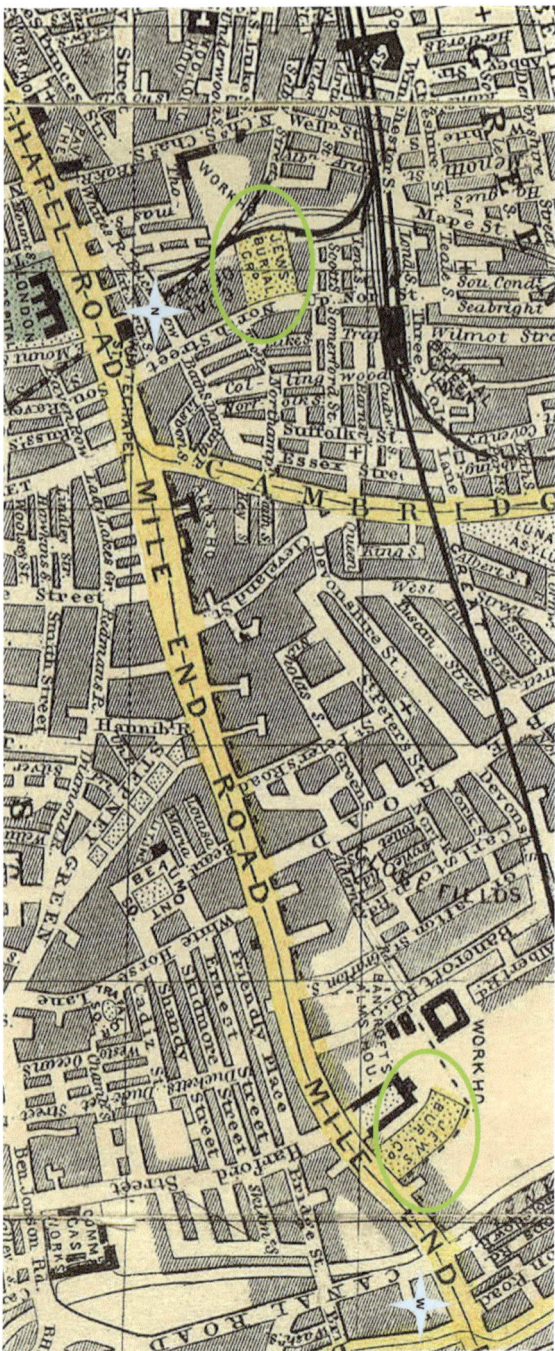

Maidman Street relative Buck's Row: the sites of the Wilson and Nichols attacks.

End of Chapter 13 notes:
Geographic and related observations

The anti-Jewish riots which broke out on the day that Annie Chapman was killed were evidence of George Hutchinson's campaign having momentarily hit pay dirt. It was a vein he was eager to exploit, hence the clear anti-Semitic overtones on display during his next outing on the night of the double-event. While violence was the main lever he reached for, by way of ratcheting up the pressure and attempting to make his all-important narrative heard, the Berner Street and Mitre Square killings displayed an extra dimension again, notably the use of geography in service of his scheme.

More broadly across the series, geographic considerations offer a tantalising prospect for obtaining a better understanding of the scope of tactics the killer employed to bring method to his plan. The use of geography as a convenient means of implicating his Jewish neighbours may not have been lying entirely dormant prior to and after the night of the double-event, as touched on in various parts of the preceding study. An opportunist such as he undoubtedly was, George Hutchinson had many layers of subterfuge, dare it be called sophistication, to call upon by way of trying to achieve his objective. Nothing should be put past him.

Below are some general geographic observations relevant to the sites of his attacks. An interesting repetition or echo, appears to be at work, effectively pairing off locations bearing a degree of similarity with one another. In many instances, a relationship to the intersection of Commercial and Wentworth streets also comes to the fore.

Maidman Street (28 March, 1888) and Buck's Row (31 August, 1888)

Maidman Street: The immediate neighbourhood contained the Jews' New Burial Ground situated on the northern side of Mile End Road (the easterly continuation of Whitechapel Road). Maidman Street was **one street back and parallel** to this highway, and practically around the corner from the cemetery. The victim shared her residence, at number 19, with a Jewish family. In 1915, number 26 Maidman Street would become home to the Mile End & Bow Synagogue, although there is at least one artefact that appears to date an earlier expression of that congregation at the same site to the year 1900. That Maidman Street would soon enough come to host a Jewish place of worship could be indicative of a gathering momentum in the demographic change that was being experienced in that general neighbourhood.

Buck's Row: The most easterly location after Maidman Street, they were both further to the east than the main area of Jewish settlement. There is, however, much contemporary testimony recording migratory breakouts to the east, deeper into the East End, and along the main highways, especially Whitechapel Road. Buck's Row was **one street back and parallel**.

As far as the neighbourhood around Buck's Row, it was distinguished for its proximity to another Jewish cemetery (disused). As an aside, this burial ground features in an apocryphal and anti-Semitic episode in the Ripper tale[*][485]. Nearby, was the Saloman's Almshouses, a Jewish charity administered by the Great Synagogue[§]. It took up a row of four houses on the western side of Brady Street, which intersects Buck's Row to the east.

The immediate neighbourhood, but not Buck's Row, featured many Jewish surnames in the 1881 and 1891 censuses. This is borne out by a report in the *Echo* from the day Nichols was buried:

> There were large crowds around Buck's-row, this afternoon, the numbers being augmented by many Jews, now observing one of their special holidays.[486]

It is difficult to ascertain what role, if any, location per se may have played in the attacks in Maidman Street and Buck's Row.

---

* One of the men who found Polly Nichols' body supposedly pointed in the direction of the Jewish cemetery and said that the murderer was "probably some sneaking Yid who wouldn't pay for his fun".

§ United Synagogue.

They shared some marked points of affinity. The proximity of both to Jewish cemeteries and their relation to Whitechapel / Mile End roads, offers food for thought.

George Yard (7 August 1888) and Dorset Street (9 November, 1888):

Based on witness evidence and Arkell's 1899 map, both locations seem to have been situated in what might be described as gentile islands in a residential Jewish sea. **One lay off Wentworth Street, the other off Commercial Street**. Both murders took place away from the street, one indoors, the other on the landing of a building. The victims may each have had a second degree of personal connection to George Hutchinson, as well as a first degree in Kelly's case. Consistent with contemporary accounts, Booth's 1889 poverty map placed Dorset St in the "lowest class, vicious, semi-criminal" rank, while George Yard was described in similar terms in the media.

The racist blood narrative blaming the Jews for the murders having already been established by the time of the Miller's Court atrocity, the killing and mutilation of Mary Kelly seemed to have been focused on providing 'shock-value' and mirorring media cues about "revolting murders" and women being "frightfully mutilated" as per reports from continental correspondents in the lead-up.

Hanbury Street (8 September, 1888) and Castle Alley (17 July, 1889):

Arkell's 1899 map, supported by contemporary evidence, placed both murders in streets denoted by the highest level of Jewish settlement, 95-100%. These streets were part of larger neighbourhoods conforming to the same demographic pattern. **One lay off Wentworth Street, the other off Commercial Street**.

George Yard (7 August 1888) and Castle Alley (17 July, 1889):

Both lay one street back and parallel to **Commercial Street**. Both linked **Wentworth Street** to Whitechapel High Street. Effectively, they were geographic mirror images of one another, with the Victoria

Home in the middle.

Hanbury Street (8 September, 1888) and Dorset Street (9 November, 1888):

Commercial Street is made up of three conjoined kinks as it meanders roughly north to south: effectively, northern, central and southern components. Both Hanbury and Dorset streets lay off the central part. Hanbury, to the east; Dorset, to the west.

Dutfield's Yard and Mitre Square (30 September, 1888):

Apart from the overtly Jewish associations of the murder sites, as discussed in chapter 3 and its end of chapter notes, there is a spatial relationship between the two. Commercial Road merges at an angle into Whitechapel High Street, which continues west becoming Aldgate High Street. Both Dutfield's Yard and Mitre Square fed into streets that intersected with this broad axis, Berner and Duke streets respectively.

It is worth noting that Dutfield's Yard was the only location, among the eight attack sites, to be situated south of this important line. It is more reason to suggest that the murderer was drawn there for a very special reason: the inculpatory thematics available to him courtesy of the Jewish radical club.

Note too, Hutchinson's practical, or possibly psychological, aversion for straying south of this axis when considering that he chose to go to Commercial Street police station to give his statement (situated north of the line), rather than the station in Leman Street (south), for all that Leman Street was *considerably* closer to home.

There is another consideration to ponder in regard the double-event and its broader geographic implications. At first thought it is an almost outlandish one, but a naggingly difficult one to dismiss altogether. Catherine Eddowes was last seen near the southern side of the Great Synagogue together with her killer, on the corner of Duke Street and Church Passage. Was he lingering there with her, intentionally, hoping that they might be observed in that location? Indeed, it would seem Eddowes was whisked from the spot and taken, in a beeline, to an unlit corner of adjacent Mitre Square, straight after this final sighting; meeting her doom, but minutes later. This sequence of events unfolded within an exceptionally tight timeframe, making it difficult to dismiss the notion out of hand that being spied by the synagogue was part of the plan. By chance, the decision of the three Imperial Club patrons, witnesses Lawende, Harris and Levy, to call it a night when they did, may inadvertently have had the effect of sealing Catherine Eddowes' fate.

What provides ballast to the floating of this proposal, is that Stride's murder, about an hour earlier, conformed to some of the same benchmarks, notably:

- she was killed very soon after the final sighting
- her body was found nearby the location of that sighting
- she was last seen alive by the entrance of a locale easily recognisable for its association with the Jewish community
- the last witness to see her alive was Jewish (and acknowledged as such by the killer, with his cry of "Lipski")

It raises a concluding question regarding events in Berner Street. Whether, by directing the cry of "Lipski" at Israel Schwartz, the murderer was not mischievously intent on implicating an innocent Jewish passer-by in the homicidal assault on Elizabeth Stride, via loud and feigned association?

Consistent with such broader strategic thinking, he may even have intended to ensnarl the three Imperial Club patrons milling on Duke Street not just as witnesses of convenience, but potential fall-guys, given the inevitable and swift police dragnet that Catherine Eddowes' murder was sure to unleash.

Certainly, Jack The Ripper was a quick thinker and good on his feet – and the above scenarios may simply have been his response to things not having gone quite as he had intended them to. For the south-eastern corner of the Great Synagogue was a significant one: it constituted one of the temple's formal entrances. It is proposed here, for the first time in 130 years, that the arrival on the scene of Lawende, Harris and Levy may well have scuttled the simplest of plans: to leave a second corpse at the door of a Jewish institution that early morning.

Lawende, Harris and Levy's view: looking out across Duke Street and into Church Passage. The structures making up the right half of the illustration helped form the south-eastern corner of the Great Synagogue. The arched doorway represented the synagogue's southern entrance.

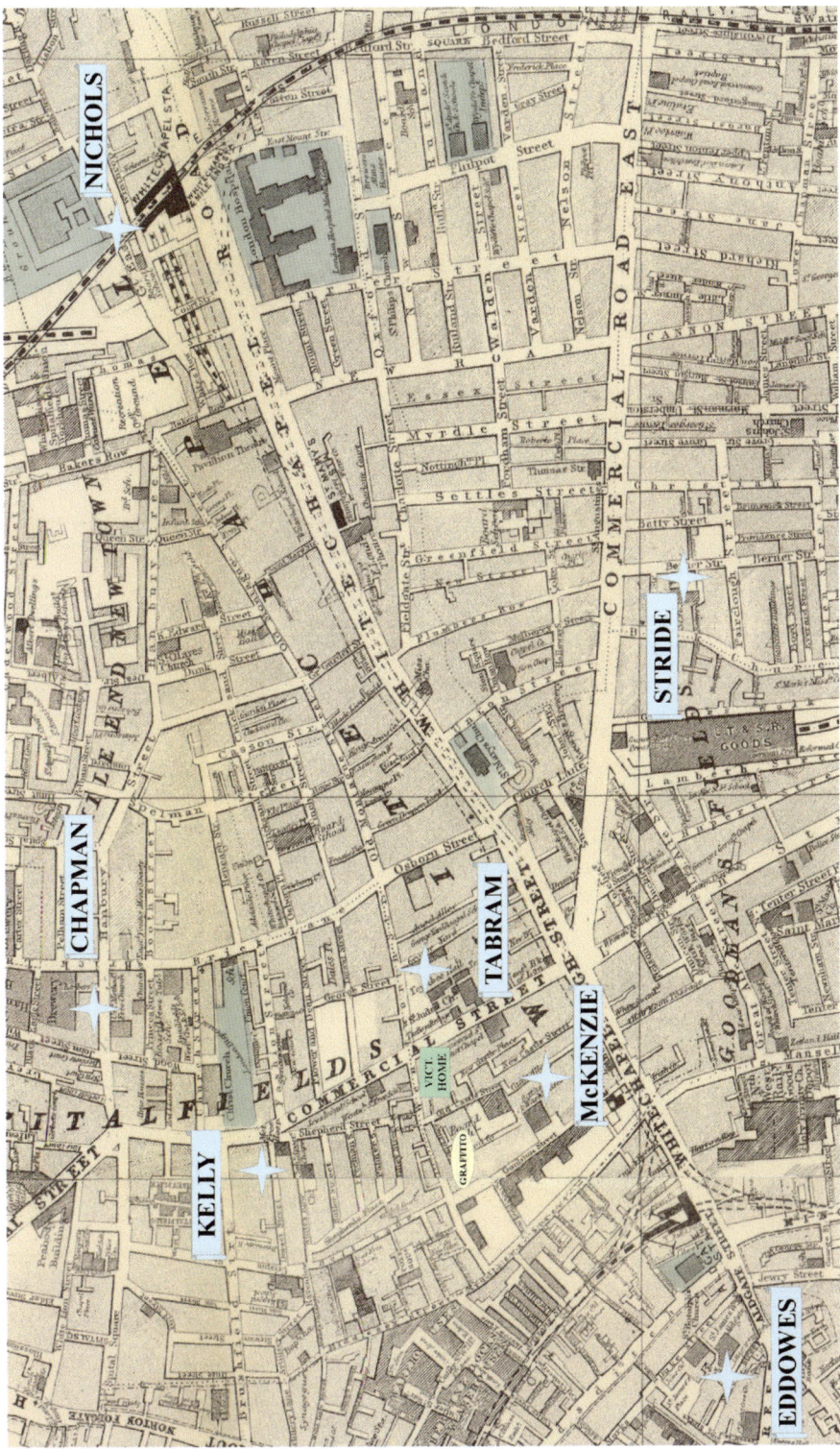

NICHOLS

CHAPMAN

STRIDE

KELLY

TABRAM

McKENZIE

EDDOWES

VICT. HOME

GRAFFITO

EPILOGUE

A PERSPECTIVE

> What is history but a fable agreed upon?
>
> Napoleon (attributed)

I am aware, that because this study is grounded in the socio-political and industrial conditions affecting Whitechapel in 1888, it might not make for the most readily appetising of offerings; the staple, for so long, having been provided by an altogether fancier, and some might argue, fanciful, fare. More to the point, it places itself outside the usual table talk: that inviting the finger of blame to be pointed at a nefarious array of dinner guests made up of members of the British aristocracy, masonic conspirators, deranged doctors (top-hat, cape and gladstone bag almost de-rigueur in this category), black magicians, mad butchers, melancholy medical students, the habitués of asylums, spouse poisoners, famous writers, poets, artists etc.. Just about the only ones missing are Professor Plum and Colonel Mustard...

I beg the reader's indulgence if I lean on rhetoric to underscore the point, motivated at heart by a belief in the need to move away from this staid narrational framework. Not that the old paradigm hasn't served a worthwhile role. It can certainly boast of having provided successive waves of interest rolling in for well over a century – but paradoxically it has driven a better understanding of what happened ever further out to sea and a historical forgetfulness, flowed in. How can it be, for example, that the case is still so often discussed in such a way as to relegate the centrality of the Jewish neighbourhoods in which the murders took place to little more than window dressing? Contemporary writers, both Jewish and gentile, had no compunction in describing Spitalfields an ethnic "ghetto", yet the full extent of it seems to have fallen beyond the modern grasp. Some renditions of the tale manage to get through the story without any mention of the then-endemic anti-Semitism. But how can such a fantastic evocation of Whitechapel be? And what price admittance, if not by abandoning any hope of catching sight of Jack The Ripper?

After spending the last several years marooned in late-19th century East London, I am mindful that the setting of the tale is no mere coincidence. It is of concern, that the study seems to have broken its moorings and drifted into a lacuna where Whitechapel, as it was in 1888, is almost reduced to an incidental consideration: history, as mere aesthetic.

I would like to imagine, that this book may help return the locale to its rightful place as a principal protagonist of the story, and bring to prominence long ignored socio-political questions. In preceding pages, their intersection with the 'Autumn of Terror' has been rendered down to inherently plausible, even likely, scenarios. I have tried to give back to the case and its setting, some small verve of immediacy, beyond any twenty-first century, mainstream preconceptions. As such, cultural clichés are hazards best avoided and clearly marked on the map by critical analysis. They are nought but imagined landscapes, dreaded mirages, prone to gobble up reality like quicksand. The study of history is particularly vulnerable to them, and Napoleon's old maxim still stands as a fair warning post.

Aware of such pitfalls, and looking through a clearer lens, the killer might be prone to reveal himself. Which is not to suggest that conventional offender profiling doesn't successfully manage to pile up the black marks against George Hutchinson. But what this study has primarily sought to propose, has been the *rationale*: the method, to the madness.

To that end, I think it was no coincidence that he was prepared to serve the cause of capital on a ship of blacklegs in mid-1889. As much as it may have been a practical one, it was a highly political decision. As was, leaving a victim in the yard of a Jewish workingmen's club as it hosted a lecture entitled, 'Why Jews Should Be Socialists' – during a moment when parliament was investigating Jewish immigration and its effect on sweated labour in the East End. Or, depositing a mangled corpse behind the Great Synagogue so soon after the anti-Jewish riots which he had sparked; or running the gauntlet to chalk anti-Semitic graffiti afterwards; or fingering a well-to-do Jew for the Miller's Court atrocity; or, for that matter, staging the murders to mirror the anti-Semitic rot he had been reading in newspaper reports emanating from the continent. From inception to escape, the picture remains an ideologically consistent one: the man wore his politics on his sleeve.

Timing too, is crucial. Key dates pertaining to the work of the parliamentary select committees provide telling chronological markers which overlay the story. Just as importantly, the timing of the dock strike which ultimately played its part in bringing the murder spree to a definitive close. Such is my holistic interpretation of events. In short, Jack The Ripper was a stark, political by-product of what was going on around him. It does not excuse him, though it provides a better understanding of what happened.

The alternative, is to declare him autonomous of his surroundings and to believe in a sequence of coincidences which defy the reality represented by the locale at that moment and during that period. Which effectively requires history to be swept under the rug. Whitechapel can then become Wembley, Weimar or Wuhan – in any meaningful sense, irrelevant – and the game of Cluedo is ready to begin, superimposed on an anodyne version of ye olde history.

As to the case's finer points, and their intersection with the broader framework discussed here, I believe that the question of luck, or rather, Jack The Ripper's occasional *bad* luck, can provide important insights. Owing to his project being such a theatrical exercise, the killer's instinctive response to things not going to plan was to ostentatiously return to his anti-Semitic script and exert control as quickly as possible* – with palpable determination. It remains a visible and telling signature. To that end, the botched attack on Stride helps explain why events transpired as they did later that morning, but his coming forward after the Kelly murder was the most revelatory by way of exposing the killer and laying bare his motivation. Even his 'Jewish gentleman' was melodramatically depicted in a manner consistent with the arc of his greater storyline (and his politics).

Being spotted at the scene, likely played an important part in Hutchinson's eventual decision to try and blind-side the police by making direct contact with them. But the looming capacity of Cox's and Lewis' testimony to undermine his anti-Semitic message should not be underestimated. Its obvious potential to take the investigation, and its reporting, in the opposite direction to that demanded by his grand scheme must have played on his mind. Indeed, neither media coverage in the immediate lead up to the coroner convening his jury, or anything coming out of that probe, would have given him cause to celebrate. Certainly, there were no spontaneous anti-Jewish riots as he had managed to set off previously – so important to him, that he had boasted of them in Goulston Street. At the first opportunity therefore, at the conclusion of the inquest, he rushed forward. After all the risks he had successfully already taken, what was another? The important thing was, to ensure that the narrative was re-established and the record set straight: the murder had been committed by a Jew. He could scarce contain himself, and the intervening four days must have been long and frustrating ones for George Hutchinson as it dawned on him that his plan might be coming undone, and his direct involvement become necessary. As it turned out, his instincts had been spot-on: it was too late. Through a combination of incidental factors, the bomb he had planned to go off, had failed to detonate.

Another point needs to be considered when weighing up his rationale for coming forward. It is maybe the greatest irony, that as the murder spree picked-up momentum, he who had broached no compunction to slice through flesh and bone to make his point, found it ever more

---

* Confirming my belief that he was a proto-fascist on a self-propelled, *false flag* operation.

difficult to 'cut through' in the modern media sense of the term, owing to all the 'background noise' he had been the catalyst of. A victim of his own success, the capacity for his message to be heard became ever more compromised as it jostled with shrill attention seekers and letter writing impersonators, hoaxers, madmen, pundits and self-declared experts who at times nearly overwhelmed police efforts and who demanded their own degree of media coverage and public attention. No wonder that, finally, he was forced to step-in personally, walking into Commercial Street police station on that cold Monday evening to have his say. Perhaps as much as anything else, this was George Hutchinson, the man, trying to take back control of the message from the burgeoning shadow of Jack The Ripper, only too painfully aware that things were slipping away from him. If ever a case, then here was Doctor Frankenstein wrestling with the Adam of his creation.

The murder and mutilation of Alice McKenzie in July 1889 can then be better seen for the half-hearted last roll of the dice that it was. No doubt, the hiatus provided by the colder months, the extra patrols and closing police net played their part in drawing out his patience until then. But there is almost a feel of despondent defensiveness in this final atrocity, by necessity conducted so close to home, which ultimately reveals a killer on the verge of giving up. The commencement of the dock strike and the publication of the immigration committee recommendations, coming so soon after events in Castle Alley, lay bare a sequence of events only too readily lending themselves to a welcome exit strategy – effectively marking a controlled hoisting of the white flag.

I believe that for 130 years this murder series has been misunderstood, which in turn has played the greatest role in stymieing efforts, not only to resolve it, but to study it – amplifying its legendary status exponentially, and feeding back into the disconnect. This book is my humble effort to try and untie the knot. I hope that it can help take us back to old Whitechapel. Even today, if you adjust your train of thought, Jack The Ripper can still be spied there. Not in the old pubs, or among the myriad of Ripper tours which every night attempt to conjure their best approximation of the tale. Look instead at the faded and less faded letters of some of the antiquated, occasionally dilapidated, shops and buildings. They can still be found, and they are part of this story too. Like the archaic shopfront lettering which faintly reads, "S.Schwartz 33A" in Fournier Street. Or the old "Soup Kitchen For The Jewish Poor" in Butler Street. Take a moment to read the plaque outside the house in Princelet Street, around the corner from where Annie Chapman was killed, and which boasts the birth in 1886 of the woman who would become the first female mayor of Stepney, Miriam Moses. Then look up at the silvery tiled minaret on the corner of Brick Lane and Fournier Street which every evening comes to life in an alternating rainbow of colours. As you pass one enticing curry restaurant after another, continue to head north a little, past the comedic banter of milling Cockney workers preparing for their shift at the Old Truman brewery, and you will eventually arrive outside two of the finest bagel bakeries in London, at the top of the lane.

And along the way you will have realised that you have come face to face with one man's utter failure before history. Marvel at his defeat, and at that moment you will see him.

AFTERWORD

Whatever happened to George Hutchinson?

It may be the subject of another study, if a trail might one day be picked up. History's last known sighting has him standing outside Darlinghurst gaol in Sydney*. That information comes courtesy of the *New South Wales Police Gazette* of 17 August 1898, which lists him as one of the prisoners recently discharged to freedom.

Interestingly, the gazette notes that he had a conviction for another, previous crime, though it does not specify what that was. At once ominous and elusive, it is an apt final entry to George Hutchinson's story. For now...

---

* The old Darlinghurst gaol still stands, but is today home to the National Art School. In what is possibly one of those historical ironies, it is within easy line of sight of the new Sydney Jewish Museum, located diagonally across the street.

Darlinghurst gaol, Sydney 1887.

On the trail of the assassin. The author today, in front of the old Darlinghurst gaol; and inset.

APPENDIX I

The leading minds of the Cork United Trades Council have not been above borrowing a hint from the Middle Ages and the enlightened practice of modern Russia. These gentle patriots have begun, we are told, a crusade against Jews and crucifying gypsies – an enterprise at once beneficent and picturesque. Crucifying gypsies one would suppose to be few and hard to know, but they are no doubt none the less good sport when run to earth. Jews, on the contrary, are a fairly well understood quarry. Apparently it is as unpleasant to be a Jew as to be a loyal subject in county Cork; for, unless report lies, it is said that ever since the Jews were stoned out of Limerick they have met with a good deal of persecution at Cork; being threatened, stoned, and swindled. But, oddly enough, the representatives of the (Irish) National League are uneasy about the matter, and (their leader) Mr. Parnell has himself ordered the Mayor of Cork to put an end to the fun. It appears Mr. Parnell "derives much valuable help from several excellent Home Rulers of the Jewish persuasion in London." This may seem a sordid motive to the simple-minded earnest men of Cork; but they will, no doubt, temporarily abstain from the pious joys of Jew-baiting. Meantime the incident is well worthy the consideration of (Orientalist) Mr. Wilfrid Blunt and other philanthropists.

St James Gazette, 14 March 1888
(author's parentheses)

APPENDIX II

On Thursday I had been to Romford, in Essex, and I returned from there about two o'clock on Friday morning, having walked all the way. I came down Whitechapel-road into Commercial-street. As I passed Thrawl-street I passed a man standing at the corner of the street, and as I went towards Flower and Dean-street, I met the woman Kelly, whom I knew very well, having been in her company a number of times. She said, 'Mr. Hutchinson, can you lend me sixpence?' I said, 'I cannot, as I am spent out, going down to Romford.' She then walked on towards Thrawl-street, saying, 'I must go and look for some money.' The man who was standing at the corner of Thrawl-street then came towards her, put his hand on her shoulder, and said something to her which I did not hear; they both burst out laughing. He put his hand again on her shoulder, and they both walked slowly towards me. I walked on to the corner of Fashion-street, near the public-house. As they came by me his arm was still on her shoulder. He had a soft felt hat on, and this was drawn down somewhat over his eyes. I put down my head to look him in the face, and he turned and looked at me very sternly. They walked across the road to Dorset-street. I followed them across, and stood at the corner of Dorset-street. They stood at the corner of Miller's-court for about three minutes. Kelly spoke to the man in a loud voice, saying, 'I have lost my handkerchief.' He pulled a red handkerchief out of his pocket, and gave it to Kelly, and they went up the court together. I went to look up the court to see if I could see them, but could not. I stood there for three-quarters of an hour to see if they came down again, but they did not, and so I went away. My suspicions were aroused by seeing the man so well dressed, but I had no suspicion that he was the murderer. The man was about 5ft. 6in. in height, and about 34 or 35 years of age, with dark complexion, and dark moustache turned up at the ends. He was wearing a long, dark coat trimmed with astrachan, a white collar with black necktie, in which was affixed a horse-shoe pin. He wore a pair of dark "spats," with light battens over button boots, and displayed from his waistcoat a massive gold chain. He had no side whiskers, and his chin was clean shaven. He looked like a foreigner. I went up the court, and stayed there a couple of minutes, but did not see any light in the house, or hear any noise. I was out on Monday night until three o'clock looking for him. I could swear to the man anywhere. I told one policeman on Sunday morning what I had seen, but did not go to the police-station. I told one of the lodgers here about it on Monday, and he advised me to go to the police-station, which I did, at night. The man I saw did not look as though be would attack another one. He carried a small parcel in his hand about eight inches long, and it had a strap round it. He had it tightly grasped in his left hand. It looked as though it was covered with dark American cloth. He carried in his right hand, which he laid upon the woman's shoulder, a pair of brown kid gloves. One thing I noticed, and that was that he walked very softly. I believe that be lives in the neighbourhood, and I fancied- that I saw him in Petticoat-lane on Sunday morning, but I was not certain. I have been to the Shoreditch mortuary, and recognised the body as that of the woman Kelly, whom I saw at two o'clock on Friday morning. Kelly did not seem to me to be drunk, but was a little bit spreeish. I was quite sober, not having had anything to drink all day. After I left the court I walked about all night, as the place where I usually sleep was closed. I came in as soon as it opened in the morning. I am able to fix the time, as it was between ten and five minutes to two o'clock as I came by Whitechapel Church. When I left the corner of Miller's-court the clock struck three. One policeman went by the Commercial-street end of Dorset-street while I was standing there, but not one came down Dorset-street. I saw one man go into a lodging-house in Dorset-street, and no one else. I have been looking for the man all day.

London Standard, 14 November 1888

APPENDIX III

BOOK NOTICES

'The Enemy in Our Midst.' By Walter Wood.
London: John Long.

"The Enemy in Our Midst" is one of the many tales with which the press may expect shortly to be deluged. It tells the story of a possible German invasion of Great Britain with many gruesome details such as have been more than fulfilled in the case of Belgium. The story begins with the experiences of an Englishman in "Alienland." These experiences are given to us in the person of John Steel, a strong British working man, who has no special trade because he has served his tame as a soldier, and finds no opening, for his untrained energies except in "casual labour," for which, however, he is well fitted. Yet he can get no work in the capital of his native land, all possible positions being occupied by aliens, who gladly work for starvation wages. Steel applies mainly for work at the docks, where he sees shiploads of these people constantly entering. He tries every other opening, but finds no place. He and his young wife and babe are reduced to a miserable attic containing nothing but a bed, a wooden trunk, and a chair. This wretched place in a dirty tenement house belongs to an alien landlord, who, when Steel can no longer pay his rent, orders him into the street. Steel, losing self restraint, knocks the man down, but not before he has been goaded nearly to madness by taunts directed against himself and his country. Steel is tried by a sympathetic magistrate, who yet cannot go against the law. He is fined, and his fine is paid by the court missionary. After this the unfortunate man joins in a demonstration of the unemployed and finds himself one of many who are in the same plight. Then he and others bring their indictment against those who have stolen their birthright; and against those legislators who have allowed it to be stolen. So the fire smoulders until a mere spark would set the train ablaze. And, of course, the spark falls. A little thing fires the train, and a war which has been secretly planned and engineered for years suddenly breaks out. It soon passes the limits of industrial unrest and is carefully fanned into an abiding flame, so that without any precise declaration of war, the Germans, finding the time ripe, take their opportunity. The fate of Belgium is to some extent the fate of England. Before any protective measures can be taken, an invading army is in her midst, largely recruited from aliens already on the spot. In the end it is her fleet which saves England; and Mr Wood's description of the various sea fights is most thrillingly and powerfully written.

Otago Daily Times, 4 December 1914, p. 9

APPENDIX IV

Castle-alley communicates with High-street, Whitechapel, and through Wentworth-street with Commercial-street. But it is not connected only with these great thoroughfares. A maze of smaller streets and alleys surround it, any one of which might have been taken by the murderer, and none of which would have been for him a much more likely route than another.

Daily News, 18 July, 1889

END NOTES

Introduction

[1]   Bloody Foreigners, R. Winder (Abacus, 2006) p.234; 'The Haunts Of The East End Anarchist', Evening Standard, 2 October 1894

[2]   Bloody Foreigners, R. Winder (Abacus, 2006) p.232; 'The Haunts Of The East End Anarchist', Evening Standard, 2 October 1894

[3]   Living London - Volume II, Chapter 'Jewish London' by S. Gelberg, (Cassell & Co, 1902), p.29

[4]   Anti-Semitism in British Society 1876-1939, Colin Holmes (Edward Arnold, 1979), p.8

[5]   ibid. p.9

Chapter 1

[6]   Sanitary Ramblings, Being Sketches & Illustrations of Bethnal Green, Hector Gavin (John Churchill, 1848), p.106 (Table X)

[7]   In Darkest England And The Way Out, William Booth (Cambridge 2014), pp.14-15

[8]   Policing The Ghetto: Jewish East London 1880-1920, David Englander, p.7; Crime, History & Societies, Vol. 14, No. 1 (Librarie Droz, 2010)

[9]   Love & Eugenics in the Late Nineteenth Century, A. Richardson (Oxford University Press, 2003), see discussion pp.23-26

[10] 'Report of the Lancet Special Sanitary Commission on the Polish Colony of Jew Tailors', Lancet, 3 May 1884, pp.817-19; cited, A Documentary History Of Jewish Immigrants In Britain, 1840-1920, David Englander (Leicester University Press, 1994), pp.85-89

[11] Bloody Foreigners, R.Winder (Abacus, 2006), p.230

[12] ibid. p.229

[13] A population of 459,873 is quoted by Charles Booth in Life & Labour Of The People Vol. II (Williams & Norgate, 1891) – note figures are for the years 1886-87 and refer to the Registration Districts and School Board Division figures for Tower Hamlets, see: 'The Inhabitants of Tower Hamlets (School Board Division), their Conditions & Occupations', Journal of Royal Statistical Society, Vol. 50, n. 2, June 1887 – see author's population table and explanatory note at end of chapter notes

[14] House of Commons Select Committee report & minutes Emigration & Immigration (Foreigners) 1888 p.112 & p.133

[15] The Politics Of Immigration 1881-1905 by Cecil Bloom Jewish Historical Studies Vol. 33 (1992-1994), p.191

[16] 'The Inhabitants of Tower Hamlets (School Board Division), their Conditions & Occupations', Journal of Royal Statistical Society, Vol. 50, n. 2, Jun 1887, p.365-366

17 The report of the 1888 Select Committee on Emigration & Immigration (Foreigners) references one observer, citing school register data who estimated a figure of 60,000, while 'Statistics of Jewish Population in London 1873-1893' by J. Jacobs (London 1894) cites a figure of between 61,000 & 106,000 – see 'The Politics Of Immigration 1881-1905' by Cecil Bloom Jewish Historical Studies Vol. 33 (1992-1994), p.191

18 In their essay, the Webbs refer to a figure of 60,000-70,000. Essay reproduced in Problems Of Modern Industry by Sidney & Beatrice Webb (Longmans, Green & Co, 1898) pp.32-33 or pp.69-70, depending on edition; the authors cite research published in Statistics of Jewish Population in London 1873-1893 by Joseph Jacobs (London 1894)

19 Studies In Jewish Statistics: Social, Vital & Anthropometric, Joseph Jacobs (D. Nutt, 1891), p.1

20 'The Inhabitants of Tower Hamlets (School Board Division), their Conditions & Occupations', Journal of Royal Statistical Society Vol. 50, n. 2, Jun 1887, p.366

21 House of Commons Select Committee report on Emigration & Immigration (Foreigners), 1888 p.53

22 The Alien Invasion, William Henry Wilkins (Methuen & Co, 1892) p.18-19

23 Living London: Vol. II Section I (edited by George R. Sims), Chapter 5, 'Jewish London', S. Gelberg (Cassell & Co. Ltd 1902), p.29

24 The Alien Invasion, William Henry Wilkins (Methuen & Co, 1892), p.14

25 Bloody Foreigners, R. Winder (Abacus, 2006), p.230

26 The Jewish Chronicle & Anglo-Jewry, 1841-1991, David Cesarani (Cambridge University Press, 1994), p.77

27 East End 1888, William J. Fishman (Five Leaves, 1988), p.180

28 The Alien Invasion, William Henry Wilkins (Methuen & Co, 1892), p.20

29 'The Jewish Colony In London', Sunday Magazine, XXI (1892) pp.16-20, 119-23; cited, A Documentary History Of Jewish Immigrants In Britain, 1840-1920, David Englander (Leicester University Press, 1994), p.70

30 The London Years, R. Rocker (Five Leaves, 2005), p.6

31 'The Haunts Of The East End Anarchist', London Evening Standard, 2 October 1894

32 Aliens and Asians: Huguenots, Jews and Bangladeshis in Spitalfields 1660-2000, Anne Kershen (Routleadge, 2011), p.141

33 Policing The Ghetto: Jewish East London 1880-1920, David Englander, p.7; Crime, History & Societies, Vol. 14, No. 1 (Librarie Droz, 2010)

34 PRO MEPO 2/733, Report Superintendent Mulvaney, Leman Street Police Station, H Division; cited A Documentary History Of Jewish Immigrants In Britain, 1840-1920, David Englander (Leicester University Press, 1994), pp.82-83

35 From London Mail, reproduced in Boston Evening Transcript, 8 April 1903

36 ibid.

37 House of Commons Select Committee report on Emigration & Immigration (Foreigners) 1888, p.52; Henry Dejonge's testimony

38 ibid. p.191; Thomas Arnold, Head of H (Whitechapel) Division testimony

39 ibid. p.189; Thomas Arnold, Head of H (Whitechapel) Division testimony

40 The London Years, R. Rocker (Five Leaves, 2005), p.26

41 The Alien Invasion, William Henry Wilkins (Methuen & Co, 1892), pp.18-19

42 'The New Community 1880-1918', I. Finestein in V. Lipman (ed.), Three Centuries Of Anglo-Jewish History (Cambridge 1961), p.108 – as quoted in Second Chance: Two Centuries of German-speaking Jews in the United Kingdom, Julius Carlebach (Mohr, 1991), p.473

43 The Heart Of London, H.V. Morton (1925); cited in Placing London: From Imperial Capital To Global City, J. Eade (Berghahn Books, 2000), p.27

44 Times, 13 July 1887

45 Retrieved Riches: Social Investigation in Britain 1840-1914, Englander, D. and O' Day, R. (Eds.) (1998) (paperback edition, 2003). Aldershot: Ashgate, page 306 – as quoted by Dr Laura Vaughan in Mapping The East End Labyrinth (University College London)

46 As quoted in, Strangers, Aliens and Asians: Huguenots, Jews and Bangladeshis in Spitalfields 1660-2000, Anne Kershen (Routleadge, 2011), pp.204-5

47 'The Inhabitants of Tower Hamlets (School Board Division), their Conditions & Occupations', Journal of Royal Statistical Society Vol. 50, n. 2, Jun 1887, p.365

48 'Policing The Ghetto: Jewish East London 1880-1920', David Englander, p.8; Crime, History & Societies, Vol. 14, No. 1 (Librarie Droz, 2010)

49 Family History to Community History, By W. T. R. Pryce, (Cambridge Univ. Press, 1994), p.202

50 The Alien Invasion, William Henry Wilkins (Methuen & Co, 1892), p.18

51 Booth notebooks, B351, pp.47-49; as quoted in City Of Cities, Stephen Inwood (Pan Macmillan 2005), p.72

52 The Jewish Immigrant in England, 1870-1914, Lloyd P. Gartner (Simon Publications, 1973), pp.156-7

53 City Of Cities, Stephen Inwood (Pan Macmillan 2005), p.73

54 Aliens and Asians: Huguenots, Jews and Bangladeshis in Spitalfields 1660-2000, Anne Kershen (Routleadge, 2011), p.205

55 East End Jewish Radicals 1875-1914, William J. Fishman (Five Leaves 2004), p.73

56 Pall Mall Gazette, February 1886; as quoted in East End 1888, William J. Fishman (Duckworth, 1988), p.144

57 The Alien Invasion: The Origins Of The Aliens Act of 1905, Bernard Gainer (Heinemann, 1972), p.43

58 East End Jewish Radicals 1875-1914, William J. Fishman (Five Leaves 2004), p.92

59 Labour Leader, 19 December 1891; as quoted in Anti-Semitism in British Society 1876-1939, Colin Holmes (Edward Arnold, 1979), p.84

60 The Alien Invasion, William Henry Wilkins (Methuen & Co, 1892), Introduction

61 Jewish Chronicle, 18 March 1887

62 Article, appearing in The Fortnightly Review entitled 'Foreign Pauper Immigration' by Samuel Jeyes, 1 July 1891, p.22 – as cited by 'The Politics Of Immigration 1881-1905' by Cecil Bloom, Jewish Historical Studies Vol. 33 (1992-1994), p.194

63 The Trials Of Israel Lipski, Martin Friedland, (Beaufort 1984), p.197; quoting The Alien Invasion, Bernard Gainer (Heinemann, 1972) p.167

64 East End News, 21 February 1888 – as quoted in 'Tower Hamlets 1888', originally published in East London Record, no.2 (1979); viewable at Casebook Jack The Ripper – www.casebook.org

65 Standard, 4 August 1888, p.5

66 British Weekly, 25 May 1888; as reproduced in Toilers In London, by the British Weekly Commissioners & edited by Margaret Harkness (Hodder & Stoughton, 1889), p.49/50

67 For a detailed discussion see, The Alien Invasion: The Origins Of The Aliens Act of 1905, Bernard Gainer (Heinemann, 1972), Chapter 3; 'The Englishman's Castle, and Chapter 4: 'Anti-Alien Societies in East London'

68 The Alien Invasion: The Origins Of The Aliens Act of 1905, Bernard Gainer (Heinemann, 1972), p.61

69 East End Jewish Radicals 1875-1914, W. Fishman (Five Leaves 1904), p.74

70 Politics, Religion and Love: The Story of H.H. Asquith, Venetia Stanley and Edwin Montagu, Based on the Life and Letters of Edwin Samuel Montagu, Naomi Levine (New York University Press 1991), pp.19-20

71 Eastern Post, 25 June 1892; as cited in East End 1888, William J. Fishman (Five Leaves, 1988)

72 Politics, Religion and Love: The Story of H.H. Asquith, Venetia Stanley and Edwin Montagu, Based on the Life and Letters of Edwin Samuel Montagu, Naomi Levine (New York University Press 1991), pp.19-20

73 ibid. pp.19-20

74 The Alien Invasion: The Origins Of The Aliens Act of 1905, Bernard Gainer (Heinemann, 1972), p.59

75 East End 1888, William J. Fishman (Five Leaves, 1988), p.367

76 St James's Gazette, 9 March & 14 March 1888

77 East End 1888, William J. Fishman (Five Leaves, 1988), p.368

78 East London Advertiser, 14 July 1888 – as quoted in East End 1888, William J. Fishman (Five Leaves, 1988), p.368

79 Jewish Immigrants in London, 1880–1939 by Susan Tanabaum (Routledge, 2014) Chapter 4 Notes (n. 151); and East End Jewish Radicals 1875-1914, William Fishman (Five Leaves 2004)

80 Die Tsukunft, 12 August 1887, quoted in The Trials Of Israel Lipski, Martin L. Friedland (Beaufort Books 1984), p.118

81 The Alien Invasion: The Origins Of The Aliens Act of 1905, Bernard Gainer (Heinemann, 1972), p.57

82 Cited: A Documentary History Of Jewish Immigrants In Britain, 1840-1920, David Englander (Leicester University Press, 1994), pp.94-96; see also, Family History to Community History, By W. T. R. Pryce, (Cambridge Univ. Press, 1994), p.202

83 Family History to Community History, By W. T. R. Pryce, (Cambridge Univ. Press, 1994), p.202

84 East End Jewish Radicals 1875-1914 (Five Leaves, 2004) William J. Fishman, p.47

85 95%-100% Jewish residents, according to Arkell's 1899 demographic map

86 The London Years, Rudolf Rocker (Five Leaves, 2005), p.26

87 East End 1888, W.J. Fishman (Five Leaves, 2005), p.195

88 Policing The Ghetto: Jewish East London 1880-1920, David Englander, p.8; Crime, History & Societies, Vol. 14, No. 1 (Librarie Droz, 2010)

89 East London Observer, 14 July 1888; cited in East End 1888, William J. Fishman (Five Leaves, 1988), p.195
90 Commonweal, 5 May 1888; cited in East End 1888, William J. Fishman (Five Leaves, 1988), p.195
91 Guardian, 5 March 2015
92 Jewish Museum London, pamphlet exhibit
93 For a detailed discussion on the British Brothers League and the extent of the anti-Semitism motivating its agenda, refer to Anti-Semitism in British Society 1876-1939, Colin Holmes (Routledge, 2016) Chapter 6: 'Movements & Measures Against Jews'
94 Anti-Semitism in British Society 1876-1939, Colin Holmes (Routledge, 2016), p.28
95 ibid. p.91
96 Jews In Twentieth-Century Ireland, Dermot Keogh (Cork University Press, 1998), p.40
97 A Documentary History Of Jewish Immigrants In Britain, 1840-1920, David Englander (Leicester University Press, 1994), pp.288-296
98 PRO HO 45/10822/318095/478, 'Anti-Jewish Demonstration' report by Superintendent J. Best, Hackney Police Station, J.Div. 24 September 1917; cited in A Documentary History Of Jewish Immigrants In Britain, 1840-1920, David Englander (Leicester University Press, 1994), pp.296-297
99 PRO HO 45/10810/311932/56; Anti-Semitic Riots In London & Leeds; cited in A Documentary History Of Jewish Immigrants In Britain, 1840-1920, David Englander (Leicester University Press, 1994), pp.296-297
100 East London For Mosley: The British Union Of Fascists In East London and South-West Essex, by Thomas P. Linehan (Frank Cass, 2003)
101 City Of Cities, Stephen Inwood (Pan Macmillan 2005), p.73
102 East End 1888, William J. Fishman (Five Leaves, 1988), pp.195 & 220 (see Chapter 6, 'The Ghetto')
103 A Jew Went Roaming, A Goldberg (1937) pp.3-4; quoted in A Documentary History Of Jewish Immigrants in Britain 1840-1920, D. Englander (Leicester University Press, 1994), pp.93-94
104 Pall Mall Gazette, 26 February 1886
105 Pall Mall Gazette, 9 March 1887
106 Times, 23 July 1887; cited in The Trials Of Israel Lipski, Martin Friedland (Beaufort, 1984), p.197

Chapter 2

107 aged 47
108 Times, 14 September 1888
109 National Archives: HO 144/221/A49301C, ff. 137-45 Chief Inspector Swanson's report to the Home Office, 19 October 1888
110 HO/144/220/A49301C, f 8g
111 HO 144/221/A49301C, ff. 137-45 Chief Inspector Swanson's report to the Home Office, 19 October 1888
113 The Complete Jack The Ripper, Donald Rumbelow (Virginia Books 2013)

[114] Pall Mall Gazette, 8 September 1888
[115] Star, 4 September 1888; New York Times, 4 September 1888
[116] 15 September 1888
[117] Edition of 9 September 1888
[118] East London Advertiser, 15 September 1888
[119] East London Advertiser, 15 September 1888
[120] Jewish Chronicle, 14 September 1888
[121] For a more detailed discussion, see: Anti-Semitism in British Society, Colin Holmes (Edward Arnold, 1979), p.7
[122] Rambles In An Old City, Susan Swain Madders (Cautley Newby, London 1853) p.44
[123] Sheffield Daily Telegraph, 1 January 1889, p.6
[124] North London News & Finsbury Gazette, 5 January 1889
[125] The Complete History of Jack The Ripper, Philip Sugden (Robinson Publishing, 1995), p.122
[126] Anti-Semitism in British Society, Colin Holmes (Edward Arnold, 1979), pp.49-57
[127] Anti-Semitism: Myth & Hate from Antiquity to the Present, F.Schweitzer & M.Perry (Palgrave MacMillan, 2002), p.68
[128] Can Faiths Make Peace? Holy Wars and the Resolution of Religious Conflicts, Philip Broadhead & Damien Keown (I.B.Tauris & Co, 2077) p.110
[129] http://religiousstudiesblog.blogspot.com.au/2011/04/reviewof-popes-against-jews-by-david.html
[130] 'Limerick 1904: An Anti-Jewish Pogrom In Ireland', International Business Times, 18 February 2013
[131] Blood Will Tell: Anti-Semitism & Vampires in British Popular Culture, 1875-1914, Sara Libby Robinson (2009, as reproduced in GOLEM: Journal Of Religion & Monsters); viewable at: www.osservatorioantisemitismo.it
[132] London Evening News, 6 September 1882
[133] 'The Ritual Murder Accusation in Britain', Colin Holmes, Ethnic and Racial Studies, Volume 4, (University of Sheffield, 1981), pp.267-8
[134] ibid. p.267
[135] Anti-Semitism: Myth & Hate from Antiquity to the Present, F.Schweitzer & M.Perry (Palgrave MacMillan, 2002), p.61-2
[136] Spectator, 23 June 1883
[137] History Of The Jews In Russia & Poland - Volume I, S.Dubnow & I.Friedlaender (Avotaynu, 2000), p.238
[138] Times, 1 August 1883
[139] Birmingham Daily Post, 19 July 1883 reproducing the report by the Times' correspondent
[140] Spectator, 7 July 1883
[141] London Evening Standard, 30 March 1888
[142] York Herald, 22 September 1888; Manchester Courier and Lancashire General Advertiser, 22 September 1888
[143] Southern Reporter, 16 October 1884
[144] The Oxford Dictionary of National Biography – citation for "Jack The Ripper (1888)", Richard Davenport-Hines (Oxford University Press 2004)

[145] 14 September 1888
[146] Daily News, 11 September 1888
[147] Pall Mall Gazette, 8 September 1888, p.8
[148] eg. Lloyd's Weekly, 9 September 1888
[149] Encyclopaedia Britannica; see, entry for G.W.Pabst at: www.britannica.com

Chapter 3

[150] Abberline, Ref. MEPO 3/140/221/A49301C, ff. 204-6
[151] Star, 1 October 1888
[152] Ref. MEPO 3/140/221/A49301C, ff. 204-6
[153] Die Tsukunft, 12 August 1887, quoted on p.118 The Trials Of Israel Lipski, Martin L. Friedland (Beaufort Books 1984)
[154] Ref. HO 144/221/A49301C, ff. Ref. MEPO 3/140/221/A49301C, ff. 148-59; 204-6; MEPO 3/140/221/A49301C, ff. 207; Ref. HO 144/221/A49301C, ff. 199
[155] Edward Spooner's inquest testimony; Daily Telegraph, 2 October 1888; also, cited The Complete History Of Jack The Ripper, Philip Sugden (Robinson Publishing 1994) p.169
[156] Star, 1 October 1888
[157] Daily News, 1 October 1888
[158] Ref. HO 144/221/A49301C, ff. 220-223
[159] Evening News, 1 October 1888
[160] Daily News, 12 October 1888
[161] Daily News, 2 October 1888
[162] Daily Telegraph, 12 October 1888
[163] Chief Inspector Donald Swanson Ref. HO 144/221/A49301C, ff.184-94
[164] Superintendent Thomas Arnold, H Division, Ref. HO 144/221/A49301C, ff. 197-98
[165] Metropolitan Police commissioner, Sir Charles Warren, Ref. HO 144/221/A49301C, ff. 173-81
[166] Times, 12 October 1888
[167] Daily Telegraph, 12 October 1888
[168] Daily Telegraph, 12 October 1888
[169] Pall Mall Gazette, 4 November 1889
[170] Detective Inspector Henry Moore, Ref. MEPO 3/142, ff. 157-9
[171] From the City to Fleet Street, J. Hall Richardson, (S. Paul & Co. 1927) Chapter XV
[172] From Constable To Commissioner, Sir Henry Smith, (Chatto & Windus, 1910) Chapter XVI
[173] Metropolitan Police commissioner, Sir Charles Warren, Ref. HO 144/221/A49301C, ff. 173-81
[174] Chief Inspector Donald Swanson Ref. HO 144/221/A49301C, ff. 184-94
[175] Jewish Chronicle, 12 October 1888
[176] Daily News, 15 October 1888
[177] As quoted by Metropolitan Police commissioner, Sir Charles Warren, Ref. HO 144/221/A49301C, ff. 173-81
[178] London's East End - Point Of Arrival, Chaim Bermant, (New York 1975), p.117

[179] Sir Charles Warren, Ref. HO 144/221/A49301D, ff. 23-6
[180] Pall Mall Gazette, 15 October 1888
[181] Times, 12 October 1888; Auckland Star, 27 November 1888
[182] A Documentary History Of Jewish Immigrants In Britain, 1840-1920, David Englander (Leicester University Press, 1994), p.66
[183] Children Of The Ghetto, Israel Zangwill (Black Apollo, 2004), p.15
[184] Jewish Chronicle, 22 March 1889
[185] Whitby Gazette, 22 March 1889
[186] East End 1888, William J. Fishman (Five Leaves, 1988), p.346
[187] Jewish Chronicle, 22 March 1889
[188] Lloyd's Weekly, London 24 March 1889
[189] Freedom – A Journal Of Anarchist Socialism, as quoted in East End Jewish Radicals 1875-1914, W.J. Fishman (FiveLeaves, 2004) p.167

Chapter 4

[190] Times, 2 October 1888
[191] Pall Mall Gazette, 2 October 1888
[192] Pall Mall Gazette, 2 October 1888
[193] Manchester Guardian, 4 October 1888
[194] Jewish Chronicle, 12 October 1888
[195] Jewish Chronicle, 5 October 1888
[196] Times, 16 October 1888
[197] Eg. London Standard, Daily Telegraph, 26, October 1888
[198] Daily Telegraph, 26 October 1888
[199] eg Galveston Evening Tribune, 27 November 1888; Maitland Mercury, 15 December 1888; McIvor Times & Rodney Advertiser, 25 January 1889; Otago Witness, 14 December 1888

Chapter 5

[200] I Caught Crippen, W. Dew (Blackie & Son, 1938)
[201] Daily Telegraph, 13 November 1888
[202] Times, 13 November 1888
[203] The Globe (Canada), 13 November 1888
[204] Daily News, 10 November 1888; Daily Telegraph, 13 November, 1888
[205] Observer, 18 November 1888
[206] Lloyd's Weekly, 11 November 1888
[207] Kelly's post-mortem examination notes reproduced in The Complete Jack The Ripper A to Z, Begg, Fido, & Skinner (John Blake Publishing 2010), p.60
[208] Times, 12 November 1888
[209] Kelly inquest testimony, Mary Ann Cox
[210] Illustrated Police News, 17 November 1888
[211] Inquest notes & police notes.
[212] Daily Telegraph, 13 November 1888
[213] Daily Telegraph, 13 November 1888
[214] The Complete History Of Jack The Ripper, Philip Sugden (Robinson, 2006),

p.417

215 I Caught Crippen, W. Dew (Blackie & Son, 1938)
216 MEPO 3/140, ff. 227-9
217 MEPO 3/140, ff. 230-2
218 From Hell: The Jack the Ripper Mystery, Bob Hinton (Old Bakehouse,1998)
219 Echo, 19 November 1888
220 Washington Evening Star, 14 November 1888, p.4
221 Star, 12 November 1888
222 Pall Mall Gazette, 24 & 31 March 1903
223 I Caught Crippen, W. Dew (Blackie & Son, 1938)
224 Daily News, 17 October 1888; cited, The Complete History Of Jack The Ripper, Philip Sugden (Robinson Publishing 1994)
225 Quoted by Sir Melville Macnaghten, Days Of My Years (1903)

Chapter 6

226 Daily Telegraph, 10 November 1888
227 Star, 10 November 1888
228 Illustrated Police News, 17 November 1888
229 Media version of Hutchinson's statement
230 Police version of Hutchinson's statement
231 Daily Telegraph, 10 November 1888
232 Report by Chief Inspector Swanson to Home Office, 19 October 1888, HO/144/221/A49301C 8a
233 I Caught Crippen, W. Dew (Blackie & Son, 1938)
234 Likely Detective Inspector Reid, interviewed by Evening News, 23 July 1889
235 Cassell's Saturday Journal, 28 May 1892
236 Kelly Inquest papers & K. Skinner (Carroll & Graf Publishers, 2000), p.373
237 Other editions published on 12 November 1888, include Gloucestershire Echo and Sheffield Evening Telegraph
238 (London) Echo, 12 November 1888
239 Times, 14 November 1888
240 The Complete Jack The Ripper A to Z, Begg, Fido, & Skinner (John Blake Publishing 2010), p.216
241 I Caught Crippen, W. Dew (Blackie & Son, 1938)
242 ibid.
243 Western Mail, 13 November 1888
244 Penny Illustrated Paper (London), 17 November 1888
245 Elizabeth Prater police witness statement
246 Daily Telegraph, 13 November 1888
247 ibid.
248 ibid.
249 Kelly Inquest papers
250 Echo, 9 November 1888
251 St James's Gazette, 8 November 1888
252 London Evening Standard, 8 November 1888
253 Daily Telegraph, 21 September 1888

[254] The People Of The Abyss, Jack London (1st World Library, 2004) pp.188 & 191
[255] sighted during author's visit to Salvation Army Heritage Centre (William Booth College, London), November 2016; file VH

Chapter 7

[256] Cox's inquest testimony, Daily Telegraph, 12 November 1888
[257] Cox's police statement; MJ/SPC, NE1888, Box 3, Case Paper 19, (London Metropolitan Archives)
[258] op. cit. Dr Bond's report
[259] "... the opinion of Dr. George Bagster Phillips, the divisional surgeon of the H Division...when he was called to the deceased (at a quarter to 11) she had been dead some five or six hours"; Times, 12 November 1888
[260] Daily Telegraph, 13 November 1888
[261] Echo, 10 November 1888
[262] Star, 10 November 1888
[263] Echo, 14 November 1888
[264] 101 Amazing Facts About Jack The Ripper, by Jack Goldstein, Frankie Taylor (Andrews UK Ltd, 2014), Ch: 'Mary Kelly' fact n. 4
[265] John McCarthy's inquest testimony
[266] I Caught Crippen, W. Dew (Blackie & Son, 1938)
[267] Illustrated Police News, 17 November 1888; Morning Post, 10 November 1888
[268] Evening News, 12 November 1888
[269] Subject: Jack The Ripper, FBI investigation, J.E. Douglas, 1988, p.6; viewable at: https://vault.fbi.gov/Jack%20the%20Ripper/Jack%20the%20Ripper%20 Part%201%20of%201/view; also, The Cases That Haunt Us, John Douglas & Mark Olshhaker (Scribner, 2000), pp.65-66
[270] 'Light On The Ripper Murders', The Chronicle (Adelaide, South Australia), 30 May 1896, p.46
[271] I Caught Crippen, W. Dew (Blackie & Son, 1938)
[272] Cox told the inquest that she "should know the man again"; in her original police statement such a supposition is absent.
[273] Illustrated Police News, 24 November 1888
[274] HO 144/221A49301C, ff. 220-3
[275] I Caught Crippen, W. Dew (Blackie & Son, 1938)
[276] Illustrated Police News, 24 November 1888

Chapter 8

[277] www.mindhuntersinc.com/why-killers-take-trophies/
[278] The Complete History Of Jack The Ripper, Philip Sugden (Robinson, 2006), p.417
[279] Star, 1 October 1888
[280] HO 144/220/A49301, f 16
[281] Times, 24 October 1888, p.3
[282] For Morris Eagle and Joseph Lave's evidence, see Chapter 3
[283] Times, 24 October 1888

284 Times, 24 October 1888; Times, 6 October 1888
285 Star, 1 October 1888
286 HO 144/220/A49301, f 16
287 Coroner's inquest (L), 1888, N. 135, Catherine Eddowes inquest, 1888 (Corporation of London Record Office)
288 HO 144/221/A49301C, ff 184-94
289 Daily Telegraph, 12 October 1888
290 Evening News, 9 October 1888
291 Times, 2 October 1888; also, Police Gazette, 19 October 1888
292 op. cit. Subject: Jack The Ripper, FBI investigation, J.E. Douglas, 1988, p.4
293 I Caught Crippen, W. Dew (Blackie & Son, 1938)
294 Days Of My Years, Sir Melville Macnaughten, (1914) Chapter 5 'Laying The Ghost Of Jack The Ripper
295 Star, 10 November 1888
296 News Of The World, 12 April 1896; cited, Ripperologist n.147, December 2015
297 London Evening Standard, 12 November 1888
298 Inquest testimony
299 I Caught Crippen, W. Dew (Blackie & Son, 1938)
300 Jack The Ripper: A Suspect Guide, Christopher J. Morley (e-book, 2005), viewable at casebook.org; also, On The Trail Of A Dead Man, C. Miles (Milestone Press, 2003) pp.103-104 & 120-121
301 1891 Census, England, Wales & Scotland, archive ref. RG12, piece n. 281, folio 86, p.1
302 Jack The Ripper: The Simple Truth, B.Paley (Headline, 2004), p.176
303 Star, 10 November 1888; Lloyd's Weekly, 11 November 1888
304 Star, 10 November 1888
305 www.mindhuntersinc.com/why-killers-take-trophies/

Chapter 9

306 Children Of The Ghetto, Israel Zangwill, (Black Appollo, 2004), p.20
307 A Rough Guide To London, Rob Humphreys (Rough Guides, 2003), p.234
308 Our East End: Memoires Of Life In Disappearing Britain, Piers Dudgeon (Headline Review, 2008), Ch.3 'Cockney Wide Boys'
309 House of Commons Select Committee report on Emigration & Immigration (Foreigners) 1888, p.53; H.D.'s testimony
310 Living London: Vol. II Section I (edited by George R. Sims), Chapter 5 "Jewish London", S. Gelberg (Cassell & Co. Ltd 1902), pp.30-31
311 House of Commons Select Committee report on Emigration & Immigration (Foreigners) 1888, pp.52-53; H.D.'s testimony
312 Children Of The Ghetto, Israel Zangwill, (Black Appollo, 2004), p.51
313 'The Jewish Colony In London', Sunday Magazine, XXI (1892) pp.16-20, 119-23; cited, A Documentary History Of Jewish Immigrants In Britain, 1840-1920, David Englander (Leicester University Press, 1994), p.70
314 Children Of The Ghetto, Israel Zangwill, (Black Appollo, 2004); note - Zangwill uses the Yiddish word for synagogue, "shool"
315 www.jewishgen.org/JCR-UK/London/EE_old-castle/index.htm

[316] House of Commons Select Committee report on Emigration & Immigration (Foreigners) 1888, p.189; T.A.'s testimony

[317] ibid. p.188; T.A.'s testimony

[318] A Documentary History Of Jewish Immigrants in Britain 1840-1920, D. Englander (Leicester University Press, 1994), p.90

[319] House of Commons Select Committee report on Emigration & Immigration (Foreigners) 1888, p.188; T.A.'s testimony

[320] House of Commons Select Committee report on Emigration & Immigration (Foreigners) 1889, p.45; T.A.'s testimony

[321] House of Commons Select Committee report on Emigration & Immigration (Foreigners) 1888, p.188; T.A.'s testimony

[322] Jewish Chronicle, 19 October 1888; cited in East End 1888, William J. Fishman (Five Leaves, 1988), p.192

[323] House of Commons Select Committee report on Emigration & Immigration (Foreigners) 1888, p.192; T.A.'s testimony

[324] Report of the Select Committee on Emigration & Immigration (Foreigners) 1889, testimony of Superintendent Arnold pp.43-45; also, cited, A Documentary History Of Jewish Immigrants in Britain 1840-1920, D. Englander (Leicester University Press, 1994), pp.95-96

[325] Otago Daily Times, 4 December 1914, p.9

[326] The People Of The Abyss, Jack London (Macmillan & Co. 1903), p.243

[327] 'Light On The Ripper Murders', The Chronicle (Adelaide, South Australia), 30 May 1896, p.46; Lloyd's Weekly, 4 February 1912

[328] Subject: Jack The Ripper, FBI investigation, J.E. Douglas, 1988, p.6

[329] HO 144/221/A49301C, ff. 220-3

[330] Times, 12 October 1888

[331] Daily Telegraph, 12 October 1888

[332] Chief Inspector Donald Swanson Ref. HO 144/221/A49301C, ff. 184-94

[333] correspondence dated 13 June 1918, between the owner of the Commercial Street property, Miss Amelia Levy and the lessee Lord Radstock, sighted during author's visit to Salvation Army Heritage Centre (William Booth College, London), November 2016; file VH

[334] Star (NZ), 7 September 1889, issue 6644, p.2; described it as "matchless audacity"

[335] Star, 10 November 1888

Chapter 10

[336] Ripper & The Royals, M.Fairclough (Duckbacks, 2002), p.246

[337] See any of the numerous on-line forums discussing Sue Iremonger's findings (as presented at the 1993 WADE Conference, in her paper 'Jack The Ripper Revisited'); also see, The Complete Jack The Ripper A to Z, Begg, Fido & Skinner (John Blake Publishing 2010), p.435, re: the telephone conversation with Martin Fido

[338] New South Wales Police Gazette, 11 November 1896

[339] Edition Fri 30 Oct 1896, p.2 - article dated 29 October 1896; edition Tue 3 November 1896, p.2 - article dated 30 October 1896; edition Fri 4 December 1896, p.2 - article dated 1 December 1896

340 State Records Authority of New South Wales: NRS1998, [3/5960], Bathurst Gaol photographic description book, 1874-1930, No. 1166, p.19, reel 5085.

341 State Records Authority of New South Wales: Shipping Master's Office; Passengers Arriving 1855-1922; NRS13278, [X201] reel 493.

342 July, 1887; March 1888; November, 1888; March 1889; March 1890; July, 1890; November 1890; March 1891; July 1891; November 1891; July 1892.

343 Forbes & Parkes Gazette, 30 October 1896; New South Wales Police Gazette, 17 August 1898

344 City Of Cities, Stephen Inwood, (Pan Macmillan 2005), pp.101-103

345 www.portcities.org.uk/london/server/show/ConNarrative.77/chapterId/1855/ The-Great-Dock-Strike-of-1889.html

346 Dundee Courier, 12 September 1889, p.3

347 The Advertiser (Adelaide), 13 September 1889, p.4

348 Argus (Melbourne), 13 September 1889, p.5

349 City Of Cities, Stephen Inwood, (Pan Macmillan 2005), pp.101-103

350 City Of Cities, Stephen Inwood, (Pan Macmillan 2005), p.22; see also: Chris Jenks, Urban Culture: Critical Concepts in Literary and Cultural Studies, Volume 4, Routledge 2004, pp.156-7

351 Hansard, House Of Commons, 24 February 1891, vol. 350 – cc 1510-34

352 British Railways: Their Passenger Services, Rolling Stock, Locomotives, Gradients & Express, Speed, J. Pearson Pattison (Cassell & Co, 1893) pp.225-27

353 ibid.

354 East End Chronicles, Ed Glinert (Allen Lane, 2005), pp.27-8

355 ibid. pp.235-6

356 Cited; City Of Cities, Stephen Inwood (Pan Macmillan 2005), p.103

357 City Of Cities, Stephen Inwood, (Pan Macmillan) 2005, p.103

358 Reading Mercury, 7 September 1889, p.7

359 Herald, 23 September, p.3

360 Essex Newsman (Herald), 21 September 1889, p.3

361 Old Thunder: A Life Of Hilaire Belloc, Joseph Pearce, Ignatius Press, San Francisco 2002

362 www.portcities.org.uk/london/server/show/ConNarrative.77/chapterId/1865/ The-Great-Dock-Strike-of-1889.html

363 Guardian, 18 September 1889

364 The Alien Invasion: The Origins Of The Aliens Act of 1905, Bernard Gainer (Heinemann, 1972), p.59 & pp.56-59

365 ibid, p.59 & pp.56-59; Chapter 4, 'Anti-Alien Societies In East London', provides an expanded discussion of these questions, in broader terms; City Of Cities, Stephen Inwood (Pan Macmillan 2005), p.74; perusal of the weekly, Commonweal, during the general period in question is also illuminating

366 https://historyhackblog.wordpress.com/tag/ship/

367 Melbourne Daily Telegraph, 21 November 1887; cited, https://historyhackblog. wordpress.com/tag/ship/

368 State Records Authority of New South Wales: Shipping Master's Office; Passengers Arriving 1855 - 1922; NRS13278, [X201] reel 524. ; also, Ancestry. com UK, Outward Passenger Lists, 1890-1960 [database on-line].

369 New South Wales, Unassisted Passenger Lists, 1826-1922; UK, Outward

Chapter 11

[370] Illustrated London News, 13 July 1889
[371] Pall Mall Gazette, 17 July 1889, p.4
[372] MEPO 3/140, ff. 294-7
[373] MEPO 3/140, ff. 263-71
[374] Times, 19 July 1889
[375] The Lighter Side Of My Official Life, Sir Robert Anderson (Hodder & Stoughton, 1910), p.137
[376] MEPO 3/140, FF. 263-71
[377] Daily News, 18 July 1889
[378] ibid.
[379] Trenton Times, 18 July 1889
[380] Pall Mall Gazette, 17 July 1888
[381] HO 144/221/A49301G, ff. 24-5
[382] HO 144/221/A49301G, ff. 28-9
[383] East London Observer, 20 July 1888
[384] Times, 19 July
[385] South Wales Echo, 17 July, 1889
[386] Star (NZ), 7 September 1889, issue 6644, p.2
[387] Lloyd's Weekly, 21 July 1889
[388] Times, 19 July 1889
[389] Times, 17 July 1889
[390] Times, 18 & 19 July; 15 August 1889
[391] Manchester Times, 20 July 1889
[392] Times, 19 July 1889
[393] Lloyd's Weekly, 21 July 1889
[394] Times, 18 July 1889
[395] Lloyd's Weekly, 21 July 1889
[396] Times, 18 July 1889
[397] Manchester Times, 20 July 1889
[398] Times, 19 July 1889
[399] Evening News, 23 July 1889
[400] The Man Who Hunted Jack The Ripper, N. Connell & S.P. Evans (Rupert Books, 2000) p.83
[401] Evening News, 23 July 1889
[402] Lloyd's Weekly, 21 July 1889
[403] London Mid Surrey Times & General Advertiser, July 20 1889; Blackburn Standard, 20 July 1889
[404] Sheffield Evening Telegraph, 18 July 1889; Cambridge Daily News, 18 July 1889; Gloucestershire Echo, 19 July 1889; Blackburn Standard, 20 July 1889; Northern Echo, 19 July 1889
[405] HO 144/221/A49301C, ff. 217-23; HO 144/221/A49301C, ff. 217-23
[406] Based on later media interviews by the pair

407 East London Observer, 20 July 1889
408 Star (NZ), 7 September 1889, issue 6644, p.2
409 'Twenty-five Years Headmaster At The Old Castle Street Board School', Jewish Chronicle, 10 November 1899; quoted in A Documentary History Of Jewish Immigrants In Britain, 1840-1920, David Englander (Leicester University Press, 1994), pp.222-225
410 From Family History To Community History Vol. 2, W.T.R. Pryce (Cambridge Univ. Press 1994), p.193
411 Northen Echo, 19 July 1889
412 Subject: Jack The Ripper, FBI investigation, J.E. Douglas, 1988, p.4
413 Pall Mall Gazette, 17 July 1889, p.4; HO144/221/A49301I Ref. ff. 7-10; Walthamstow and Leyton Guardian, 20th July 1889
414 Dundee Courier & Argus, 12 September 1889
415 Pall Mall Gazette, 4 November 1889
416 Morning Advertiser, 30 March 1903
417 Pall Mall Gazette, 24 March 1903
418 Morning Advertiser, 30 March 1903
419 East London Observer, 1 June 1901
420 Chronicle (Adelaide, South Australia), 30 May 1896
421 Daily Telegraph, 12 October 1888; Dr Sequeira's inquest testimony
422 East London Observer, 14 May 1910
423 HO 144/221/A49301/21
424 Southern Reporter, 16 October 1884
425 Jewishencyclopedia.com/articles/14407-tisza-eszlar-affair
426 Birmingham Daily Post, 19 July 1883
427 Jewishencyclopedia.com/articles/14407-tisza-eszlar-affair

Chapter 12

428 In the New South Wales Police Gazette of 17 August 1898, which provided rudimentary details of prisoners upon their release, Hutchinson's eyes are described as "brown" and hair "dark brown". There is no accompanying photo or any other descriptive details proffered; his height and complexion were left blank, so too details of nose, mouth and chin.
429 Subject: Jack The Ripper, FBI investigation, J.E. Douglas, 1988, p.5
430 www.casebook.org/forum/messages/4922/6536.html#; & http://jtrforums.com/showthread.php?t=13917
431 I Caught Crippen, W. Dew (Blackie & Son, 1938)
432 Times, 12 October 1888
433 Subject: Jack The Ripper, FBI investigation, J.E. Douglas, 1988, p.6
434 Blackwood's Edinburgh Magazine, 1901; relevant quote viewable at: http://webarchive.nationalarchives.gov.uk+/http://www.movinghere.org.uk/galleries/histories/irish/working_lives/docks_shipcanal.htm
435 The Alien Invasion: The Origins Of The Aliens Act of 1905, Bernard Gainer (Heinemann, 1972) p.58
436 Police Review, 11 July 1913; cited The Complete Jack The Ripper A to Z, Begg, Fido, & Skinner (John Blake Publishing 2010), pp.356-7

437 Pall Mall Gazette, 4 November 1889
438 Similarly reported in Pall Mall Gazette, 24 March 1903
439 Cassell's Saturday Journal, 28 May 1892
440 Times, 24 August 1888, p.4
441 London Magnet, 13 August 1888, p.1; North-Eastern Daily Gazette, 10 August 1888, p.4; 'The Case For Re-Canonizing', Q.L. Pittman; viewable at Casebook Jack The Ripper – www.casebook.org; 'Martha Tabram: The Forgotten Ripper Victim?', Jon Ogan, Ripperologist, March 1996, n.5
442 Times, 10 August 1888
443 North-Eastern Daily Gazette, 10 August 1888
444 MEPO 3/140, ff.44-8
445 Times, 24 August, p.4
446 I Caught Crippen, W. Dew (Blackie & Son, 1938)
447 East London Observer, 11 August 1888
448 Pall Mall Gazette, 24 March 1903
449 I Caught Crippen, W. Dew (Blackie & Son, 1938)
450 Times, 10 August 1888

Chapter 13

451 Hitler, Ian Kershaw (Penguin 1998), p.64
452 British Weekly, 25 May 1888; as reproduced in Toilers In London, by the British Weekly Commissioners & edited by Margaret Harkness (Hodder & Stoughton, 1889), p.49/50; also viewable at: www.victorianlondon.org/publications3/newtoilers-3.htm
453 East End 1888, William J. Fishman (Five Leaves, 1988), pp.88-9; The Social Question And The Jewish Question In Late Victorian London (in Imagination & Commitment - Representations of the Social Question - Groningen Studies in Cultural Change Leuven: Peeters 2010), Seth Koven, pp.47-8
454 The Alien Invasion: The Origins Of The Aliens Act of 1905, Bernard Gainer (Heinemann, 1972) p.57
455 'The Sweating System', Report Of The Committee (By Cable Message), London 5 May; Brisbane Courier, 7 May 1890, p.5
456 'Cable Messages From Our London Correspondent'; 'The Sweating Committee - London 10 May'; Brisbane Courier, 12 May 1890, p.5
457 Fifth & final report (1890) of the House Of Lords Select Committee on the Sweating System
458 Echo, 4 August 1889, p.2
459 Standard, 4 August 1888, p.5
460 ibid.
461 Star, 12 November 1888, p.1
462 East London Observer, 31 March 1888
463 Eastern Post & City Chronicle, 31 March 1888
464 Sheffield Daily Telegraph, 30 March 1888, p.5
465 ibid.
466 Illustrated Police News, 7 April 1888
467 The Complete History Of Jack The Ripper, Philip Sugden (Robinson 2006),

p.471
[468] East End 1888, William J. Fishman (Five Leaves, 1988), p.192
[469] St James's Gazette, 15 March 1888; Huddersfield Daily Chronicle, 16 March 1888; East London Observer, 17 March 1888
[470] Scotsman, 15 March 1888, p.6
[471] The Complete History Of Jack The Ripper, Philip Sugden (Robinson 2006), p.370
[472] Dracula, Bram Stoker (Country Life Press, 1897)
[473] 'The Jewish Colony In London', Sunday Magazine, XXI (1892) pp.16-20, 119-23; cited, A Documentary History Of Jewish Immigrants In Britain, 1840-1920, David Englander (Leicester University Press, 1994), p.70
[474] Dracula, Bram Stoker (Country Life Press, 1897)
[475] ibid.
[476] 'Blood Will Tell: Anti-Semitism & Vampires in British Popular Culture, 1875-1914', Sara Libby Robinson (2009, as reproduce in GOLEM: Journal Of Religion & Monsters); viewable at: www.osservatorioantisemitismo.it
[477] 'Dracula, Jack the Ripper and A Thirst for Blood', Robert Eighteen-Bisang, Ripperologist n.60, July 2005
[478] As reproduced in 'Letter From Castle Dracula' (news bulletin of the Transylvanian Society of Dracula), April 2014, pp.10 & 12; viewable at: www.mysterious-journeys.com/pdf/letter_easter_2014.pdf
[479] 'Blood Will Tell: Anti-Semitism & Vampires in British Popular Culture, 1875-1914', Sara Libby Robinson (2009, as reproduce in GOLEM: Journal Of Religion & Monsters)
[480] Times, 13 July 1887
[481] Antisemetism: Myth and Hate from Antiquity to the Present, Marvin Perry & Frederick M. Schweitzer (Palgrave MacMillan, 2005); see Chapter 3, 'The Diabolization of Jews: Demons, Conspirators, and Race Defilers', pp.73-118
[482] Apostates, Hybrids Or True Jews: Jewish Christians & Jewish Identity In Eastern Europe 1860-1914, R. Lillevik (Pickwick, 2014) pp.117-18
[483] Dracula, Bram Stoker (Country Life Press, 1897)
[484] Antisemetism: Myth and Hate from Antiquity to the Present, Marvin Perry & Frederick M. Schweitzer (Palgrave MacMillan, 2005); see Chapter 3, 'The Diabolization of Jews: Demons, Conspirators, and Race Defilers', p.72
[485] cited in, The Identity of Jack the Ripper, Donald McCormick (London, 1959), p.26
[486] Echo, 6 September 1888

Printed in Great Britain
by Amazon

16223895R00161